ISVOLSKY AND
THE WORLD WAR

ISVOLSKY AND THE WORLD WAR

BASED ON THE DOCUMENTS RECENTLY PUBLISHED BY THE GERMAN FOREIGN OFFICE

BY

FRIEDRICH STIEVE

Translated by

E. W. DICKES

BOOKS FOR LIBRARIES PRESS
FREEPORT, NEW YORK

First Published 1926
Reprinted 1971

940. 3112
StSi
14 5783
Jan. 1989

INTERNATIONAL STANDARD BOOK NUMBER:
0-8369-5862-4

LIBRARY OF CONGRESS CATALOG CARD NUMBER:
78-160994

PRINTED IN THE UNITED STATES OF AMERICA

PREFACE

DR. FRIEDRICH STIEVE, the writer of this book, is the author of a number of historical works ; some years ago he joined the staff of the German Foreign Office, in which he holds the post of Vortragender Legationsrat.   He was responsible for the publication on behalf of the German Foreign Office of four volumes containing the diplomatic correspondence of A. P. Isvolsky, Russian ambassador in Paris, between 1911 and 1914 (*Der diplomatische Schriftwechsel Iswolskis 1911–1914*), and the following pages are based on that collection of documents.

The great majority of the documents were taken from the collection published by the Soviet Government in 1922, under the title of *Material for the history of Franco-Russian relations, 1910–1914.   Collection of secret diplomatic documents of the Imperial Russian Ministry of Foreign Affairs.* A French translation of this " Material " was published by René Marchand (*Un Livre Noir. Diplomatie d'Avant-Guerre d'après les Documents des Archives Russes, November 1910–Juillet 1914*, 2 vols., Paris, 1922 and 1923).   Dr. Stieve writes as follows in his preface to *Der diplomatische Schriftwechsel Iswolskis* :

In the following publication it was possible almost everywhere to refer back to the original Russian text, which shows a few small variations from the French edition.   There are a few documents which are given only in the *Livre Noir*.   These were also accepted, as the checking of this publication had shown its great reliability. . . . The items published by the French newspaper *Humanité* concerning the influencing of the French Press by means of Russian funds may also be regarded as a safe source, since the former Russian Prime Minister, Mr. Kokovtsov, said recently in giving evidence in a Paris law suit that they were undoubtedly genuine.   It has also been possible to add to the documents already made public over five hundred new items, which have been translated direct from the Russian originals.

Dr. Stieve does not state the source of these last documents, but it may be assumed that they are from originals in the Russian embassy in Paris.   Two facsimiles of draft telegrams of a later date, in Isvolsky's handwriting, and on the blue paper used by the Russian embassy in Paris, are included in Dr. Stieve's later work, *Iswolski im Weltkriege* (*Isvolsky in the World War.   Isvolsky's diplomatic correspondence during the years* 1914–1917), published by the instructions of the German Foreign Office in 1925.

E. W. D.

CONTENTS

Isvolsky and the World War

I

ISVOLSKY'S EARLIER CAREER

ALEXANDER PETROVITCH ISVOLSKY was born in 1856. We know comparatively little of his career before 1911, when he was appointed Russian Ambassador in Paris. His intended autobiography did not get beyond its first volume, as death overtook him at Biarritz, in his sixty-fourth year, while he was engaged on the work. But this volume [1] contains data which are of importance in forming a judgment as to the character of the man.

The foreword, addressed to Isvolsky's daughter Helen, gives us the following details of his career. He was educated at the Imperial Lyceum at St. Petersburg (now Leningrad) and entered the Russian Foreign Office at the age of nineteen. Three years later he was sent to Philippopolis as secretary of an international commission, and here he first came into touch with the problems of the Near East. Diplomatic appointments in Bucarest and Washington followed, and while still comparatively young he was commissioned to represent his country at the Vatican, where he remained for six years, enjoying specially good relations with Cardinal Rampolla. Later he was Ambassador in Belgrad, Munich, Tokyo, and Copenhagen. In 1906 he was appointed Russian Foreign Minister.

Up to this date only two incidents of his career are

[1] *Mémoires de Alexandre Iswolski, Ancien Ambassadeur de Russie à Paris* (1906–1910). Préface de M. Gabriel Hanotaux, Paris, Payot.

known, both belonging to the Copenhagen period. The unfortunate Russo-Japanese War produced a current of opposition at the Court of the Tsar Nicholas II against Count Witte, the Minister of Finance, who was advocating an alliance between Russia and the other Continental Powers, particularly Germany. Russia's representatives abroad were asked their views as to this idea, and Isvolsky joined Benckendorff in London and Nelidov in Paris in declaring against it. The main argument of Witte's opponents was that France would refuse to join in and that nothing should be done to alienate this Ally.[1] The other incident we have from Isvolsky's own pen ; he relates that during a stay made by King Edward VII in Copenhagen he " had the opportunity of sketching to the British sovereign, in the course of long conversations, the essentials of the agreement arrived at later, in 1907, between Russia and Great Britain, which has so greatly influenced the course of events in Europe." [2]

We shall deal later with this agreement. Suffice it for the moment to note that Isvolsky was a convinced supporter of those in Russia who advocated co-operation with the Western Powers, Great Britain and France. Similarly, in Tokyo, to quote his own words, he was opposed to any embitterment of relations with Japan, and he tells us that he persisted in this attitude even to the point of drawing upon himself the displeasure of his monarch, who, under the influence of Bezobrazov and of Admirals Abaza and Alexeyev, decided on war against Japan.[3] Towards the end of the Russo-Japanese War there was some talk in St. Petersburg of appointing Isvolsky ambassador in Berlin, but it came to nothing. Nor was he sent to negotiate peace at Portsmouth ; he had himself expressed unwillingness to go. However, Isvolsky's advice against the Far East adventure had been justified by the unhappy

[1] H. Friedjung, *Das Zeitalter des Imperialismus*, ii. p. 66. *Mémoires du Comte Witte* ; Introduction de François Rousseau, Paris, pp. 360 sqq.
[2] *Mémoires de A. Iswolski*, p. 24.
[3] Ibid., p. 25.

issue of the war, and he came back into favour and in May 1906 was placed at the head of the Foreign Office.

Shortly before this, in March, he went to Paris, where he met three other Russian diplomats : Count Benckendorff, ambassador in London; Nelidov, ambassador in Paris; and Muraviev, ambassador in Rome.[1] There was an exchange of views between the four concerning the programme which Russia should follow, and the new Foreign Minister informed the Tsar of its results when he took over the seals of office. Isvolsky himself describes it as the programme " of which the further development led to the system known as the ' Triple Entente.' "

In his book [2] he mentions the considerations which pointed to this course, in dealing with the German-Russian treaty of alliance which was concluded in 1905 at Björkö between the German Emperor and Tsar Nicholas II, but not subsequently ratified :

Russia's position in Europe was determined by the fact that for fifteen years she had been bound by a formal treaty of alliance with France. For a moment Tsar Nicholas had yielded to the urgent pressure of Emperor William, who aimed at engaging Russia in a political system which must, from its nature, if not dissociate her completely from France, at all events put her into an infinitely more complicated and insecure situation. The error of the Tsar was only momentary ; his feeling of honour and his sound instinct had prevented him from persisting in it, and with the aid of Count Lamsdorff he succeeded in evading the trap which had been laid for him. The alliance with France was intact ; meanwhile, in the two years which were just ending, there had been important changes in French policy. Great Britain and France had set a term to their old quarrel, and the way had been paved for an era of mutual trust and friendship between these two Powers. During the war with Japan, Russia had already felt in no small measure the benefit of this entente ; but if she were to draw full and permanent advantages from it it was clear that she must herself come nearer to Britain. This, however, was only possible if, following France's example, she found means of removing the various differences which separated her from that Power. Moreover, a *rapprochement* with Great Britain was not in itself enough ; it was essential that it should be accompanied by a sincere reconciliation with Japan. By following such a policy Russia would be

[1] *Mémoires*, p. 39.   [2] Ibid., pp. 60 sqq.

certain not only to strengthen her position as France's ally but to provide a fresh and sounder basis for the whole edifice of the Dual Alliance.

Isvolsky then refers again to the discussion in Paris between the four Ambassadors, and remarks :

We came unanimously to the conclusion that Russia's foreign policy must continue to rest on the indestructible basis of her alliance with France, but that this alliance should be reinforced by agreements with Great Britain and Japan.

The words quoted here are significant as describing a moment of crucial importance to the fate of Europe—that in which Russia turned her face away from the Far East and towards Europe, and in which her pressure towards the sea was relaxed on the Pacific coast and directed west-wards. The man who effected this historic deflection of Pan-Slav Imperialism was Alexander Isvolsky.

A short survey of the public events of his career as Foreign Minister will show at once that he remained faithful to his programme. Almost immediately after taking office he began to work towards a *rapprochement* with Great Britain and her ally Japan.[1] The former was the more easily influenced, for the Japanese victory had largely removed the fear of Russia so far as concerned Britain's Asiatic interests. But Tokyo also had an incentive to a reconciliation with Russia in the threatening conflict with the United States, which were now Japan's principal rival in the Pacific. On July 30, 1907, a convention was concluded between Russia and Japan clearing up all existing differences and defining the respective spheres of interest of the two Powers in China. Now was Isvolsky's opportunity for a rapid settlement of matters at issue with Great Britain. On August 31, 1907, a convention was concluded at St. Petersburg between Great Britain and Russia covering all points at issue between the two Powers in regard to Afghanistan, Tibet, and Persia. Recognition was accorded to the *status quo* in Afghanistan, Tibet was

[1] Friedjung, *Das Zeitalter des Imperialismus*, ii. pp. 142 sqq.

freed from influence by either party, and Persia was divided into three zones, the north being recognized as a Russian and the south a British sphere of influence.

For the Foreign Minister of a recently defeated country these were great achievements. They had come so easily mainly because Isvolsky's aims harmonized with the London policy of encircling Germany. The plan agreed on with King Edward VII at Copenhagen had thus quickly been carried through. The Entente with Great Britain was cemented by the meeting of the British King and the Tsar at Reval in June 1908.

A necessary result of the new course at St. Petersburg soon showed itself : the good relations with Austria, which had been maintained for years, especially in regard to the Balkans, began to grow less intimate. Here again we may detect the hand of Isvolsky. When the moment came to begin to put into execution the juridical reforms in Macedonia which had been agreed on between Russia and the Dual Monarchy, Isvolsky suddenly declared that all the Powers must be associated in the work, and in the course of the subsequent negotiations it became clear that here again he was making a point of working with Great Britain. Very slowly there began to open that fatal gulf which was soon to separate Europe into two sharply divided camps—that of the Entente Powers and that of the Central Powers.

The gulf first revealed to the full its ominous depth when Isvolsky precipitately passed from the defensive side of his programme, the settlement of existing differences with Great Britain, to the offensive, by developing the Russian claim to the Straits. As already mentioned, since Japan's defeat of Russia the pressure of the latter towards the open sea had been deflected from Far Eastern waters to the Continent of Europe. The way to the relief of this pressure was through the Turkish Dardanelles into the Mediterranean. Russia already maintained an important naval force in the Black Sea, but the Bosphorus had been closed to ships of war by the treaty of 1841, and Russia had felt this disability keenly in the Russo-Japanese War.

Isvolsky now endeavoured to obtain an agreed settlement of this question in his country's favour.[1] He first knocked at the door of the Vienna Cabinet. In a Memorandum of July 2, 1908, he offered the Dual Monarchy Russia's assent to the annexation by Austria-Hungary of Bosnia, Herzegovina, and the Sandjak of Novibazar in return for the assent of the Dual Monarchy to the free passage of Russian ships of war through the Dardanelles. Count Aehrenthal, the Austrian Foreign Minister, readily entertained the proposal, making only two conditions—that Roumania and Bulgaria, which also border on the Black Sea, should have the same right as Russia, and that the security of Constantinople must be assured. Moreover, he would content himself with the incorporation of Bosnia and Herzegovina in the Empire and would make no claim to the Sandjak.

The two statesmen met on September 15 in Count Berchtold's Schloss at Buchlau, and after thorough discussion concluded an agreement on these lines. They agreed to proceed in close co-operation, and contemplated calling a European conference in order to obtain its covering sanction on the completion of their negotiations. On one point, however, there appears to have been a misunderstanding : Isvolsky imagined that before putting the agreed resolutions into action he had time to win over the Italian, French, and British Governments to his Dardanelles plan, but Aehrenthal, under the pressure of the growing risk of the Serb designs on Bosnia and Herzegovina, took action on October 6. After this, though Isvolsky went personally to Paris and London, he was unable to obtain any satisfactory result. He complained that Aehrenthal had stolen a march on him, and the controversy between the two assumed an acute form and led to an estrangement between them that was to have grave

[1] Friedjung, pp. 218 sqq.

results. Isvolsky was irreconcilable ; the opportunity of a solution of the Dardanelles question had been spoilt and Russia had been left empty-handed, and for this Aehrenthal was to blame.

Nevertheless, it is very improbable, especially as regards Great Britain, that Russia would have secured the assent needed, even if Austria had not acted prematurely ; for the greatest importance was attached in London to the maintenance of Turkish sovereignty over the Dardanelles intact ; this was known in Paris, so that the French reply was cautious and non-committal.[1] The annexation of Bosnia and Herzegovina had merely made it easier to veto or put off the Russian schemes.

That solid fact, at all events, Isvolsky brought home from his journey—that Great Britain had vetoed his Dardanelles ambition. The effect of this on his plans was certainly more lasting even than his indignation against Aehrenthal. Together with the now complete estrangement between Russia and Austra-Hungary, it beckoned him, and Russian policy, over to a path which was exceedingly perilous for the peace of Europe. The attempt to find a solution of the question of the Straits through international agreements had failed. Was there, then, no other method remaining ? That was the reflection which came naturally from the rebuff experienced.

In the absence of sufficient reliable documentary material from this period it is, of course, quite impossible to follow up every link in the chain of Isvolsky's thought. None the less, certain facts are of pregnant significance and give ground for quite definite conjectures.

Three things are specially noteworthy. Shortly after the annexation of Bosnia and Herzegovina, Isvolsky as Foreign Minister made a speech in the Duma in which he advised the Balkan States to federate.[2] Immediately

[1] See pages 40 and 44 below, where Isvolsky, referring to the year 1908, speaks of French verbal assurances in regard to the future, but of " very definite objections " in England. This supersedes Friedjung's account. [2] Friedjung, ii. p. 264.

afterwards he associated himself with the Greater Serbia policy, which aimed at the expulsion of Austria from the Balkan peninsula.[1] And in December, 1909, a secret military convention was concluded between Bulgaria and Russia,[2] of which the fifth article laid down that

The realization of the high ideals of the Slav peoples in the Balkan peninsula, which are so close to Russia's heart, is only possible after a fortunate issue of the struggle of Russia with Germany and Austria-Hungary.

These words show very clearly the direction of the train of Isvolsky's thought.

Now, if the expression may be allowed, he was preparing a solution on the grand scale of the question of the Straits, after the small-scale one had come to grief. This solution aimed at securing Russian predominance, through the Balkan States, in the south-east corner of Europe, and, following that, domination of the Straits. That Constantinople remained always Isvolsky's ultimate objective is clear from the agreements concluded with Italy on October 24, 1909. Under these Italy promised to maintain a benevolent attitude should Russia decide to raise the question of the Straits, while Russia declared her acquiescence in Italian action against Tripoli.

Three obstacles lay directly in the way of this grand-scale solution. These were Turkey herself, Austria-Hungary, and the friend of both countries—Germany. There are indications that Isvolsky more than once considered the possibility of detaching Germany from Vienna ; this would, of course, have very greatly simplified the attainment of his purpose. But there were no prospects of success in this direction, and Germany, as the principal obstruction in his path, gradually became the actual point of application of the lever for the execution of his whole plan. From this point of view the entente with Great

---

[1] Friedjung, ii. p. 266.
[2] Ibid., p. 282. The text of the convention is given in translation in Bogitchevitch, *Causes of the War*, p. 89—George Allen & Unwin, 1920.

Britain and France gained steadily in importance, as it offered the means of shifting the Central European bulwark. These were without doubt the political considerations which produced the fatal association of Russia's ambitions in the Straits with the British tactics of *Einkreisung* (encirclement) against Germany and the French lust for *revanche* for Alsace-Lorraine. Three perils to peace directed their spear-points in unison against the heart of the Continent.

As already mentioned, during the Bosnian crisis Isvolsky found deaf ears turned in London to his Dardanelles project. The reason was, no doubt, the importance to vital British interests in Asia of giving support to Turkey, especially in Asia Minor. France was lukewarm from disinclination to work against her British ally. Was it not logical, from the Russian point of view, to begin work in Paris, to work against the opposition of Russia's friends at the point where it was weakest? Was there not reasonable hope of shifting the Central European block in the path to Constantinople by whipping up French vengefulness against Germany? Does not this logically follow from the facts we have been able to establish?

Isvolsky retired from office on September 28, 1910, and went to Paris as Russian ambassador. A letter in the Paris *Humanité* of January 17, 1924, from M. Ernest Judet, throws valuable light on this development :

He [Isvolsky] appeared to me at once in his true colours, which were only revealed to the world later—burning to transform the Franco-Russian alliance and to debase its original character, turning it from a purely defensive treaty into a weapon of offence. M. Isvolsky had come here as his country's representative to make soundings in France and to play as ambassador the part on which his heart was set. A former candidate for the post he held had pointed out to me the purpose which might have lain behind this choice of a fresh scene for Isvolsky's activity : Count Muraviev, who died later in Rome. After an ample breakfast in the Hotel Maurice, Count Muraviev said confidentially to me : " To bring the healing crisis, to direct European politics to a breach, can be more effectively achieved in Paris than St. Petersburg."

This witness confirms what we have suggested above. The healing crisis, the turning-point in European politics, was to be the smashing of the great barrier—Germany, Austria-Hungary, and Turkey—which blocked the way to Constantinople. And Paris was the best point from which to operate, since the assault could there be mobilized against the centre of the barrier, Germany.

Do these assumptions and the dictum of Muraviev correspond with the facts ? This can be determined only from Isvolsky's own papers of the period during which he was ambassador in Paris. These are now available.[1] Let us leave them to speak ; they will give us a glimpse into the hidden origins of the World War.

[1] *Der Diplomatische Schriftwechsel Iswolskis*, 1911–1914 (Isvolsky's diplomatic correspondence 1911–1914, from the Russian Secret State Archives). Edited for the German Foreign Office by Friedrich Stieve, four volumes, Deutsche Verlagsgesellschaft für Politik und Geschichte m. b. H., Berlin, 1924.

II

THE YEAR 1911

ISVOLSKY'S first reports date from January 1911; he had taken up his appointment as Russian Ambassador in Paris shortly before. His first impressions are not difficult to divine from his reports and letters—especially the latter, since they had not to pass under the eyes of a clerk or subordinate. The signs of distinct depression are unmistakable. Even in externals the situation was comfortless; his predecessor had left the embassy building in a state of neglect and disrepair. He pours out his troubles in a letter to Sazonov, his successor at the Foreign Ministry, on February 2 [13] : [1]

I am still busy with getting the Embassy into order; I found it in a fearful condition; the dirt and damage and disorder are beyond description; if I do not get some help at least from the Ministry Mme. Nelidova's management (she ordered and saw to everything) will have been a very expensive business for me. I have to provide fresh curtains and carpets for the whole of the lower floor, and must have the walls and friezes repainted—they have ten years' dirt on them; and these no doubt are the state rooms. There was hardly a stick of furniture, but I do not mind buying this as I can take it with me and sell it when I leave the Embassy. Argutinsky will be able to confirm the desolation I found. It is a shame to see the condition of our Embassy building and to compare it with those of other countries, even of the poor Italians, who have bought a house near us and are furnishing it anew. The offices of the Embassy, too, and of the Consulate-General, are indescribable. They will have to have another story added to make them respectable.

Even when one remembers that diplomats are often inclined to be critical of their predecessors, and of their

[1] The figures in brackets denote the numbers of the documents reproduced in *Der Diplomatische Schriftwechsel Iswolskis, 1911–1914* (Berlin, 1924, Deutsche Verlagsgesellschaft für Politik und Geschichte).

successors for that matter, and when one makes allowance
for Isvolsky's personal position—he was far from rich,
and his highly coloured account certainly aimed at softening the heart of the close-fisted authorities at home—even
so his complaint was probably both sincere and justified.

But in other matters he found equally little cause for
satisfaction. The whole political atmosphere in France
was uncongenial to him. The last months of 1910 had
brought hopes of lessening tension in Europe. In
November, Tsar Nicholas II had been engaged in conversations at Potsdam, with the result that a number of
agreements had been concluded with Germany, removing
many points of friction, especially in the East. Russia
was to be undisturbed in the exercise of her influence in
northern Persia, and would make no opposition to German
progress with the Bagdad Railway. This Potsdam meeting
awakened suspicion and mistrust in France, and the Paris
Press was constantly declaring that there had been a
political re-orientation in St. Petersburg to the disadvantage
of the Franco-Russian Alliance. On January 9, 1911 [4],
Isvolsky telegraphs to his Foreign Minister about this,
adding the news of a speech in Parliament by M. Pichon,
the French Foreign Minister, designed to counter the
rumours. Then follow on January 18 [6] a report and
several letters concerning this speech and the debate which
followed it :

These last words brought M. Pichon to the main point of his
speech, and raising his voice he emphatically reaffirmed the
inviolacy and the vitality of the Franco-Russian Alliance, which
was free of all aggressive aims and directed exclusively to the
maintenance of universal peace. . . . Summing up, the Minister
of Foreign Affairs rejected the contention that France was isolated,
and recounted a whole series of agreements which France had
concluded in recent years as offshoots of her alliance with Russia,
which forms the basis of her international relations. M. Pichon
expressed the intention of further developing these agreements
in the future, and remarked that the disharmony which unfortunately characterizes home policy must not be allowed to extend to
foreign policy. Reminding his hearers that diplomacy, to be equal

to its task, must have the support of adequate military force, he
concluded his speech with an appeal to the patriotism of the representatives of the nation for the strengthening of the military power
of France.

In the debate M. Jaurès, the Socialist leader, laid special
stress on Russia's omission to inform her ally beforehand
of her approach to Potsdam.   In connexion with this,
M. Pichon expressed to Isvolsky the desire " to be kept
informed of any substantial changes in the project of our
agreement with Germany, or any fresh questions touched
on in our conversations with Berlin " [8].

According to the Russian Ambassador, however, the
effort to silence criticism did not entirely succeed.   He
finds that there is still dissatisfaction, and describes his
difficulties in a letter to Sazonov on February 15, 1911 [19] :

I do not think that in my successive letters I have exaggerated
the excitement that has grown up here.   Since my arrival I have
met a large number of people in all grades of society, as I have
made a point of getting into touch not only with the leaders of
society but with the widest possible circles, political, literary,
scientific, and so on.   This is not only interesting but useful, for
it is simply incredible how ill-informed even serious people here are
concerning Russia and Russian affairs.

He suggests that the Russian Foreign Minister should
make a public statement, and advises him to come to
Paris as soon as he can for personal discussion :

Finally, I will mention one further way of convincing the public
that nothing can disturb the Franco-Russian military convention,
though I do not feel certain that the step is to be recommended.
Several people have been sent in secret to me to remind me that
there was a talk a few years ago of sending special French and
Russian military representatives to St. Petersburg and Paris, as
has been done between St. Petersburg and Berlin.

It is nothing unusual for a diplomat, on taking up a
new post abroad, to paint conditions in the gloomiest
possible colours, so as to be able in the course of time
gradually to report an improvement, not unconnected
with his own efforts.   Making all allowance for this,

Isvolsky's various communications of this period give the impression that France was indeed far from what he would have desired and expected. His report of February 5, 1911 [14], describing the attitude of public opinion in France towards " the discussion in the German Reichstag of the bill for a revised constitution for Alsace-Lorraine," concludes on a note of decided melancholy :

There has been no mistaking the very reserved tone of the French Press on this matter.   This is plain evidence of the development which has taken place in French opinion in recent decades in regard to the Alsace-Lorraine question.   The thought of the lost territories is still wounding to the national pride of the French, who would naturally welcome an opportunity to recover them ; nevertheless, as memories fade and the dream of the possibility of a *revanche* grows fainter among the new generations, the subject has lost some of its poignancy.

In such an atmosphere, what can be done to awaken at least sympathies for Russia ? That, as we have seen, is the question which at this period is constantly exercising Isvolsky. One important method is, of course, direct operation on public opinion. On February 8 [15] he writes to his Foreign Minister to recommend M. Reinach, the French Deputy, " who is going for a fortnight to St. Petersburg to gain acquaintance with our problems through his own observation." He is, " no doubt, of Jewish extraction," but must be cordially received because he " occupies a very important position in the political world here and is very influential, especially in matters affecting military questions and foreign politics." At the end of the note we hear the familiar plaint once more :

It is a matter of daily concern to me to note the astonishing ignorance of Russia and things Russian evinced by politicians here.   This in part explains the unconcealed consternation awakened in Paris by the Potsdam meeting and the fables of our military change of front.   In view of all this it seems to me very desirable that M. Reinach should gain a good impression from his journey to Russia.

The spectre of the Potsdam meeting and its implication of a measure of *rapprochement* between St. Petersburg and Berlin pursues Isvolsky for a considerable time. A new Ministry takes over the helm in France in March, and Isvolsky has to see the new Foreign Minister, M. Cruppi, in regard to railway construction in Turkey. Once more, according to his letter of March 16, 1911 [36], he has to explain that there is nothing in the Russian agreements with Germany either to injure French interests or to weaken the position of Great Britain in the East. And again, on April 13 [51], he reports the Opposition in the French Chamber as declaring that :

At Potsdam Russia has finally abandoned France and Great Britain and gone over to the camp of the Triple Alliance. In view of this and of the fickle nature of British friendship, France, they conclude, is in a dangerous and utterly helpless situation.

Thus Isvolsky, the founder of the Entente and the outright opponent of the Central Powers, found very real disappointments in his new sphere of action. He seems to have found the whole political atmosphere uncongenial and rather disconcerting. It must be remembered that at that time Socialism played a very important part in France, and that things were in consequence going on in France which must fill the Tsar's representative with mistrust. Again and again he deals in his reports with internal conditions in the country, and for all the objectivity which he is careful to preserve the reports frequently reveal unmistakable signs of amazement, mistrust, and impatience.

The first crisis which he witnesses is the fall of the Briand Cabinet at the end of February and beginning of March 1911. The Left was up in arms against this Government's attempted programme of " appeasement," and Briand, who in the autumn of 1910 had energetically suppressed the railway strike, had to give way before his opponents. In dejection Isvolsky reports on February 28 [21] :

It is impossible not to regret deeply that, however the present crisis may end, M. Pichon, tired out with the intensive work of

five years and discouraged by the continual attacks of the extreme
parties, is unlikely to retain the portfolio of Foreign Affairs. We
shall lose in him a sincere friend of Russia and a convinced supporter
of the closest union between Russia and France.

The new Monis Cabinet had a strong Radical infusion
[24] :

Its two characteristic features are an extreme anti-clericalism
and a disposition to satisfy the Socialist demands revealed in the
recent railway strike.

Only one ray of light is at first seen : the appointment
of Delcassé as Minister of the Navy. Delcassé had already
shown his anti-German bias, and quite recently, as chairman of the committee on the development of the French
Navy, had come forward with a comprehensive programme
of new construction. On March 3 [27] Isvolsky telegraphs
to Sazonov that Delcassé called on him and declared that :

His entry into the Ministry implied a guarantee of the special
concern which would be shown for France's military strength.
His first task was the provision of a strong fleet, and he hoped to
have at his disposal not later than August or September six new
armoured ships. He would answer for it that the new Cabinet
would redouble its efforts in regard to the land forces. While he
had no intention whatever of overstepping the limits of his com-
petence and awakening distrust in Germany, he assured me that
he was ready to use all means of setting up the most intimate
relations between France and Russia, and he asked me to lay at
the feet of H.M. the Tsar his feelings of sincere devotion for Russia.

A letter of March 14 [30] mentions that the general
opinion is that the new Navy Minister will undoubtedly
influence the Foreign Minister, M. Cruppi, the latter being
poorly versed in foreign affairs. This view of Cruppi is
frequently repeated, and there are several references to
the unfortunate French habit of appointing " civilian "
Ministers of War. Isvolsky looks with no favour on the
Parliamentary system.

Under the Monis Ministry, Isvolsky keeps a specially
sharp watch on the Socialist movement. On the occasion

of the debate in the Chamber concerning the workers dismissed on account of their participation in the railway strike already mentioned, he notes as a French peculiarity the tendency to assume that " the State, as the representative of the highest interests of the nation, has the right to intervene in the administration of undertakings of a public character as a sort of co-partner in the undertakings ; and that from this point of view it must bring its influence to bear in the direct settlement of the conditions of labour in this field." On the other hand, he sees just cause for the anxieties of financial circles, " which are finding expression in a considerable fall in railway stocks." It is certainly interesting to note how the diplomat from Tsarist Russia follows the first beginnings of modern State Socialism. He sees in it a symptom new to him, for which he is unable to feel any sympathy. He gives a very full description of the events of May Day, the day of the demonstrations of organized Labour in Paris. He praises the attitude of the Government, which, " despite the warning of the Socialist leader (Jaurès), whose political creed M. Monis actually shares, remained convinced of the necessity of taking energetic measures for the maintenance of order in the State, a necessity which exists under all conditions and all forms of government " [68]. With reference to the Socialist Congress at St. Quentin, he writes on May 11, 1911 [90] :

For the moment the political situation is very favourable for the Socialists. The Radicals have paved the way for them. The slackening of the power of the State in their hands, the strikes of postal workers and railwaymen, the mutual rivalries of the bourgeois parties, the prevailing tendency in elementary education—all this favours the aims of the Socialists.

Despite this, they are seriously incapacitated by internal disunion, which was clearly discernible even during the proceedings of this Congress. He concludes, with ironic satisfaction :

After the St. Quentin Congress the party of the " United " Socialists remains divided and weakened, and one may rest assured that its sympathy will not be so useful to the Monis Ministry as might have been supposed.

From further reports on matters of internal politics it is equally clear that Isvolsky has no love for the Left-wing Government and the forces behind it. When Monis comes to grief, Demidov, the ambassador's deputy, recounts once more, on June 22, the errors of the falling Cabinet ; in his view it lacked decision in home and knowledge in foreign affairs. On the same day [94] Demidov reports growing discontent in France, one result of which is a growth of royalist propaganda ; " in Conservative circles of the bourgeoisie there is evidence of increased activity in favour of a change from the hated demagogic regime."

One consideration was, of course, paramount in Isvolsky's attitude to the Left-wing parties in France ; his own words give frequent confirmation of it : the Socialists and Radical Socialists were no friends of France's alliance with Russia. They took every opportunity to represent co-operation with the reactionary Tsardom as a danger to their own country. They were thus of necessity opponents of Isvolsky.

The incomplete harmony between those in control in the two countries may be instanced from the negotiations between Cruppi and Isvolsky concerning railways in Asia Minor. France was busily trying to obtain concessions from Turkey for the construction of considerable lengths of line in Asia Minor. When the Russian Ambassador proposed to discuss this question, and that of the Bagdad Railway, the French Foreign Minister at first declared, on March 16, 1911 [36], that he had not had time to master the material, which was new to him. Ten days passed before the desired discussion could take place. Isvolsky then, according to his own account, declared " in very definite terms " that Russia could only oppose the construction of railways which would threaten her strategic position on the Caucasian frontier. "The construction of lines of this nature," he added [41], "would compel us to adopt very extensive military measures in the Caucasus, and this would weaken our position on our western front, which could not be a matter of indifference to France." To this plain language Cruppi at first replied evasively, but later, at Sazonov's request, a compromise was arrived at, Russia making concessions in regard to the zone west of the Samsun-Sivas line.

There was also difficulty with France in China. Leading French banks were associated with British, German, and American banks in the so-called Four-Power Consortium, which proposed to grant the Chinese Government a loan of 250 million francs. On March 15 Isvolsky asked for information as to the attitude of the Monis Cabinet on this question, pointing out that part of the loan was to be expended in Manchuria, where Russia had special interests, and recalling M. Pichon's assurance that the French Government would not allow quotations on the Paris bourse for Chinese loans with a political aim directed against Russia and Japan. A letter had already been sent on this matter by Sazonov, and Isvolsky had made inquiries of the French Foreign Minister concerning it. Cruppi's written answer [34] declares that special attention is being paid in France to ensuring "that the capital investments . . . in Manchuria are not applied under conditions which could give rise to objections on the part of Russia and Japan." On April 25 [60], Isvolsky transmits a Memorandum from the French Government communicating the terms of the loan, which had in the interim been arranged. Its purposes were, first, the reform of the currency of the Chinese Empire, and, secondly, industrial development in Manchuria. The memorandum states that it is unlikely that plans obnoxious to Russia will be put forward, and in any case there will be a period of six months during which any objections can be represented. On May 11 [69] Sazonov telegraphs that the French

chargé d'affaires has informed him that the Chinese
Government has asked the Four-Power Consortium for an
advance of £400,000 on account of the loan, and that he
has replied :

Russia is interested in an equal degree both in the definition
of the purpose and in the guarantees of the loan in question, since
part of it is to be expended on requirements in Manchuria, where
Russia has important special interests, and since, according to the
information available, certain Manchurian revenues are to serve
as guarantees. This opens the possibility of foreign intervention
in the internal affairs of this territory, and perhaps also of foreign
control of them.

This time Cruppi replies, as Isvolsky telegraphs on May 20,
that the British-German-American group has already
approved the advance in question, and that it is therefore
advisable that Russia should take energetic steps in Peking
and London. On July 20 Isvolsky reports that negotiations on the whole matter are being begun over again with
Cruppi's successor in the Foreign Ministry, De Selves, who
is trying to leave open until later the question of the
financing of Chinese undertakings in Manchuria. On this
Russia demands in a Memorandum that a special syndicate
shall be formed, with Russian, French, and Japanese
participation, for financial operations in those Chinese
territories in which Russian and Japanese rights and
interests predominate. Isvolsky regards this plan as
hardly practicable, and recommends " energetic diplomatic
pressure " on France. Towards the end of the year
M. Verstraete, the Chairman of Directors of the Russo-
Asiatic Bank, came to Paris to negotiate with the French
banks. Russia refused their proposal that Japan and
Russia should participate each to the extent of one-sixth
in the Syndicate, and made a counter-demand that the
French group should retire from the Syndicate. This
the French Government declared to be impossible, reaffirm-
ing at the same time that France would take care that the
activities of the Four-Power Consortium should not do
injury to Russian interests. Isvolsky now describes this

as "wholly inadequate," as Russia is determined to participate in the financing of China. In a letter of December 27 [175], Sazonov sums up Russia's position as follows :

We are working for the destruction of this Syndicate by inducing France to retire from it, and we regard our participation as only possible if it is so reconstructed that we have predominant influence north of the Great Wall.

The whole course of the negotiations briefly summarized above reveals a concealed and ultimately an open rivalry between the two allies, France and Russia, though it is not allowed to disturb their mutual friendship, since St. Petersburg stands in need of Paris as the main avenue for her ambitions. The events sketched are also a reminder that we are immersed in an epoch in which the Great Powers were busily engaged in competition for the domination of distant parts of the earth. The striving after political power was the obverse of the rivalry of commercial and financial interests.

In 1911 there occurred an event of the utmost importance in this precise respect, the second Morocco crisis. A division of French troops had been attacked, Colonel Marchand murdered, and a rising attempted against the Sultan Muley Hafid. These events were made the occasion of armed intervention, the investment of the Moorish capital, Fez, and finally, in open breach of the Act of Algeciras of 1905, the declaration of a protectorate over the greater part of Morocco. This was colonial conquest on the grand scale in close proximity to Europe, and, as we shall see, it entailed important consequences in the general political situation. It is interesting to watch the various phases of this development as reflected in Isvolsky's reports.

In one of the earliest communications on this subject (March 16), sent shortly after the decision of the Monis Cabinet to send reinforcements to Morocco and to give

financial support to the Sultan, Isvolsky reports [36] :
" In reply to my question whether difficulties were not
anticipated from Germany, M. Cruppi said that he thought
there was no occasion for concern in regard to this."
Spain also was aroused in March by the action of the Paris
Government, and put forward claims to Moroccan territory.
Sazonov commissioned Isvolsky to co-operate in the settlement of the differences between the two countries.   Isvolsky
replies on March 28 [43] :

In these disputes it is very difficult to discover who is right and
who is wrong.   In any case, in discussions with M. Cruppi I have
carefully avoided expressing any opinion as to this, and have
confined myself to pointing out the importance, in the general
political interest both of France and Russia, of giving Spain just
satisfaction.   Not to do so would be to throw her into the
arms of Germany and the Triple Alliance.   Since the period of
the Algeciras Conference Germany has been very cool and even
unfriendly towards Spain, who on her part has tended towards
friendship with the Triple Entente.   It would be very regrettable
if the matter now at issue were to lead Spain to begin to seek
support and protection from Germany.

In April the situation grows so acute that France announces
active steps for " the restoration of order " in Morocco.
Isvolsky's first question [53] as to this is " what position
the Governments which had signed the Act of Algeciras,
and especially Germany, had taken up in regard to this
communication."   The French Foreign Minister announces
the probability of the investment of Fez, and Isvolsky
writes on April 24, 1911 [58] :

According to M. Cruppi, Germany has as yet made no sign of
any intention to raise objections against any of the French measures,
or to demand compensation ; but the public here is seriously
concerned at the tone of the German Press.   In her action in
Morocco, France is stepping beyond the bounds of the Act of
Algeciras, and is placing the Morocco question on a completely
new footing.   The French Press, which is demanding that the
Government shall adopt energetic measures, is no longer relying
on the Act of Algeciras, but on the right and duty of France as a
sovereign Power to come to the aid of the French officers and of
the foreigners in Fez. . . .   Everything depends, of course, on the

attitude of Berlin and the extent to which the German Government will determine to take advantage of this state of affairs for its own ends.

Thus, from the very beginning Isvolsky has no word of disapproval for France's arbitrary and unquestionably illegal action, but merely fears that it may give Germany the opportunity of making claims on her own account. Of special significance in this regard is his letter of May 11 [72]. He declares that the situation into which France has come through the Moroccan adventure is very serious, " as the French Government has to reckon, not only with the delicate problem of the pacification of the Shereefian Empire, but still more with the very complicated diplomatic situation," and he continues :

In the latter regard I am very much afraid that M. Cruppi, who is entirely without diplomatic experience, is permitting himself a dangerous and insufficiently grounded optimism. You will no doubt have noticed that M. Cruppi's constant reply to my questions concerning the course of conversations in Berlin is that there is no sign of any inclination of the German Government to raise objections to France's action or to demand any sort of compensation. He is no less optimistic in his judgment of the Spanish attitude, though in this case he shows a certain irritation. The ground he gives for this optimism is that in view of France's fixed intention of not overstepping the limits set by the Act of Algeciras, and in any case of avoiding any permanent or even lengthy occupation of Fez, neither Germany nor Spain would have any occasion for protest or active intervention.

For my part I see the situation in a rather different light. Judging from the information which I have, the Berlin Cabinet has chosen a very strong and subtle position : as yet it has raised no objection to the French method of proceeding, but it is reserving its liberty to declare at any time that there has been an infringement of the Act of Algeciras. It is very probable that at the same time it is surreptitiously encouraging Spain and so preparing the ground for complications between the two Powers directly interested in Morocco. Thus German diplomacy is in control of the situation and is able suddenly to bring the Moroccan question to a head as may suit it in connexion either with developments on the spot or with the general course of Germany's home or foreign policy. It is here that the danger seems to me to lie, and M. Cruppi does not seem fully to appreciate it. The danger seems to me the more serious since M. Cruppi, so far as I am able to judge, has not a thoroughly clear and definite programme in regard to Morocco. His action is influenced by changing currents and conditions. From this point of view one can but regret the resignation of M. Pichon. M. Pichon is now being very sharply criticized by the Press here, but he knew exactly what he wanted in Morocco, and was not under the influence of the Chauvinists, who exist here as everywhere.

Finally I may mention that my apprehensions are fully shared by those Ambassadors here who are most open in their relations with me, namely, the representatives of Great Britain and Italy. It is interesting that Sir Francis Bertie is personally convinced that Germany is simply awaiting the most suitable moment for announcing that the Act of Algeciras has ceased to exist, and for then occupying one or two ports (including Mogador) on the Atlantic coast. This, in the words of the British Ambassador, would deal a distinct blow at the interests of Great Britain, since it would endanger her security of communication with South Africa.

A week later Isvolsky telegraphs [74] : " It seems to me very desirable that moderating influence should be brought to bear on the Madrid Cabinet, which is unquestionably being secretly worked upon by Germany." And after the news of the occupation of Fez has become public property, Germany still remaining inactive, he writes on May 24 [78] that he is still doubtful whether Cruppi's " optimism is justified." Now, he thinks, is beginning the still more delicate second phase of the French operations, and shortly after, on June 6, 1911 [89], he concludes a statement of the further programme of the Paris Government in Morocco with the words :

The whole question is simply whether its execution will be possible and whether it will not inveigle France into an obstinate struggle against Moroccan anarchy and ultimately into definite occupation of the whole country, thus leading to international complications.

It is easy enough to see from all this that the Moroccan crisis brought very little satisfaction to Isvolsky. His boundless distrust of Germany, to whose intrigues he attributes Madrid's protests, although it was obvious that Spain was acting in defence of very real interests of her own, is not the only explanation of his disapproval of Cruppi's "optimism." The ultimate ground of his dissatisfaction was the fear of a collision between Germany and France, which would have run counter to Russia's aspirations and aims of expansion, and would have robbed St. Petersburg of the opportunity of working for them. For it was plain to him from Sazonov's telegrams that the French adventure was being followed at home with merely a platonic goodwill, and that it was not felt that Russia was directly concerned. If war had actually broken out, Russia would have had, if possible, to play the part of a spectator, and French support would have been lost for Russia's aims, which extended to quite other spheres than North Africa.

The course of events was in any case largely producing this result. At the end of June Germany sent the gunboat *Panther* to Agadir, in order publicly to emphasize her demand for compensation for France's disguised annexation of Morocco, and Isvolsky had at least the politician's satisfaction of having prophesied correctly. In reporting a conversation with the new French Minister of Foreign Affairs, M. de Selves, he writes on July 19 [100]:

You may remember that two months ago I predicted to M. Cruppi the very complicated and dangerous situation which has now been created. M. Cruppi had shown unaccountable optimism, and had no belief in the possibility of any active intervention on the part of Germany; but, as was to be expected, Germany bided her time and has now come forward with her claims on the strength of the situation created by France, and especially by Spain. It is of no importance whatever whether or not there existed any secret understanding with Madrid. Cruppi's greatest mistake, to which I have more than once drawn attention, was his cavalier treatment of Spain's desires and interests. The result was that Spain played Germany's game and has made a thorough tangle of the unlucky Moroccan question. M. de Selves, with whom I have had two long conversations, and who, as my telegrams have shown, has been keeping me informed of the Berlin negotiations, does not deny his predecessor's mistakes.

With reference to the contemplated compensation nego-

tiations between Paris and Berlin, Isvolsky tries to fore-
stall any deal at the expense of Russian interests [100] :

> I have pointed out to de Selves that if France should propose
> to offer by way of compensation to dispense with the Danube-
> Adriatic line, the assent of Russia and Italy will first be required.
> De Selves assured me that he had no such purpose, and also that
> up to the present Germany had asked for no compensation except
> in the Congo. M. Klotz, the Minister of Finance, declared to me
> that the French Government would under no circumstances agree
> to Germany's compensation taking the form of the admission of
> German State securities to quotation on the Paris Bourse.

For the rest, the conversations between Herr Kiderlen-
Wächter, the German Secretary of State, and M. Cambon,
the French ambassador in Berlin, concerning the indemni-
fication of Germany by concessions in the Congo, increase
rather than abate Isvolsky's pessimism. It becomes his
duty to report to St. Petersburg each stage reached in
these conversations, and he does not fail to paint them in
the blackest possible colours. Again and again he suspects
dark German designs, and anticipates still more energetic
proceedings on Kiderlen's part, or the occupation of Agadir
and parts of Morocco. When, in the middle of August,
the negotiations come to a standstill, he becomes extremely
agitated, and in a letter of August 19 [113] to M. Neratov,
the acting Russian Foreign Minister, he tells him that he is
asking M. Kokovtsov, the Prime Minister and Minister of
Finance, "for the moment quite privately," to provide
him,

> in view of the approaching international crisis, with adequate
> material means of influencing the Press here [in France]. It has
> only been with the very greatest efforts that I have just succeeded
> in preventing misinterpretation of the signing of the treaty with
> Germany concerning Persia, which has just taken place at this
> critical moment. But this was purely a chance success, and it
> would be of the utmost service to have a permanent and reliable
> means of giving the desired direction to the most important organs
> here, which are almost all only accessible to " clinking " arguments.
> One need only mention the important part played at the time of
> the Bosnian crisis by Count Khevenhüller's discreet distribution
> of Austrian money among the French Press. I hope that

M. Kokovtsov will let me know whether he regards my request
at the present moment as justified as an exceptional case.   In
this case I will not fail to send him my remarks as to the sums
needed and the method of their application.   If you regard my
request as justified, may I hope that you will not refuse to give
it your support with M. Kokovtsov.   I should like to ask you to
let me know by telegraph whether the Minister of Finance concurs
in principle or not, so that I may send the necessary detailed
information by the next courier.

This first evidence in the records of a proposal from
Isvolsky to bribe the Paris Press, in order to work upon
public opinion in Russia's interest, is notable as coming
at a moment when the originator of the idea believed in
the probability of an outbreak of war between France
and Germany. " God grant," he writes on August 31,
1911 [116], " that my pessimism be not justified by events,
for a failure of the Berlin negotiations would certainly
bring a dangerous crisis." We may add a crisis the
prospect of which filled Isvolsky with dismay because
Russia would not be concerned in it, and might therefore
find to her discomfiture that France would possibly take
a line of her own.   It was naturally very inconvenient in
his view that at that very moment the treaty between
Russia and Germany concerning Persia should be signed,
as it might give rise to the idea that St. Petersburg and
Berlin stood closer together at the moment than St.
Petersburg and Paris.   Clinking arguments must at least
bring the aid of the French Press in obviating this
unfortunate impression.

It is unnecessary to follow up every step of the strayings
of Isvolsky's pessimism.   On this occasion he was quite
wrong, and the judgment of the situation in St. Petersburg
was much cooler and better.   From the beginning of the
crisis St. Petersburg had had a definite plan, and had
followed it circumspectly but with decision.   Precisely
as in Germany, it was proposed to profit by the French
campaign in Morocco, but unlike Berlin the work went on
behind the scenes and more discreetly.   It was prepared for

by giving ostentatious evidence of entire readiness to give diplomatic support to the French adventure. After the occupation of Fez the Russian ambassador in Berlin was instructed to declare there [65] " that the Tsar's Government regarded France's action as entirely unobjectionable." And on May 5, 1911 [67], Isvolsky was requested to lay stress in Paris on " the fortunate result of the friendly Russian intervention in Berlin, which has produced a completely satisfactory German reply." Isvolsky was, of course, not to omit " to express confidence that should occasion occur we (that is, the Russians) should enjoy similar support from France."

As the negotiations between Paris and Berlin approached their conclusion, there came a repetition of this friendly hint. On the same day, October 5, on which the Russian embassy in Paris reported a fresh postponement of the negotiations between Cambon and Kiderlen, Neratov, the acting Russian Foreign Minister, sent the following letter [132] to Isvolsky :

There is no longer any doubt that the Franco-German conversations on Morocco are slowly approaching a successful conclusion. The agreement will apparently be in such a form that the other Powers interested in the questions touched upon in the conversations will only be able to " adhere " to the decisions come to and to declare their assent.

As we are allied with France and our relations with her are precisely defined, and as we are very little interested in North-West Africa, it is clear that we shall agree in advance to whatever France decides in these negotiations with Germany. But this, it seems to me, gives us just ground for hoping that France will feel morally bound to pay us back in the same coin should occasion arise, and to dispense in advance with opposition or intervention in such questions as are of minor interest to France but of importance to us. To this class belong two questions of a quite sharply defined character, that of the Straits and that of Manchuria.

We are far from desiring to tie France down in regard to the Straits by any concrete promise for any definite future date, but we think the time has come to assure ourselves of the agreement of our Ally not to oppose our standpoint or any steps we may take at the moment when we consider it necessary to enter upon definite conversations and perhaps even actions affecting our problems.

I assume that the agreement concerning the Straits might be given the form of letters between the two Foreign Ministers in some such form as the enclosed draft, following the lines of the declarations exchanged with Italy at Racconigi, which have just had to be formulated with the greatest precision.

With reference to the matter of Manchuria, I will write fully in a separate communication of to-day's date.

Will you please take the first opportunity of acquainting the Government of the Republic with our expectations as laid down above, and inform me in due course by telegraph of the result of your conversation on this matter.

To understand this Russian step, especially in regard to the Straits, it must be borne in mind that at about the same time another State had taken decided action on the strength of France's Moroccan adventure. On September 28 Italy addressed an ultimatum to Turkey demanding the cession of the Tripolitan peninsula. We know from the French Yellow Book concerning the Franco-Italian treaties of 1901–2, that in 1901 the two countries had defined the limits of their spheres of influence in the Mediterranean, Morocco being reserved to France and Tripoli to Italy. Now that Paris had taken action, that of Italy followed automatically. The Russian Government was informed before September 28, 1911, of the intentions of the Italian Cabinet, for two letters from Isvolsky, both dated September 26, and written in reply to a communication from Sazonov, deal with this matter. In the second [125] we read :

To begin with, you will, of course, remember that under the secret treaty concluded at Racconigi we bound ourselves to place no obstacle in the way of Italy's freedom of action in Tripoli, Italy promising on her part to take up an analogous attitude in regard to our policy in the Straits. It seems to me, therefore, that we are unable in any case to make objections of principle to the Italian intervention, and that the most that we can do is to contend that Italy has not chosen the right moment for her enterprise. Should it prove possible to localize the Italo-Turkish conflict over Tripoli, it must be confessed that the event would have undeniable advantages for us ; it would place Germany and the whole Triple Alliance in a particularly difficult position, and give Turkey visible evidence of the error of her policy of distrust towards ourselves and the Powers of the Triple Entente.

Isvolsky's proposal to prepare to open the question of the Straits with Italy finds approval in St. Petersburg, for he writes as follows on October 9 [133] to Neratov on his conversations with Signor Tittoni, the Italian ambassador in Paris :

I am very pleased that my idea of establishing Italy's obligations in regard to the Straits has met with your sympathy. Immediately after receiving your letter, I asked Signor Tittoni to enter into concrete discussions, and I have passed to him the draft which you elaborated of a letter from the Italian Minister of Foreign Affairs to the Russian Foreign Minister. Signor Tittoni has not only agreed with the procedure which you proposed, but has expressed to me his view that the draft seems perfectly acceptable, and that if he were Foreign Minister he would not hesitate to sign it. He wrote a draft letter at my dictation, and promised either himself to take it to Rome or to send it thither by a courier. He prefers the former method, as it would give him the opportunity to place in person before the King and Signori Giolitti and San Giuliano the considerations which argue for compliance with our desire. The date of his journey to Rome depends on the end of the Tripolitan crisis. If the crisis drags on, he will state the case for compliance by letter. In any case he is sure of the assent of the King and his Ministers.

Russia's parallel step with the French Government was naturally taken in close conjunction with this, though, as we see, it had undoubtedly been longer under consideration. Each step involved the next, and the Powers were drawn into the realization of long-nursed ambitions. The French annexation of Morocco had set in motion the whole perilous system of the secret expansionist ambitions of the Powers close to the borders of the European continent. This was undeniably its fatal effect on the course of European history in the final years before the World War. Already Isvolsky mentions in his letters, in connexion with Italy's aggression against Turkey, the possibility of unrest in the Balkans. Germany, with her demands for compensation in the Congo, remained some distance behind the rest, for this was a question of purely colonial acquisitions in the far interior of Africa. The noise of her clumsy entry on the scene, however, as often before, drew upon her much more indignation and disapproval from the rest of the world than did the rapid and decided action of France and Italy, or the diplomatic intrigues of Russia. But for the peace of the world it was the action of the latter States which was the real peril, for it brought the danger of war right into the foreground.

Let us, however, return to Russia's negotiations with France concerning the Straits and Manchuria. They were taken up first by Tcharykov, the Russian representative in Constantinople, who, on instructions from his Government, saw M. Bompard, the French ambassador in that city. There followed a conversation between M. Neratov, the acting Russian Foreign Minister, and M. Panafieu, the French chargé d'affaires. On the same date, October 11, 1911, Isvolsky set to work. In an interview with de Selves he began by reminding him of Russia's unchangingly friendly attitude towards every step taken by France in the Moroccan affair, and proceeded then to discuss the question of the Straits. He had no knowledge, he said, of when it would become possible to open this question, but he had instructions to draw the attention of the French Government to it without delay. We may best follow the argument from Isvolsky's own report [149] :

Recently, I said to him [de Selves], there have been very substantial political changes in Europe, and especially in the Mediterranean. France is setting up her rule over Morocco ; Italy is acquiring Tripoli and Cyrenaica ; Great Britain is consolidating her position in Egypt, and, as is evident from the arrangement for Egyptian neutrality during the Italo-Turkish War, is indifferent to any consideration of the juridical ties of that country with the Ottoman Empire. So far as we are concerned, while we are not immediately interested in these questions, we are, in consonance with the general character of our relations with France, Great Britain, and Italy, showing entire complaisance in face of all these movements, and are, in addition, making the most disinterested efforts to restrain the Balkan States from warlike activities. But we are bound also to have regard to our own interests, and to our liberation from restrictions which were imposed on us under quite different circumstances and are now completely out of date. Three years ago we received from France, on the occasion of the crisis produced by the annexation of Bosnia and Herzegovina, the most definite assurances that we might count on her sympathy in the question of the Straits. At that time, however, we voluntarily abstained from opening this question, in order not to complicate the situation and endanger the general peace. We do not, of course, for one moment doubt that we are sure also of France's sympathy in this matter in the future, all the more since the appearance of our Black Sea Fleet in the Mediterranean could but strengthen the position of the French naval forces in those waters. But, in view of the formal changes which are now taking place in this field, it is necessary for us to seek an equally formal confirmation of our rights and interests. We hope, accordingly, that the French Government will not refuse to define its position in some way in regard to the measures which we shall consider it necessary sooner or later to adopt in regard to the Straits and the adjacent territories.

Isvolsky went, he says, with about equal thoroughness into Russia's desires " in regard to railways in Asiatic Turkey, her rights in the Eastern Chinese railway question, the capitulations in Manchuria, the question of Mongolia and Chinese Turkestan, and, finally, the Chinese loan." Thus it was a respectable bundle of claims that he opened before Russia's ally as her price for support in Morocco. De Selves expressed his readiness to enter into the frankest discussion of these questions.

In a separate letter to Neratov on the following day [141], Isvolsky reminds him of the former papers, dating from his own period of office in the Foreign Ministry, concerning the Straits question, the question in which he is primarily interested :

You will, of course, have dug out from the archives what has already passed in this matter. There have twice been conversations with Great Britain, the first in Benckendorff's time, and the second on the occasion of my stay in London in the autumn of 1908 (Bosnian crisis). I believe I turned over all the papers to you, but you may find them in the secret archives in Savinsky's care. In London the British authorities raised very definite objections and showed a good deal of reluctance, but on the whole the matter was advanced a step. I remember noting a German statement of the utmost importance indicating assent to our plans, but I have completely forgotten the form and the occasion of this statement ; it may even have been contained in a letter or telegram from

Emperor William to the Tsar. These papers also are probably with the rest of the Straits papers.

I should like also to point out that it is of great importance to associate the coastal States, Roumania and Bulgaria, with the right of passage through the Straits.

On the whole he is quite taken with the plan which is being pursued in St. Petersburg, and only remarks regretfully that " M. de Selves is very ill-informed on all these questions, and, apart from this, is entirely taken up with the Morocco and Congo questions." Incidentally he uses the opportunity to renew his request for funds for bribing the French Press [141] :

If we definitely decide now to raise the question of the Straits, it is very important to have " a good Press " here. Unfortunately I am still deprived of the principal weapon for assuring this. Nothing has come of my urgent requests to be furnished with special funds for the Press. I shall of course do my utmost, but this is precisely one of those questions in which public opinion is traditionally against us.

Further conversations with de Selves reveal a certain anxiety on the French side as to the British attitude in the matter. The Foreign Minister had " no objection at all to offer either as to the substance or the timeliness of the proposed claim in regard to the Straits. . . . The only aspect of the question which seemed to disturb him was the probable attitude of Great Britain " [147]. The effort is, therefore, made to ascertain Sir Edward Grey's opinion. Still no progress is made in the negotiations, and Isvolsky takes advantage of the day on which the Franco-German agreement concerning Morocco and the Congo is signed, November 4, 1911, to send a letter [154] to de Selves repeating in writing the various requests of his Government and concluding as follows :

Summing up what I have written above, I venture once more to express the conviction that at the moment when France, Russia's friend and ally, is proceeding to establish her position in North Africa on a new and firm basis, the French Government, which has at all times accorded to the Tsar's Cabinet its sincerest diplomatic support, is prepared on its part to assure us of its recognition of our freedom of action in the sphere of the Straits and in North China, and will not deny us its assent to the measures which we may find ourselves in a position to adopt to safeguard our interests and establish our position in those territories.

The reply is some time coming. On November 23 [158] Isvolsky suspects " that the French Government will fight shy of committing itself unconditionally to a recognition of our complete freedom of action in the Straits, and that it will confine itself at first to some indefinite formula and ask us to state our desires in more precise form." And in another letter of the same day [150] we read :

It was clear from what M. Louis [1] said to me that there is a good deal of hesitation here to give an undertaking to support us in the Straits in the terms used in the latter part of my letter. M. Georges Louis is mainly concerned with the indefiniteness of the expression " freedom of action." He wanted to know definitely what we are thinking of doing in regard to the Straits, and what solution we are aiming at in the questions connected therewith.

I replied that I had used that expression precisely on account of its indefiniteness, since it is impossible at the moment to foresee what turn the question of the Straits may take. " It is to Russia's interest," I said to him, " to maintain the existence of the Turkish Empire as long as possible, but on the proviso that we are liberated from obsolete restrictions, incompatible with our interests and our dignity. Accordingly we are striving primarily for a friendly understanding with the Turkish Government on this question. Should, however, such an understanding prove unattainable, or should Turkish rule in Europe be liquidated, our standpoint in the question of the Straits would naturally change. Just as France has declared to us this summer that she cannot permit the establishment of any foreign Power in Morocco, so we are bound on our part to inform France that Russia cannot allow the Straits to pass into other than Russia's own hands. We are, needless to say, convinced in advance that in both cases we shall meet with full sympathy and support on the part of our ally, France. But it is of great importance to us to have definite confirmation of the attitude of the French Government in this question. So also with the questions connected with North China. My letters give details of some of the measures which we shall in all probability have to adopt sooner or later to consolidate our position in these countries.

[1] M. Georges Louis, French Ambassador in St. Petersburg, was at this time working at the Quai d'Orsay, and temporarily in charge of the principal questions of foreign policy.

But it is clear that this does not exhaust all the combinations and eventualities that may arise in the course of time. At the moment it is impossible to foresee how present events in China will develop. If the period of the final dissolution of the Chinese Empire is beginning, we may find ourselves compelled to extend our programme. The same result might follow from active intervention by Japan, with whom we have concluded a treaty defining our respective spheres of influence in Manchuria. In all these cases we are similarly entitled to expect sympathy and diplomatic support from our Ally."

In any case, Louis holds out the prospect of an early reply. But further weeks still pass before it arrives. At last, on January 4, 1912, de Selves sends the following note [185] :

Your Excellency was pleased to express on November 4, in the name and on the authority of the Russian Government, the conviction that France would certainly be prepared to show to Russia, in certain questions which are of specially close concern to our Ally, the same wide measure of indulgence which the Russian Government has shown on the occasion of the preliminary negotiations and the recent conclusion of the Morocco Treaty.

The questions which you had specially in view in your communication mentioned above refer, in Europe, to the regime of the Straits, and in Asia to the position of Russia in the northern territories of the Chinese Empire.

I am glad to be able to confirm anew, quite generally, to Your Excellency the declarations made by the French Government on the occasion of the events of 1908, which were concerned with the satisfaction which the Russian Government might perhaps find itself called upon to demand in the question of the Bosphorus and the Dardanelles. The French Government declares its readiness to exchange views with the Russian Government on this question, should fresh circumstances make an examination of the question of the Straits necessary.

As regards Russia's interests in North China, Your Excellency has been pleased to recall that the French Government has constantly declared its intention to support Russia in the defence of her interests in Manchuria, and has given concrete evidence of its goodwill in this regard in its recent prohibition of the quotation of the Chinese 250 million loan so long as Article 16 of the Treaty, which concerns Manchuria, is not deleted and revised in the sense of the Russian demands.

The French Government's support, thus confirmed, of all Russia's rights and legitimate interests in North China extends not only to Northern Manchuria, but also to Mongolia and Chinese Turkestan :

the policy which we have consistently followed in this region is a sure guarantee that we shall also continue it in future in these regions of special importance to our Ally.

In a covering letter of January 11 [184], Isvolsky comments :

A careful consideration of this letter will show, I think, that it is not without value and importance. Its first section contains, in the form of a reiteration, the recognition of the equivalence of our attitude towards France's interests in the Morocco question with that of France towards our interests in the questions of the Straits and North China. Moreover, M. de Selves formally confirms the assurances which the French Government gave us in 1908 in regard to the Straits. These assurances, it will be remembered, were not set down in writing at the time, but merely given in the form of promises, in quite general terms, that France would support our policy in the Bosphorus and Dardanelles. Further, M. de Selves' expression of readiness to enter into an exchange of views with us concerning the Straits gives us the opportunity, as time goes on, to secure a more detailed clearing up of this question. Should you disagree with my view and regard M. de Selves' letter as inadequate for our purposes, it is possible to treat my whole correspondence with the French Minister of Foreign Affairs as of a merely preparatory character and to initiate more formal and thorough-going negotiations.

There is no evidence in the documents as yet available that the Russian Government took any further step in the question of the Straits. It may therefore be assumed that St. Petersburg also was satisfied for the time being with the attitude of the French Government. France had not admitted without further ado her Ally's complete freedom of action ; she dared not adopt an attitude so directly aimed against Turkey, not only on account of Great Britain, but because in undertaking a protectorate over Morocco it seemed a duty to consider the feelings of the Mohammedan world. But Paris was well aware of Russia's policy. The " Notes " of the Russian Foreign Ministry [182] provide a second record of Isvolsky's declaration that " Russia cannot allow the Straits to pass into other hands than her own." Thus de Selves' note amounted to a valuable assurance, since it held out the prospect of a friendly exchange of views " should fresh circumstances make an examination of the question of the Straits necessary " [182], in other words when Russia considered that the moment had come to stretch out her hand for the object of her desire. This had certainly added to the store of inflammable matter glowing beneath the soil of Europe.

It is easy to see that Isvolsky's part in the events described was no small one. But even in these last months of feverish activity he breaks out continually into expressions of dissatisfaction. De Selves especially, as Foreign Minister in the Caillaux Cabinet, the third French Ministry of 1911, is the cause of continual complaints. At the end of December, when this Cabinet in turn begins to totter, Isvolsky declares [177] that " it is impossible not to want to see at the head of affairs in the Quai d'Orsay a personality better acquainted with its business than this unfortunate de Selves." But it may safely be concluded once more that the real trouble was not so much the inexperience of the French Ministers as the repeated realization of the gulf between French policy at this time and Russia's aims and ambitions.

Isvolsky's policy emerges plainly enough from various passages in his letters and reports : on the negative side it aimed primarily at the disastrous segregation in Europe of two main groups, the Triple Entente and the Alliance. The smallest contribution to ending this fatally perilous division, which already contained the seed of possible conflict, drives him into extreme agitation. On April 25, 1911 [63], he reports that he has been bitterly reproaching M. Cruppi for the loan just granted in France to the city of Budapest :

I made no secret of the fact that the granting of a loan to the Hungarian capital by French banks would be bound to create an extremely painful impression in Russia, as this loan would certainly be regarded as the prelude to the financing of further Hungarian loans.

To make due impression on M. Cruppi I made certain general observations arising out of this special case : " Latterly," I said, " I have more than once had occasion to draw the attention of the French Government to the severe injury which might result to Russia's most vital interests from certain financial enterprises planned by French banks. Owing to her enormous extent and the peculiarities of her geographical situation, Russia is vulnerable at very many points in her periphery, and cannot be equally strong on all fronts. Such enterprises as the Chinchou–Aigun railway or the network of railways in Asia Minor would burden us with immense expenditure on the strengthening of our Asiatic frontiers in those regions, and this would weaken our military position on our western frontier, to the detriment of the common interests of France and Russia. Every loan granted to Austria-Hungary, or even simply to Hungary, would similarly weaken the position of Russia, and consequently also of the " Dual Alliance." It is, moreover, exceedingly dangerous to harbour the illusion, prevalent here, that Hungary might form a counterbalance to set against German influence ; the last Bosnian crisis showed that at the critical moment Hungary will always range herself with Austria and Germany. Only recently we were hearing in the Chamber an eloquent appeal from M. Ribot urging increased unity and consistency in the policy of the Powers of the Triple Entente, and M. Cruppi himself has advocated making effective and, one might almost say, daily use of this political combination. It seems to me that the question of foreign loans and financial enterprises is precisely one of those in which the community of the high political interests of Russia and France needs the most emphatic assertion, and it would be exceedingly regrettable if the concern of French financiers for their personal profit were to gain the upper hand over the general aims of the two allied Powers

Towards the end of 1911 Isvolsky has even to fight against the " danger " of a loan to Austria, whose alleged intentions towards Serbia had shortly before, on November 23, been the subject of exceedingly tendencious treatment in his report [169] of a conversation with M. Milovanovitch, the Serbian Premier, at the time of the Serbian King's visit to Paris. On December 28 [176] he telegraphs :

A few days ago I had a serious talk with Louis about the proposed Austrian loan ; Demidov will take you the report of this to-morrow. On my instigation a newspaper campaign is already being carried on against it, beginning with an article by Chéradame in the *Petit Journal* of December 26. It is very desirable that the Russian papers should give attention to this question.

We saw at the beginning of this chapter how upset Isvolsky was, and was bound to be, at the Potsdam meeting, in the first days of his stay in Paris, between the Tsar and Emperor William. Equally out of harmony with his programme was the signing of the Russo-German treaty in Persia ; it had the appearance of a bridging of the gulf between the two Powers. While he dared not directly criticize his own Government, he gave very free expression in a letter to Neratov on August 17, 1911 [111], of his fears as to the repercussion of the event in France :

Hearty thanks for your interesting letter of July 27. The news of the impending signature of the treaty with Germany concerning Persia was especially valuable to me, for there is undoubtedly a danger of a fresh Press campaign and of fresh attempts to awaken mistrust here in regard to our policy. I have hastened accordingly to take preparatory measures, without losing a moment's time, and they have had their result in the enclosed articles in the *Matin* and *Journal des Débats*. I hope you will not blame me for having made this matter public ; for if the news of the signing of the treaty had come upon the public here as an unexpected event the results might have been most unfortunate. You know the difficulties of dealing with the Press here, especially when I am without the means for effective operation. I do not know whether I shall succeed in inspiring the needed policy in the other influential papers, especially the *Temps*, in which M. Tardieu is beyond question agitating against our interests.

How Isvolsky hoped to manage matters may be seen from a letter of April 13, 1911 [51], to Sazonov concerning the debate in the Chamber, which has already been mentioned, over the Potsdam meeting. He deals at length with two speeches of M. Ribot, " the founder of the Franco-Russian Alliance " :

They are a sort of synthesis of the whole of the last twenty years of French policy. Delivered with an extraordinary power of conviction, they made an encouraging impression and unquestionably contributed to an issue of the debate favourable to the Government. The public was pleased not only by the note of optimism which was struck throughout, but by the gentleness and good humour of M. Ribot's criticism of the policy of M. Cruppi's predecessors. The gist of his speeches was as follows : Yes, the Alliance between France and Russia is firm and unshakable, and the Entente Cordiale with Great Britain is to be relied on ; but in recent years French diplomacy has failed to draw adequate advantage from Alliance and Entente, either for France's own interests or for the general interests of the group of Powers associated in this union. Closer contact between the various members of the Triple Entente is indispensable, and what is necessary above all is a preparatory, almost daily examination of the various questions of the day, and of the various possibilities which they unfold.

I was able to satisfy myself that M. Ribot's ideas are shared by the most serious and influential personalities in France, and I venture to assume that they also deserve sincere sympathy and assistance on our part. At the moment when questions of such first-rate importance for us are arising, as the granting of important financial assistance to Turkey, and the development of her strategic network of railways, it is of the greatest importance to us that France shall undertake nothing without first coming to a precise agreement with us. I shall not fail to take advantage of the prevailing atmosphere to suggest to the French Government the necessity of the closest solidarity with us in all these and other matters of interest to us.

It is not Ribot but Isvolsky himself who confesses here his most intimate views, and recommends them to the serious attention of St. Petersburg. " The closest solidarity " between the Allies and the virtual daily reaffirmation of the Alliance—that is his ideal. And though at times reality is far from corresponding with it, he keeps watch to see at least that the possibility of attaining it is preserved. Interesting evidence of this is provided by the documents concerning the British-Russian conflict in Persia in December 1911.[1]

Under an agreement made in 1907 between Great Britain and Russia, Persia was divided into three zones, the northern being recognized as Russia's sphere of interest, and the southern Britain's. It was mutually agreed to respect Persia's independence ; the British attached special importance to this as they counted on so keeping other Powers, especially Germany and Turkey, at a distance. As time went on, however, Russia worked towards the conversion of her sphere into a sort of vassal State, with

[1] Compare B. von Siebert, *Entente Diplomacy and the World. Matrix of the History of the World*, pp. 95 sqq.

the result that Great Britain was more and more alienated. In November 1911 matters came to a head between the Russian consul-general in Teheran and Mr. Shuster, the American financial adviser to the Persian Government, with reference to a confiscation of properties of the ex-Shah Mohammed Ali. Advantage was taken of this collision in St. Petersburg, in Russia's familiar style, to threaten to March on Teheran. In vain did Benckendorff, the Russian ambassador in London, warn his Government that the results would be gravely to strain British-Russian relations. " If an end comes to our common action in Persia, this will inevitably mean the end of the Entente." So he telegraphs on December 2. But St. Petersburg was not to be deterred. At this moment Sazonov, the Foreign Minister, was in Paris. On December 5 he received a telegram [165] from Neratov, the temporary occupant of his office, stating that the dispatch of troops to Teheran was exceedingly likely. Two further telegrams of December 5 and 6 [166-7] show increasing tension with London. At this stage Isvolsky intervenes, with a letter to Neratov on December 7 [168] :

S. D. Sazonov arrived yesterday ; he looks well and cheerful. He expects to leave for St. Petersburg on Sunday evening. He has sent for Count Benckendorff, and the three of us are noting and discussing all your telegrams about Persia. I must not conceal from you that the affair fills me with grave anxiety as to the future of our co-operation with Great Britain, and that this makes me very concerned and disturbed. The events of the past summer have shown to the full the value of the Triple Entente as an important factor in the maintenance of peace and of equilibrium in Europe. For there can now be no doubt, after Sir Edward Grey's speech and Bethmann-Hollweg's weak reply, that Germany only drew back from her intention of gaining a footing in Morocco because it meant coming into conflict with France, Great Britain, and ourselves. I quite realize the difficulty of bringing our action in Persia at the present moment into line with Great Britain's desires. But none the less I urge you not to lose sight of the incalculable consequences which would follow on a break with Great Britain in Persian affairs. I think Great Britain will go a very long way with us, but it is dangerous to stretch the bow too tight. Matters will be put to the crucial test if we march into

Teheran.   In this case will it be possible to continue to reconcile
our demands and actions with the British ?   In this connexion
your telegram of yesterday is rather obscure, not to say incon-
sistent.   You begin by saying that we shall put forward no claims
of a general nature without prior agreement with Great Britain ;
at the end you assume that if our troops enter Teheran the result
will probably be the dissolution of Parliament, the appointment
of a new Government, and so on.   It is clear that such measures, if
taken by us off our own bat, would end the British-Russian Entente,
and this, I repeat once more, would have incalculable results
throughout the whole field of European politics.

I have just come from breakfast at the Palais d'Elysée with the
President of the Republic and MM. Caillaux and de Selves.   All
three are very concerned at the possibility of an issue of this sort,
which would gravely affect France's international position.

We have no precise news of what subsequently happened.
What is certain, however, is that no breach came between
Russia and Great Britain ;   Russia must, therefore, have
shrunk from overstretching the bow.   In this respect, at
all events, Isvolsky gained his object, and the faithful
guardian of the Entente system succeeded in contributing
by his advice to the averting of a very grave crisis.

We have been able to show above that he had before
him as the foremost aim of his policy an uninterrupted
activity of this Entente system, a common, "almost
daily examination of the questions of the day and of
possible eventualities."   Did this refer only to the field of
diplomatic work, or did he envisage the ultimate consequences which might ensue from the complete unity of
action between the three Powers—Russia, France, and Great
Britain—amid the growing unrest close around Europe ?
In other words, was he occupied with the idea of a war of
the Entente against the Central Powers ?   At the back of
his thoughts and calculations he quite certainly was.
Everything which lay in the direction of such a possibility arouses his keen interest.   Let us take a few specially
important instances.

On February 2, 1911, he gives a detailed report [11] of
the new shipbuilding programme of the French Admiralty,
providing for new construction of 16 battleships, 6 cruisers,

20 torpedo-boat destroyers, and 50 submarines over a period of ten years. He adds :

In general there are reasons to assume that, in the event of a conflict between the Powers of the Triple Alliance and Great Britain and France, the British naval forces will have principally to fight against the German fleet in the North Sea, while the French will probably have the task of dealing in the Mediterranean with Germany's two Allies.

Of great interest is a letter of the same day [12] to Sazonov, dealing with the question of the fortification of Flushing, then being undertaken by the Dutch. The principal passage runs as follows :

From various conversations which I have had with M. Pichon on the above question, I have gained the impression that he views it quite calmly and has no desire to attach excessive importance to it. He has not yet had an opportunity of thoroughly studying the juridical side of the question, which he has referred for examination to experts in international law ; but his personal feeling is that Holland has an incontestable right to fortify the estuary of the Scheldt ; this seems to him to be confirmed by the fact that fortifications exist already, and are merely being converted and extended at present. On the other hand, apparently neither M. Pichon nor the French Government in general have any doubt that the idea of the construction of these fortifications was suggested to Holland by Germany, and that the Dutch Government is acting, if not under a direct treaty, in any case under the pressure of fear for the independence of Holland in the event of a European war. If, despite this conviction, M. Pichon and his colleagues are keeping cool and undisturbed, the reason, it seems to me, is that the conclusion has long been reached here that in the event of a fresh Franco-German war Germany must in any case and without question infringe Belgian neutrality. Consequently, the fortifications of Flushing are being treated here as merely a secondary detail in the general plan of the German offensive operations against France. None the less, according to news which has reached me, the Press campaign, for which the signal was given by certain Belgian newspapers, thanks to French subsidies and with the secret participation of the French military attaché in Belgium, has been started in the hope of frustrating in this indirect way the realization of the Dutch Government's plan. So far as I am able to observe, it is still expected here that this campaign will succeed, and it is hoped that Holland will either abandon the plan altogether or at least postpone or modify it.

" The conclusion has long been reached that in the event of a fresh Franco-German war Germany must in any case and without question infringe Belgian neutrality." Be it noted in passing how violently this statement of Isvolsky's conflicts with the wild shout of indignation staged in August 1914 when this infringement of Belgian neutrality, already assumed as a certainty, became fact. What is quite specially noteworthy is the fact that the definite anticipation of Germany's line of action is quoted here as the reason why the French Government was " cool and undisturbed," while from the propaganda on the outbreak of war one could only draw the opposite conclusion. What is the explanation ? Why were the men at the head of affairs in Paris so unconcerned about the possibility of an advance of the enemy through Belgium ? Had they already made counter-dispositions ?

An indication of the answer to this question is given by a letter from Isvolsky dated February 16, 1911 [20], dealing with the military relations between France and Great Britain. In a conversation with M. Pichon, Isvolsky asks whether exchanges of view concerning various military questions were or had in fact been proceeding between the French and British Governments. He learns that :

There does, in fact, exist no military convention between France and Great Britain. At the same time, the higher French and British military authorities have, said M. Pichon, exchanged views concerning the various military possibilities, and are continuing to do so. It is, he said, entirely natural that this exchange of views should take place, principally between the naval staffs and commanders of the two Powers, who have determined in advance the parts to be assigned to the British and French fleets in the event of a war against the Triple Alliance. It is very well known in Germany, he said, that in that event the British fleet would turn its attention to the German naval forces, while the French fleet would operate in the Mediterranean ; this, indeed, is the explanation of the strengthening of the Austrian navy.

We shall see later that the " various military possibilities " discussed between London and Paris included the case of Belgium.

The course of events in high politics still frequently ran counter to a complete alignment of the forces directed against the Central Powers ; disagreements still cropped up from time to time between Great Britain and Russia and between Russia and France to hinder progress along the path along which Isvolsky was pushing. The principal obstacle was the attitude of the French Governments of 1911. In foreign affairs the Briand, Monis, and Caillaux Cabinets were all taken up entirely with the Morocco affair, which was to provide France with a conquest free of blood-letting on the Continent ; in home affairs they were at grips with a powerful current of opinion among the Left-wing parties, averse to Chauvinist adventures. But at the beginning of 1912 there began the critical reaction, representing a great step forward for Isvolsky's secret efforts, but for the peace of Europe a disaster : Raymond Poincaré came to the head of affairs in France.

III

ISVOLSKY AND POINCARÉ

On January 14, 1912, M. Poincaré became Prime Minister and Minister of Foreign Affairs of the French Republic. On the 15th, according to Isvolsky's telegram of that date [186], Poincaré called on him and expressed to him his fixed intention " to maintain the most sincere relations, and to pursue the foreign policy of France in the fullest accord with her Ally." In this declaration Poincaré at once goes very decidedly beyond the ordinary assurances to the Russian embassy from French Foreign Ministers newly entered into office. It has a strong flavour of intimate solidarity. We understand, therefore, how from the first moment Isvolsky feels entire trust in the new Cabinet and especially its head. On January 16 [187] he writes to Sazonov :

As to the new Ministry, which has already received the high-sounding title of " national," two circumstances have especially contributed to its formation : the increase of French national feeling produced by the Moroccan complications, and the conservative feeling in the country evinced in the last elections to the Senate. The two preceding Cabinets, those of MM. Monis and Caillaux, were deeply tinged with Radicalism and leaned mainly on the extreme parties in Parliament ; the new Ministry embraces the more moderate elements of the Republican majority. The effort of M. Poincaré to give satisfaction to the conservative tendencies is already noticeable in the distribution of portfolios. Having assured himself of the co-operation of such eminent men as Briand, Léon Bourgeois, Millerand, and Delcassé, he offered them Ministries at the head of which they would not feel bound by their earlier Radicalism. The only concession made to the Radicals seems to be the appointment of M. Steeg, who was Minister of Education under Caillaux, to be Minister of the Interior. This concession is more than set off by the promise to M. Briand, who about a year ago was supported by the extreme groups in Parliament, of the special position in the new Cabinet of Vice-President of the Council of Ministers. It is, moreover, a notable circumstance that the Ministers mentioned above, any of whom is of sufficient importance to head a Government, have been prepared to take a subordinate position in the Poincaré Cabinet. Such a composition of the Cabinet makes the new Government extraordinarily strong, and it is being compared with the famous " Grand " Ministry of Gambetta. M. Poincaré himself enjoys the reputation not only of an admirable speaker and writer (he is a member of the French Academy) but of a conciliatory, moderate, and discreet politician and financier. His assumption of the portfolio of Foreign Affairs indicates that he intends above all to ratify the Franco-German treaty and quickly to conclude the treaty with Spain. The decision has also no doubt been contributed to by the fact that the Ministerial crisis arose through the belief that M. Caillaux intended to change the direction of French foreign policy.

A passage in the telegram of January 15, 1912 [186], referred to above, shows that M. Poincaré had no intention whatever of changing French foreign policy by loosening the bond between France and Russia, but the very opposite :

I also took the opportunity of acquainting him [Poincaré] with your proposal in telegram No. 2267. He promised me to examine this proposal, but expressed the view that a joint step by France and Germany, immediately after the signing of the Morocco agreement and after the well-known episodes in the Senate Commission, might create false ideas of the degree of the Franco-German political *rapprochement* and of a weakening of the Triple Entente. I shall probably receive a definite reply next Wednesday, but I foresee that the joint step referred to is hardly likely to be agreed to here.

The reference here is to a suggestion from Sazonov that Germany and France should jointly bring pressure on Turkey ; for what purpose is not revealed by the documents which have been made public. According to a telegram of January 17 [188], M. Poincaré maintained his refusal on the grounds here given.

We learn from a report of February 15 [203] that an interpellation was made in the Chamber concerning a loan for Cuba, and in reply to it M. Poincaré declared that in such matters the national interest must come before financial interests; accordingly, when application is made for permission for foreign securities to be quoted in France, the Finance Minister must first consult the Foreign Minister. It will be remembered how Isvolsky protested against the French loan for Budapest, but had then to admit that the government of the Republic was almost powerless against such intrigues of the bankers. Clearly the new Foreign Minister intended to keep a tighter control of financial circles, to prevent any manœuvres which might upset his programme in foreign politics.

A letter of Isvolsky's, also of February 15 [207], indicates very clearly the nature of this programme. The letter deals with the debate in the Senate on the Franco-German Congo agreement, and describes the part played by the French Premier as follows :

M. Poincaré declared with special emphasis that, contrary to current rumours, the treaty with Germany could not bring the slightest change in the general direction of France's foreign policy. As an answer to the attacks on his predecessors, he declared that the Alliance with Russia and the Entente Cordiale with Great Britain were inviolate first principles of France's political programme, and that if ever a Government were so blind as to depart from them, it would be bound to collapse at once under the public indignation. These words were submerged in loud applause, and were greeted with the liveliest sympathy throughout the French Press.

Their effect on Isvolsky himself is described farther on in his letter. He points out the material and moral success which France has achieved in the second Morocco crisis, and then proceeds :

In this respect there is a complete contrast between the crises of 1905 and 1911. The contrast brings back to my mind a phrase used by Emperor William in conversation with me shortly after Algeciras, a phrase which greatly astonished me : " The Alsace-Lorraine question is finally settled ; France has rejected the offered duel, and in doing so has made formal and unconditional submission to all the consequences of the Peace of Frankfurt." Now, after the events of last summer, Emperor William will have to revise his opinion, for France, as I have said more than once in my letters to you, has shown her unshakable resolve not to shrink from defending her rights and interests even at the cost, if need be, of resort to arms. This state of mind is traceable like a red thread through every speech which was made in the two Chambers during the discussion of the treaty, and must beyond question be taken account of in dealing with such fresh disagreements with Germany as may occur. I know from perfectly reliable sources that, despite the happy ending of the Morocco crisis, fresh international complications are expected in the spring in military cricles here, and that the War Ministry is energetically continuing its preparations for military operations in the very near future.

What a change in the tone of Isvolsky's reports ! What a change from that subdued report in 1911 on the apathetic attitude into which public opinion had fallen in France in regard to Alsace-Lorraine !

No wonder that the new guide of France's destiny and the Tsar's diplomat rapidly joined in close collaboration. " The present Prime Minister and Minister of Foreign Affairs," writes Isvolsky on February 29 [216], " has great force of personality. . . . In the time of M. Cruppi and M. de Selves it was a profitless task to discuss questions of general policy with France ; with the French Government as at present composed such conversations have become valuable and even essential. . . . So far as I am concerned, he (M. Poincaré) shows great cordiality towards me, and gives clear indications of his desire to discuss matters with me as frequently and as thoroughly as possible."

So, in the very first weeks the two had come to an understanding. Their rapid approach to intimacy was hardly due to personal sympathy ; Isvolsky frequently refers to certain defects in Poincaré. He is, says Isvolsky [216], " with all his great qualities, extraordinarily pushing, and very touchy about any neglect which he may imagine to have been shown to his views or his collaboration." On another occasion he speaks of his " obstinacy " ; and, in short, there is no lack of criticism. But what brought the two men together so quickly was their common political directive. The few quotations made above are evidence of that. The proof will be clinched by an examination of their joint operations.

In the first months of 1912 the diplomatic world was primarily concerned with the Italo-Turkish war over Tripoli. In January a proposal came from Sazonov for joint mediation by the Great Powers, but Poincaré objected that according to news which had reached him " Germany had declared a week before in Constantinople that she had no intention of joining in any general move " [191]. In February St. Petersburg renewed its proposal, but M. Poincaré regarded it as still far from hopeful, first because " the minimum Italian conditions are still very wide of the maximum concessions which Turkey could accede to at present," and secondly because he was convinced that the fact that Berlin had hastened to agree to Sazonov's plan was far from guaranteeing Germany's participation later on in the proposed mediation,

for as soon as the minimum of the Italian demands proves unacceptable to Turkey, Germany will withdraw, on the usual pretext, from participation in the collective step at Constantinople. For this reason M. Poincaré expressed to me, in a tone of mild reproach, his regret that before informing Berlin and Vienna of your proposal you did not make sure of unity of view with Paris, in order to avoid even the appearance of a difference of opinion between Russia and France. For his part he is keeping strictly to the rule of seeking before all else a complete agreement with the Russian and British Governments, and accordingly he is telegraphing his counter-proposal for the present only to St. Petersburg and London. [Isvolsky's letter of February 28, 1912,—211.]

Sazonov's indulgence in independent action was the beginning of a certain coolness between Poincaré and himself, and a fortnight later, on March 14, 1912, Isvolsky writes [233] :

The causes of the present disharmony are, so far as I can ascertain, two : a part is certainly played in it, as I have already mentioned to you, by the wounded self-esteem of M. Poincaré, due to your omission throughout this affair to take him into your counsels, first consulting London and then Berlin and the other Cabinets without a preliminary exchange of views with him. Account must be taken of this peculiarity of his character, and I am of the opinion that our alliance with France does in fact impose on us the obligation to consider, in important questions like the present one, how to make sure in advance of avoiding any troublesome difference of opinion with the French Cabinet.

Sazonov takes the moral to heart, and hearing that Italy and Turkey are more inclined for mediation he asks Isvolsky on March 17 [235] to ascertain " whether the French Government shares our view that it would now be useful to authorize the representatives of the Powers jointly to offer the Porte friendly advice to give way." The tele-gram concludes, " As soon as we know the view of the French Government on this question we shall at once take steps with the other Cabinets." But despite the concession to his self-esteem, Poincaré is still unable to warm to the St. Petersburg plan. He has no belief in success at Con-stantinople, and has all sorts of objections to offer to the formula proposed by Sazonov. His attitude shows no substantial change even when, in April, Russia protests against the Turkish prohibition of the passage of foreign ships through the Dardanelles ; according to Isvolsky's letter of May 9 [276], Poincaré " is not entirely convinced of the legal justification of the thesis maintained by Russia."

A little later the idea emerges of ending the Tripolitan war by a conference, and this does gain the sympathy of the French Premier [293]. In connexion with this he gradually gives freer expression to his views. According to a report from Isvolsky on May 30, 1912 [303], Poincaré considers that Russia, France, and Great Britain should have a thorough discussion " and must be ready to seize the favourable moment for putting forward a plan for a conference ; for he is especially afraid that the Emperor William might suddenly take a similar initiative." Thus, instead of the method first recommended by St. Petersburg of joint action towards mediation on the part of all five of the Great Powers, Poincaré proposes close consultation in the Entente camp ; and while at first he suspected that Berlin would not join in Sazonov's proposed action, his first concern now is to prevent a German movement to restore peace.

His plain effort to split up Europe in this whole question into two separate groups is best seen in connexion with the controversy which breaks out between him and Sazonov over the formula of mediation which he advocates. As to this Sazonov telegraphs to Isvolsky on June 13 [325] :

> I hasten to communicate to you a few ideas about the proposal which the French Ambassador has made to me. We find the formula proposed by Poincaré acceptable with the exception of the words " The Powers must before all . . . make written declaration of their disinterestedness." That is hardly practicable, and might be construed by Germany and Austria as open mistrust of them. We consider also that while Russia, France, and Great Britain must of course proceed on the basis of mutual agreement, we should not bring into prominence their division from the two Powers named, as we are compelled to fall back on their co-operation.

The text of the formula was as follows, according to a telegram from Isvolsky dated June 17 [332] :

> The Governments of France, Russia, and Great Britain are agreed as to the conditions under which, at a given moment, they would be able to undertake effective action in favour of the conclusion of peace between Italy and Turkey. They are of the opinion that a friendly intervention of the Powers could only succeed if it is confined exclusively to the question which occasioned the present conflict. The mediating Powers should, therefore, before entering into discussion, make written declaration of their disinterestedness. In addition, the three Governments express the conviction that the five Powers should, in order to secure their peaceful aim, first come to an understanding among one another before they undertake a collective step.

It was thus against a separate step on the part of the Entente Powers that St. Petersburg raised objections. Great Britain agreed, but Grey also, according to a report from Benckendorff, the Russian ambassador in London, considered that " a grouping (of Powers) aimed at securing a definite line of action will continually come up against

difficulties which may interfere with their purpose." [1] In
this case, at all events, Sazonov did not abandon his
objection. On June 18, 1912 [337], he repeats once more
that under the procedure proposed by the French Foreign
Minister " the Powers are divided into two groups, whereas
it is most desirable that all five Powers should jointly take
part in the reconciliation of Italy with Turkey." Poincaré
is " extraordinarily agitated " at this reply, and now con-
tends (according to a letter from Isvolsky dated June 20)
that it is perfectly clear from his own proposals that he too
is in favour of the idea of joint working by the five Powers.
Finally, he agrees to omit the sentence concerning disinterestedness, and also accepts Sazonov's reservation
" that there shall be special agreement before any publication in this matter " [347]. The controversy thus ends
with a compromise which at least breaks off the most
dangerous spikes in Poincaré's plan. In July St. Petersburg has once more to try to calm Poincaré. He fears,
as before, independent mediation on Germany's part ; of
this the Russian Foreign Ministry can find " no indications "
[367].

The whole process here briefly summarized had virtually
no influence on the course of events in Europe, as in the
end Turkey and Italy preferred to enter into direct peace
negotiations with one another ; but it is not unimportant
historically as giving a first example of Poincaré's political
methods. For, just as Isvolsky had done during the second
Morocco crisis, so during the Tripolitan crisis we find the
French Premier from the very first stretching out the
feelers of his mistrust towards Berlin. No separate step
must be allowed to be taken from that quarter, lest Germany
should gain influence over the belligerents. It would be
preferable that the Entente Powers should proceed independently, even though they should so increase the gulf
between the Triple Alliance and Triple Entente. There
is no need to define the line of thought revealed by this

[1] Retranslated.

procedure. It was of the most dangerous nature in the conditions then prevailing in Europe, where the strong differences already existing could very easily be exacerbated by an ill-considered step on any side. What, however, deserves special note is the circumstance that this line of thought is very reminiscent of the political faith which the documents of 1911 revealed as Isvolsky's. Here we meet with a significant example of the attempt to work the Entente on the principle of Ribot, so warmly espoused by the Russian diplomat—an attempt at the definite splitting of the Continent into two opposing groups of interests, not only in the theory of treaties but in the practice of diplomatic intercourse.

The main lesson which this attempt provided was that the resistance came from St. Petersburg. It was there, then, that there were obstacles to be removed, and work was begun at once, ruthlessly and deliberately, to remove them. Advantage was taken of a personal intrigue, of the real nature of which there can no longer be any doubt, although the person involved in it published no word in his defence during his lifetime.

France's representative in St. Petersburg at this time was Georges Louis, the diplomat with whom Isvolsky had found it so pleasant to deal at the time of his temporary service at the Quai d'Orsay in 1911, owing to his close knowledge of affairs. Louis had, however, one fault : he was a warm advocate of a moderate and peaceful policy, and accordingly it was now suddenly discovered that he was not satisfactorily fulfilling the duties of his post.

On the occasion of the first " misunderstanding " between Sazonov and Poincaré in regard to the simultaneous communication of the Russian proposal of mediation to Paris, Berlin, and Vienna, we find Isvolsky already beginning to set St. Petersburg against his French colleague there. " Considering," he writes on February 29, 1912 [216], to the Russian Foreign Minister, " that M. Georges Louis does not always convey with entire accuracy what is said to him in St. Petersburg, I do not understand why you prefer to negotiate with Paris in this matter through him rather than through me." This first attempt to supplant Louis is followed by further and still more energetic representations. On March 2 [218] Isvolsky telegraphs to Sazonov :

It must be assumed that Louis has not conveyed the substance of your present statements here with entire accuracy and impartiality. I venture to think that if Poincaré had learned of these statements not through Louis but through me, I should probably have succeeded in averting the present misunderstanding.

That is going a step farther, for the suggestion that Louis' reports are not impartial is a very grave one. On March 14 there follows a letter [233] which has hardly any other purpose than to attack Louis. He is first accused of inexact reporting, and examples are given of alleged misrepresentations and mistakes. A very significant indication of the political background of the whole affair is contained in a sentence added by way of warning to Sazonov :

Do not forget that I have obtained the wholly undeserved reputation of an anti-German—I am charged in Germany with having tried at Reval to conclude an offensive alliance against Germany with Great Britain : that is the authentic phrase of Emperor William—while you are regarded as Teutophile and as cool towards France and the Triple Alliance.

When this argument is brought into the field to detach Sazonov from Louis, it is easy to understand the purpose of the intrigue. About the same time, on March 13, there appeared in the *Temps* a telegram from Berlin reporting that the French ambassador was expected to be transferred shortly from St. Petersburg, and that Deschanel was regarded as his probable successor. The report was premature, but it shows the efforts that were being made to bring down the inconvenient diplomat. On March 28 [242] Isvolsky renews his complaints to his chief :

I do not want to influence you to no purpose against M. Georges Louis, but I cannot refrain from pointing out the results that must follow from the distorted way in which, I am convinced, he is representing your action and your views. It is very difficult for me to battle against these results, especially if one or another of your communications arrives here through Georges Louis before I am able myself to convey it.

Gradually this agitation begins to bear fruit, for in a further very full letter from Isvolsky to Sazonov on April 11 [254] we read :

I see from your letter that you are more and more dissatisfied with M. Georges Louis and the way he conveys here the information given to him. It seems to me that your dissatisfaction is entirely justified, and in my view the present method of intercourse with the French Government must inevitably lead to grave disharmony and misunderstandings. I shall, of course, do everything to impress on Poincaré the desirability of replacing M. Georges Louis by a more suitable personality.

Then follow comments on possible successors, and finally, as a temporary measure, the recommendation :

1. In your discussions with Louis, to avoid all verbal communications as far as possible, and where they are necessary to confirm them in writing.
2. To keep rather more strictly to the general rule that French communications to us (even public ones) should be made in St. Petersburg, and our communications to France in Paris. Formerly this rule was more systematically observed than now, and in my time it was the regular custom, for example, in our relations with the Vienna Cabinet.

Isvolsky was thus near to gaining his point : he felt that he had his Foreign Minister with him in his contention that Louis ought to be removed. The further course of events is not revealed in his papers, but is to be gathered from some French newspaper comments.[1] On May 17, 1912, the *Echo de Paris* published an article by a well-informed journalist, Marcel Hutin, stating that in the last Cabinet meeting M. Poincaré had reported on the situation in the embassy at St. Petersburg, and had stated that Sazonov and Isvolsky were demanding Louis' recall. Ten days before, said Poincaré, the Russian ambassador had

---

[1] F. Gouttenoire de Toury, *Poincaré a-t-il voulu la Guerre ?* Paris, 1920, pp. 21 sqq.

told him that his Foreign Minister feared that the Russian plans in regard to the Italo-Turkish war and to the East had not been understood in Paris ; it seemed as though Louis had been unwilling to report Sazonov's views. M. Poincaré had protected his ambassador, but Isvolsky had made further complaints about him, saying that he did not go into society, received no one—in short was living in a style that by no means corresponded with the position of a French ambassador. Consequently the question of removing Louis was under consideration.

The probability of the correctness of all this is borne out by the quotations already made, and it is particularly interesting to observe the skill with which the French Premier and the Tsar's representative had defined their parts in their joint action. M. Poincaré represented himself as besieged by Isvolsky, and left with no alternative but to give way. Actually Louis had already received a telegram from Paléologue, then head of the political section at the Quai d'Orsay, recommending him as a patriotic duty to apply for recall. Louis first went to see Kokovtsov, the Russian Premier, who protested emphatically against Isvolsky's action, and assured Louis that he and his Government would not accept responsibility for it. On this Louis went to Paris to make personal representations. He mobilized his friends in the Press, and Isvolsky had, in his own words, to go through " a very unpleasant incident." In a letter of May 17, 1912 [285], he tries very significantly to shift the responsibility off his own shoulders; speaks of the " pushfulness of M. Poincaré, who knows nothing whatever of diplomatic forms and methods," and, in his defence, gives the following account of the course of events :

You know that I felt, from the first, that this was a very delicate and difficult matter, and delayed mentioning it to M. Poincaré for a long time. It was only when I received your letter in which you told me that " the cup of your forbearance was brimming over " that I decided to raise the matter. I was careful to approach the matter as delicately as I possibly could, and to embark on it with the utmost caution. I began, as though on my own initiative, to talk of expected appointments in the high French diplomatic posts, and to draw his attention to certain superficial defects of M. Georges Louis. Finding that this failed to make the intended impression, and fearing that in the new appointments and transfers St. Petersburg was going to be left alone, I decided, with a heavy heart, to acquaint Poincaré in the strictest confidence with the friction and misunderstandings between you and Georges Louis, without putting pressure on Poincaré or demanding Louis' recall. I merely pointed out the desirability in the interest of Franco-Russian relations of replacing him sooner or later by another personality, preferably a diplomatist.

With our knowledge of all that happened, this may fairly be described as a disingenuous account. Obviously, it is an attempt at evading responsibility. Not that Isvolsky gives up the hope of success in his intrigues—far from it : he writes farther on :

All this still further complicates the question of the recall of M. Louis and the appointment of his successor. As I have already telegraphed to you, his recall is decided in principle, but it is absolutely necessary to find another post for him. The idea of nominating Deschanel for St. Petersburg has been dropped. I am assured that he was sounded about it but declined, in order not to have to give up his Deputy's mandate and his prospect of becoming President of the Chamber and later President of the Republic. The most probable candidate is Barrère, especially as this would enable Louis to be sent to Rome. You knew Barrère well in Rome, so that I need not characterize him. He has worked very successfully in Rome, but his part there is played out at present. His stormy past of the time of the Commune is now entirely forgotten, and he is incomparably better suited to diplomatic life and work than Georges Louis. I should be very indebted to you if you would let me know your view as to his candidature. The idea of appointing the Marquis de Breteuil is unfortunately impracticable.

In view of the incident described above the recall of M. Louis, which was to have taken place at once, will probably be postponed for a time, and he will have to return to St. Petersburg, which will naturally be unpleasant under existing circumstances both for you and for him. Please do not judge me too harshly, for I do not see how I could have set the ambassador's recall in motion and, on the other hand, have escaped from the inevitable indiscretions in view of the diplomatic morality ruling here. I am now threatened with hostilities from the side of M. Georges Louis and his many friends, and the journalists loyal to him, whom I am unable to influence for lack of the necessary means.

The anticipated Press attacks were not long in coming. A telegram [286] on the following day reports :

Some of the papers, especially those of the extreme Right and the Opposition, which have always shown an unfriendly attitude towards Russia, are continuing their attacks against Russia and against myself. There is evidence at the same time of efforts to give the affair a political complexion and to interpret our dissatisfaction with Louis as a sign of Russian designs of an adventurous nature against Turkey, which are meeting with opposition from the French ambassador.

Once more Isvolsky adds his regret at being without financial means of influencing the Press.

Meanwhile, Louis returned to St. Petersburg. For the moment at all events the victory was on his side, though, as we see, his chief antagonist regarded it as but a pyrrhic victory. In any case, the blow aimed against the French diplomat brought not a few anxieties to his assailant. In a further letter of May 23, 1912 [296], Isvolsky writes :

Now I have to consider carefully all the consequences of this storm. My personal relations with Poincaré are, I am sure, not spoilt. But the present affair has brought into the light various intrigues and movements of which I must take count. I even suspect a personal feeling against my wife and myself in certain quarters in society. It is very possible that we are charged with too great intimacy with the leading circles and the aristocracy here ; it is true that we have been very cordially received in these circles. You are aware that our embassy here has always openly shown its sympathy with the nationalist and anti-republican circles. I am carefully avoiding this, and have formed a circle of acquaintances including the most varied grades of society. Despite this, our popularity among the " upper three hundred " may have been little to the taste of one or another of the ministerial *salons*. There is no help for this, and that is one of the chief difficulties and unpleasantnesses of public life here. Still more serious is the fact that it is impossible for me to exert adequate influence over the smaller organs of the Press, which live on bribery and extortion. I wrote at length about this to V. N. Kokovtsov about a year ago, but without result. In normal times this would not greatly matter, as I have got on excellent terms with the serious papers, and at the present juncture this was of very great advantage to me. But it is essential to be in possession at critical moments of the means of rapidly influencing the hungry horde of the small papers.

It is really remarkable how efficient an advocate Isvolsky is where his personal interests are involved. His unquestionable failure gives him the opportunity of pluming himself on his excellent connexions. Not only that, but he tries also to take advantage of it to secure the weapon against his enemies in Left-wing circles in France for which he has so long been sighing—namely, a fund for purposes of bribery. After the little intrigue against Louis was to come the larger one against public opinion in this allied country. So ruthlessly did this man pursue his dark course.

When he expresses his confidence that his relations with Poincaré are not spoilt, he may certainly be believed. It seems clear that the whole of his action was taken in intimate agreement with the French Premier, who had lent a ready ear to his complaints of Louis. Later in 1912, when fresh differences arose between Sazonov and Poincaré, Louis had once more to pay for them. Thus when disagreement arose over the formula for mediation between Italy and Turkey, Isvolsky concluded a long letter to Neratov [July 18, 371] with the words " There is nothing left but to assume that M. Georges Louis has once more misrepresented the sense of S. D. Sazonov's words, either deliberately or through a fatal misunderstanding."

It has been shown that the attack on Louis arose naturally out of the experience of Poincaré and Isvolsky in their pursuit of their common aim. They had found that it was at St. Petersburg that difficulties were met with in the pursuit of Entente solidarity ; accordingly they had tried to remove one source of them, the French ambassador. A second source of difficulty was the Russian Foreign Minister himself, with his urgent warnings against the cleavage of Europe into two groups. It was hoped to get at him in another way—to bring personal influence to bear on him. Thus arose the plan of a visit of Poincaré to Russia. It emerged just when differences were at their height, and re-emerges at every moment of crisis. But before dealing with this, it is necessary to devote further attention to the policy that had been pursued in Paris.

It will be remembered that in 1911 there had been some disagreement between the two Governments in regard to the loan to China from the Four-Power Consortium, formed by British, French, German, and American banks. It ended in a Russian attempt to upset the Consortium. The attempt failed, however. Instead, as we learn from a letter from Poincaré on March 8, 1912 [221], to the French chargé d'affaires in St. Petersburg, Russia and Japan were invited at the beginning of 1912 to take part in the Chinese loan, in other words to join the Consortium. The grounds which M. Poincaré advances for accepting the invitation are very significant : to quote his own words,

Admittance to the Consortium would not only not weaken the position of Russia and Japan, but, subject to complete equality of rights, would enable them to participate in every advantage won. The alliance of Russia and France on the one part and of Japan and Great Britain on the other, as well as the friendship uniting the four Powers, should ensure them a majority which will enable them to make themselves heard for or against the operations planned.

Needless to say, this line of thought corresponded entirely with Isvolsky's, and we find him soon occupied in urging Sazonov's agreement. The latter first put forward certain conditions for Russian participation (secret telegram of March 14). But on the same day [232] Isvolsky writes that Poincaré has assured him that Russia " might count absolutely on France's vote, and on help from Great Britain and Japan—that is, on a majority." This brings no result, and on March 28 [242] the advocacy grows more urgent. Isvolsky " ventures " " to express the view that under existing circumstances it is better for us to enter the Consortium than to sulk." At the beginning of April, St. Petersburg notifies the Russian Government's agreement, accompanying the notification with an express reminder of the assurances given by France to Russia on January 4 of support of her interests in northern Manchuria, Mongolia, and Chinese Turkestan. Isvolsky is, of course, gratified by this step, and reports on April 25 [260] that it has been very sympathetically received in Paris.

In this connexion [he continues] I think it my duty to draw your attention to an article of April 2/15 in the *Temps*. Even if the article is not directly inspired by the Ministry of Foreign Affairs, it undoubtedly reflects the views of Government circles here, and brings forward the same arguments and considerations which have been put to me in the course of my conversations with the Prime Minister and other Ministers.

The writer of the article examines the matter of the Chinese loan, not from the financial but from the purely political standpoint, and welcomes Russia's entry into the Consortium ; in this decision of ours he sees an intention of extensive application of the Alliance in future.

The necessity of bringing the operations of the Allies into complete harmony is, in the view of the writer, the indispensable first condition of success. Russia might, he says, have had a perfectly legal justification for dissatisfaction with the formation of the foreign Four-Power Consortium, whose influence threatened to extend to territories in which Russian special interests were bound to predominate. The same dissatisfaction would certainly have been felt in France, and with reason, if a consortium had been formed with the support of Russian banks, and without French participation, to finance Morocco. Both in Russia and France there has often been insufficient realization of the importance of making full use at every opportunity of the whole force which lies in the unity between the two countries. Such omissions have been of frequent occurrence, especially in the early years of the Alliance, and again latterly in regard to the Bagdad Railway. Despite M. Pichon's assurances that in regard to this enterprise no agreement would be concluded without prior reference to Germany, Russia, and Great Britain, Russia has bound herself by a separate agreement with Germany. In the view of the writer, the errors and vacillations of France's policy in the East have played into the hands of her rivals in the Triple Alliance and made possible their separate understanding with Russia.

Here, then, we have a fresh and almost a literal repetition of the familiar theme of the need for making effective use of the Entente. The semi-official article of the *Temps*, written at the instance of M. Poincaré as Foreign Minister of France, might equally well have come from Isvolsky's pen. Thus, the joint programme had been carried through in regard to the Chinese loans, and it was quickly acted on. On May 9 the Russian Foreign Ministry announced that an Austro-Hungarian capitalist group was seeking admission to the Consortium. The French Government set to work at once to defeat this Viennese " intrigue." According to Isvolsky's telegram of May 11 [282] Poincaré told the Austrian ambassador, when the latter communicated his Government's proposal, " that in this case there would be an obligation also to admit Italy and Belgium, which might arouse opposition both of a financial and political nature, and that in any case France could only act in this matter in full agreement with Russia." He also, true to his methods, proposes [288] that Russia, France, Great Britain, and Japan should give Austria a joint reply, refusing in terms to be agreed on between them. This is accordingly done, although the Consortium had itself decided against Austria. In regard to Russia's concern for consideration of her special interests in China in the application of the moneys lent to the Chinese Government, Sazonov receives a further special memorandum from Poincaré holding out the prospect of every assistance from France. Its terms, according to a telegram of July 8, 1912 [364], are as follows :

The Prime Minister has noted with interest the views of the Russian Government. With reference to M. de Selves' letter of January 4 and that of M. Georges Louis of March 31, he gladly gives the assurance that the French Government will continue to give its support to the Russian Government in the Chinese Consortium. It will use its influence both with French bankers and with foreign Cabinets, and will make special efforts to secure the effective operation of the fundamental agreement existing between the four Governments, in the matter of the application of the moneys advanced and of the questions connected therewith, such as those of guarantees and of the reliable control of the stocks, questions to which in its view every loan must be subordinated.

Thus in this affair a solution entirely agreeable to Isvolsky was secured. The group of four Powers, France, Russia,

Great Britian, and Japan, was opposed, apart from America, only by Germany, who had been placed definitely in a minority by the exclusion of Austria. France had done everything to bind her Slav ally to her by her ready assistance. Another step had been gained towards the ideal of a political regrouping.

It may be imagined, therefore, with what feelings the news was received in Paris, at the beginning of June, of an impending meeting between Tsar Nicholas II and the German Emperor in the Finnish fjords. Sazonov, taught by experience, chose a form of communication designed to silence all objections in advance. He writes to Isvolsky [311] :

Add that the bonds which unite us with France are too firm for it to be necessary to suggest that the French Government or public can feel the slightest uneasiness about this event. So far as concerns the preparation of public opinion in France, will you please ask the French Government to undertake this, so that the Press may be informed in the best way, as local circumstances may require, that the impending meeting can in no way interfere with our relations with France?

But of what avail were all efforts to calm opinion? Isvolsky replies next day [312] that he has gained the impression " that Poincaré is thoroughly concerned about the impending event, which will undoubtedly be exploited to the utmost by the enemies of the Triple Entente." Sazonov replies with some energy on June 9, 1912 [322] :

As regards his [Poincaré's] apprehensions about the impending meeting in the Fjords, I am entirely unable to understand the nervousness expressed by the French ; this would only be intelligible if changes were taking place in our mutual relations which might destroy the solidity of our alliance. We have for our part given no occasion for such apprehensions, and regard the mistrust expressed by the French as entirely without foundation and even dangerous.

At this Isvolsky shrinks back a little ; he reports on June 14 [326] that the French Premier also has no doubt of the infrangible nature of the bonds between Russia and

France, but that he foresees attempts on Germany's part to " make capital " out of the impression created by the meeting. On the following day Poincaré saw fit in a speech in the Chamber emphatically to underline the solidity of the Entente, and to make a point of declaring that " the Franco-Russian Alliance, which had been consecrated by positive agreements and by the experiences that time had brought, was being applied at every point of the globe to the benefit of both countries."

Despite these confident declarations, the doubts are still not smoothed away. Isvolsky writes on June 20 [345] :

As regards the coming meeting in the Fjords, thanks to the steps taken by M. Poincaré and to my daily and hourly efforts, the French Press is looking on calmly. But this may change at any moment. It is very regrettable that so far the papers here have received news of the affair only from Germany, and so, of course, in a German light. The papers are reproducing the comments of the *Kölnische Zeitung*, the *Berliner Lokalanzeiger*, and so on, all representing the meeting in the Fjords as a political event of the greatest importance. It is very desirable that for the information of the Press here the Russian newspapers should give it a more correct interpretation.

In the end it was found necessary at St. Petersburg to proceed to a quite extraordinary step. On July 2 the Russian Foreign Minister telegraphs [358] :

His Majesty the Tsar has graciously accorded an audience to the French ambassador. His Majesty was pleased personally to assure the ambassador of the infrangibility of the Franco-Russian Alliance, and to point out the baselessness of the concern evinced in France with regard to the impending meeting at Baltic Port.

Immediately after the meeting had taken place Paris was informed, on July 7 [363], how well everything had gone :

The meeting of the two Emperors at Baltic Port proceeded very satisfactorily. There was great cordiality on both sides, and it was shown by open declarations on both sides on political questions that no intention exists of attempting any sort of change in the grouping of the European States. Nor were any proposals made on the German side in the matter of the termination of the Italo-Turkish war. This, together with the entirely correct semi-official announcement in the Press, is the best proof of how right we were when we told the French that the apprehensions they developed were void of all foundation. Will you please speak to Poincaré in this sense ?

A confidential letter of July 8, 1912 [366], gave a further short survey of the subject of the conversations between the two monarchs, and between Bethmann-Hollweg and the Russian Foreign Minister. It was specially emphasized that Germany " is making no attempt whatever to introduce any sort of change in existing international groupings in the sense of detaching any Power from the group which it has joined in virtue of the historic development of its environment."

At last Isvolsky is content. He reports on July 18 [371] a conversation with M. Paléologue, the head of the political section at the Quai d'Orsay :

The French Government is very satisfied with the result of the meeting of the monarchs at Baltic Port. The French Ministers have been entirely convinced, both by the joint Russo-German communiqué issued on the occasion and especially by the information and explanations given by MM. S. D. Sazonov and V. N. Kokovtsov to the French ambassador, that the meeting in question has added to the guarantees for the maintenance of general European peace, and in doing so has produced no change of any sort in the relations between the Powers. For my part I have not failed to convey to M. Paléologue the substance of the telegram, No. 1620, which S. D. Sazonov sent me on June 24, with some of the contents of his letter of June 25. I chose especially those passages best calculated to strengthen the optimistic view held by the Government here concerning the event which has taken place. On the whole it seems to me that, thanks to the timely explanations given to M. Georges Louis and, through me, also to M. Poincaré, the nervousness at first shown by the French Ministers and their mistrust have entirely disappeared, and that we have no longer any reason to fear a repetition of misunderstandings such as have shown themselves since the Potsdam meeting. On the present occasion, moreover, it has been possible to take precautions against a false interpretation of this affair to the French public. This result has been achieved through energetic pressure on my part on the principal organs of the French Press, while M. Poincaré on his part took similar and, of course, still more effectual measures.

At the same time, the whole affair was fundamentally

disturbing to the political plans of MM. Poincaré and Isvolsky. There must not be the very shadow of a disturbance of the Entente, that great constellation of Powers aiming at the hemming in of the Central Powers. The definite cleavage between Triple Alliance and Triple Entente must remain, and no bridge must be thrown over from either side.

This applied not only to Russia, but to Great Britain. Towards Great Britain Poincaré pursued the same tactics which we have seen him use in regard to the Tsardom. He sought a continually more intimate union, but his love was masterful and permitted no dallyings. At the very beginning of his term of office there was organized one of those splendid ceremonies in which the Imperialist period was so rich ; ceremonies readily laughed at as empty shows, but always serving some political purpose. The peoples did not dream how fateful for them were some of these junketings of the great. On February 1, 1912 [195], Isvolsky reports the welcome given by some units of the French fleet to the British King and Queen on their arrival at Malta, homeward bound from India. Every possible honour was paid on both sides, and Isvolsky concludes his account with this remark :

After recounting every detail of the stay of the French fleet at Malta, the Paris Press lays stress on the importance of this mutual declaration of Franco-British friendly feeling, and of the fraternization of the two fleets in the Mediterranean, under the existing political conditions, immediately after the conclusion of the Franco-German Morocco agreement and in the midst of the Tripolitan crisis.

On April 25 [261] Isvolsky reports the recent unveiling at Nice and Cannes of statues of Queen Victoria and King Edward VII, in the presence of M. Poincaré and of the British ambassador in Paris. In his speeches on these two occasions Poincaré drew attention to the great service done by the late British monarch towards the creation of the Entente Cordiale :

With the insight of the " great realist " that he was, King Edward [said Poincaré] regarded it as entirely superfluous to set down in writing the understanding between the two Powers ; for him it was enough that, after disposing of passing misunderstandings which had divided them, the two peoples had learned to understand one another and to appreciate one another better.

The Russian grand duke Michael Michailovitch was also present, and Poincaré, after his return from Southern France, said to Isvolsky that " these ceremonies had given him the impression that under the surface they had plainly strengthened the mutual solidarity between the three Powers of the Triple Entente."

Is it chance that a few weeks later, on June 6, 1912 [318], Isvolsky was able to report that the question of converting the Entente into a formal alliance, launched by the British Press, had aroused lively interest in France ? Was this a kite flown by the Quai d'Orsay in order to overtrump the " great realist " Edward VII ? In any case, Poincaré showed a platonic attitude. In his view a change in the existing system was not to be desired :

Recent events [he said] have shown that in the existing situation in Europe the community of interest between France and Great Britain and the understanding based thereon are so great and so undisputed that the common action of the two States in any serious complications is thereby sufficiently guaranteed. The signing of this or that formal treaty, even supposing such a treaty to be compatible with the French or British constitution, would in no way strengthen this guarantee, since even in the event of the existence of such a treaty the public declaration recently made by Asquith that the British Government would, at the critical moment, only take the course which the will of the British nation indicated, would retain its full force.

As regards the question, touched on by the Press at the same time, of a change in the British military organization and the introduction of conscription, Poincaré is of the opinion that it would be very ill-advised of France to touch on this question, even in the most cautious way, since the matter is a purely national concern of Great Britain's. As regards the French Press, the leading papers have shown great tact in this delicate question, and have in most cases adopted the standpoint that the question of Great Britain's alliances and of her military organization must first of all be examined by the British themselves, and that the French Press must refrain from all pressure in one direction or the other [318].

These statements give the impression of being based on actual negotiations between Paris and London concerning the conclusion of a formal treaty, and of reflecting something like a reply from the British Government to a proposal from the French Government. In any case, they sound a little like well-concealed disappointment. But be that as it may, one thing is clear : the head of the French Republic was trying to complete in regard to Great Britain also his system of the utmost possible solidarity.

But, as already pointed out, this solidarity had its rough reverse side. If the wooed country ventured to cast a glance elsewhere, the wooer adopted a very sharp tone.

In February 1912, as is well known, Lord Haldane, the British Minister of War, was in Berlin, discussing a possible agreement in regard to German naval armaments. A German proposal of a neutrality agreement was put forward, but nothing came of it. While the negotiations were in progress Isvolsky, according to a letter of February 29 [214], learned from Poincaré that in French Government circles there had at first been " a certain nervousness," but that this feeling had been completely dissipated by the public declaration of the British Government that Lord Haldane's journey " would have no effect on the solidity of the political bonds between Great Britain, France, and Russia, and that both the Paris and St. Petersburg Cabinets would be fully informed of its result." At the same time, Isvolsky added on his own account :

I cannot help remarking, however, that in military circles here a rather different impression predominates. The military are afraid that in the event of an understanding between Great Britain and Germany with regard to the cessation or at least mitigation of their rivalry in naval armaments, the German Government would pursue the strengthening of the army with redoubled resources, which would result in similar measures on the part of France and Russia.

Poincaré's unconcern must shortly afterwards have changed into its opposite, since we find the following report in a letter from Isvolsky on December 5, 1912 [608] :

In my conversations with Poincaré and Paléologue I was able to learn in strict confidence that on the occasion of the well-known journey of Lord Haldane to Berlin (in February of the present year) Germany made to Great Britain a quite definite proposal, as follows : the London Cabinet should engage itself in writing to maintain neutrality should Germany be drawn into a war which was not provoked from her side. The London Cabinet informed M. Poincaré of this, and apparently delayed sending either an acceptance or a refusal of this proposal. M. Poincaré expressed himself most emphatically against such an undertaking. He pointed out to the British Government that the signature of such a treaty with Germany by Great Britain would end at a blow the existing Franco-British relations, since no written agreement of a general political character existed between France and Great Britain. This objection had its result : the London Cabinet declined Germany's proposal, to the lively dissatisfaction of Berlin.

Thus, with his threat of a breach with Great Britain, the French Premier succeeded in defeating a German proposal for a step of the utmost importance to the maintenance of European peace. Once more he had refused to countenance any bridging of the gulf. He kept suspicious watch over the maintenance of the Entente absolutely intact as an instrument against the Central Powers, while doing his utmost to improve and complete it. No further explanation is needed of his curt rejection in April 1912 of German overtures to France, in an instruction to his ambassador in Berlin, with the words : " We should lose all the advantages of the policy which France has been pursuing for years." [1]

The relations of the Republic with Italy were temporarily overclouded by the Tripolitan war. Several incidents occurred which momentarily brought the rivalry of the two Latin States in the Mediterranean to a rather acute pitch. Isvolsky expresses regret on February 28, 1912 [212], that " a good part of the years of work of French and Italian

[1] *Rapport de la Commission d'Enquête sur les Faits de la Guerre*, i. p. 363.

diplomacy for a *rapprochement* between the two sister nations " is being destroyed.   A certain personal incompatibility between Poincaré and Signor Tittoni, the Italian ambassador in Paris, added further to the difficulty of abating the tension.   In a letter of May 30 [304] to Isvolsky, Sazonov expresses the view that the coolness which has arisen between the two countries cannot remain a matter of indifference to Russia :

> As Your Excellency is well aware, we do not regard it as in our interest to work for the formal withdrawal of Italy from the Triple Alliance, but we regard it as very desirable that under the superficial maintenance of the existing state of affairs the friendly relations of the Kingdom with us and France should be cultivated. In this regard the conditions are exceptionally favourable for us. We are, of course, gladly ready to take advantage of this situation to render to France, if she desires, such services as we can, and to make every effort to smooth away her differences with Italy.

In this connexion Sazonov wants to know whether the 1902 Convention between France and Italy is to be renewed, and whether Russia can be of assistance.   In his reply of July 6 [316] Isvolsky reports that Poincaré categorically declared to him that the treaty in question, which contained a delimitation of Italian and French spheres of interest in the Mediterranean, and had had the practical results of both parties abstaining from concentrating their armies on the Franco-Italian frontier, contained no time limit.   Poincaré added that he " had reason to believe that Italy was firmly convinced of France's friendliness," and that she expected from France and Russia " much more help than from her allies."

> As to the formal withdrawal of Italy from the Triple Alliance, Poincaré shares your view that there is no reason to work for this, as it could only lead to dangerous complications. The best, he considers, would be to maintain the existing situation, since Italy is the repressive element in the Triple Alliance. At the same time, France must not forget that Italy belongs to the rival political group. Consequently the French Government must watch lest Italy should gain predominance in the Mediterranean. As the naval strengths stand at present, a simple mobilization of the French fleet would suffice to render impossible any hostile attempt on

Italy's part. " You may rest assured," said Poincaré, speaking
with emphasis, " that France is firmly resolved to continue to
preserve preponderance over Italy in the Mediterranean in the
future."

This is certainly a specially interesting contribution to
the picture which we are trying to sketch of the political
system of Poincaré and Isvolsky. The Entente must not
be deformed by any sort of concessions to the Central
Powers, but by the aid of secret agreements a member of
the Triple Alliance had been so far drawn into the opposite
camp as to be already utilizable as a " repressive element "
in its own camp. This completed the isolation of Germany
and Austria, and Italy, the supposed friend of these two
countries, failed in emergency even to do them the small
service which Bismarck had expected of her—that of holding
troops on her French frontier by the rattle of her drums.
Watching this careful piling of stone upon stone to
complete the wall round the two Central Powers, one
involuntarily asks, what was the ultimate purpose of it all ?
Was it merely a clever diplomatic game, working towards
the checkmate and subjugation of the opposing group of
interests ? If so, the calculation was conceivably on the
dissolution of the Dual Monarchy, which would leave
Germany completely alone and helpless.

But a further review of the documents of these days
shows that that was not the line of thought ; every political
step was taken ultimately from a military standpoint, the
purpose being not a diplomatic contest of strength but
quite simply, as ultimate goal, war.

The reader of Isvolsky's reports during 1912 feels at
once the growing good spirits and confidence of this man,
whose attitude we know exactly from his own statements
in 1911. In his descriptions now of internal conditions
in France it is plainly evident how he has escaped from
the nightmare of Socialist influence. Under Poincaré's
" national " Cabinet he no longer has any fear of the
victory of the tendencies which are repugnant to his line

of thought. A few instances from the mass of material available will suffice to show this.

A report of February 29, 1912 [213], describes the Socialist Congress at Lyons as " entirely colourless "— " owing mainly, no doubt, to the existing growth of nationalist feeling in the French public." Another report, dated May 9 [278], gives the result of the communal elections and sums it up as follows :

> The broad result is that, despite their efforts and their active propaganda, the Socialists have been unable, even in the great industrial centres, to gain any fresh seats. The general political situation in France is not at present in their favour. These municipal elections are evidence, to a certain extent, that the public feeling has grown more conservative ; they show the effort of the population to maintain order, which suffered recently under the unexampled criminal activities of a band of terrorists, and its determination not to abandon itself to the destructive forces of extremism.

In the franchise reform question, then one of the major issues in internal politics in France, a " splendid parliamentary victory " of Poincaré over the Radicals and Radical Socialists is reported on June 20 [344]—a victory which has greatly strengthened the position of the Cabinet. On August 29 [416] a detailed description is given of the conflict between the French Government and the Socialistic teachers, whose activities, especially in view of their anti-militarist nature, are described as " criminal."

The complete contentment of the Russian ambassador with Poincaré's France is evidenced by a very characteristic communication of March 14, 1912 [231] :

> More than once recently I have had occasion in my reports and letters to Your Excellency to refer to the growth of national feeling among wide circles of the French people under the influence of the recent crisis in foreign politics, and especially the revival of interest in the military strength of the country. This movement is shown, among other things, by the splendid success of the national subscription for the purchase of aircraft for the army, recently organized on the initiative of the *Matin*. In less than a fortnight it has brought in more than a million and a half francs. The object of the subscription is to preserve at all costs the French

6

predominance in military aviation over Germany, independently of the material resources which can be assigned to this purpose out of State funds.

The new War Minister, M. Millerand, must certainly be credited with great services to the revival of public interest in the army. Among other things he has broken altogether with the traditions of certain of his predecessors, whose actions sometimes betrayed mistrust of the army and its leaders.

I have already had occasion to inform the Imperial Ministry of the abolition of the system of secret lists recording the degree of political trustworthiness of the officers.

M. Millerand has since seen fit to revive certain military traditions which had for some time been allowed to go into abeyance, such as the ceremony of the Saturday Tattoo, which now attracts a large part of the population of the capital.

Finally, last Sunday there took place once more, for the first time after a long lapse, the spring parade of the Paris garrison at the Champs de Vincennes. On this day the streets of Paris showed extraordinary vivacity from early in the morning. Every means of conveyance to the parade ground was packed with people, and a great crowd accompanied the regiments to Vincennes on foot, singing national songs. The regiments were in field uniform, with full equipment, giving the whole a particularly impressive and warlike character. The parade itself was different in some respects from the usual programme. After the march past, the whole of the infantry formed up and undertook a mock attack on the grand stands, making a deep impression on all present. The parade was brought to an end by a cavalry attack, while several aeroplanes and two dirigibles flew above. Throughout the day the troops were the object of the heartiest ovations from the people, who were present to the number of about a million. The cry of " Vive l'armée ! " followed the troops back to barracks.

Isvolsky had his reasons for jubilation at the increasing popularity of the French army. This was just the atmosphere that he needed for secret military plans of his own. In 1911 [20] he had already mentioned a proposal " to secure direct contact between the Russian and French Naval Staffs." This proposal was now in 1912 to be realized. On February 29 [125] Isvolsky was able to report to his Foreign Minister that the naval attaché at the Russian embassy in Paris, Captain Kartzov, had been commissioned to get confidentially into touch with the French Minister of the Navy, to make preparations for the arrival of the new Chief of the Russian Naval Staff. Definite results rapidly emerged from the consultations thus initiated. We learn from a communication of Isvolsky's of July 18, 1912 [375], that a conference had taken place shortly before between the Chiefs of the Naval Staffs on the two sides, Prince Lieven and Vice-Admiral Aubert, which ended with a resolution that there must be added to the existing Franco-Russian military convention a corresponding naval convention. The text of this new convention was worked out with the collaboration of M. Paléologue, head of the political section at the Quai d'Orsay, and ran as follows :

Article 1. The naval forces of France and Russia operate jointly in all eventualities in which the Alliance foresees and provides for the co-operation of the land forces.

Article 2. Provision is made in time of peace for the joint operation of the naval forces.

To this end the Chiefs of the two Naval Staffs are henceforth empowered to correspond direct with one another, to exchange all news, to study all possibilities of warfare, and to agree together on all strategic plans.

Article 3. The Chiefs of the two Naval Staffs confer personally together at least once a year ; they draw up minutes of their conferences.

Article 4. This convention is to be identical with the military convention of August 17, 1892, and the treaties arising out of it, in regard to its duration, elaboration, and secrecy.

PARIS, *July* 16, 1912.

In connexion with this, various details were agreed on as to action in the event of war ; Isvolsky is able to give the following information as to these [375] :

Having thus laid down the basis of their exchange of views, Prince Lieven and Vice-Admiral Aubert had a number of conferences in which they thoroughly examined the various questions arising out of the contemplated joint operation of the Russian and French fleets. The results of these conferences were set down in a special protocol which was signed by both admirals. I have only had the opportunity of studying the text of this comprehensive document quite cursorily, but, needless to say, it will be communicated in due course to our Foreign Minister.

Prince Lieven told me, in communicating the contents of this document, that he was convinced that the exchange of views just concluded had had very advantageous results for us. The Chief of the French General Staff had entirely agreed that it was necessary in the common interest of the two Allies to help us to maintain our predominance in the Black Sea by putting pressure as required on the fleets of our conceivable enemies, especially, that is, Austria-Hungary, and possibly Germany and Italy. To this end France had declared her readiness to concentrate her naval forces in the Mediterranean even in time of peace more towards the East, that is, towards Bizerta. This decision, which is recorded quite clearly in the protocol, represents in Prince Lieven's view a great success for us, all the more since it is not conditioned by any undertaking on our part. Prince Lieven is warm in his praise of the openness, sincerity, and helpfulness shown throughout by his French colleague.

So Isvolsky's desires had been realized with unexpected completeness.

Immediately after the completion of this technical naval agreement between Russia and France came Poincaré's journey to St. Petersburg. We shall soon see how closely connected it was with the military agreements.

As pointed out above, the plan of this journey had arisen out of various disagreements between Paris and St. Petersburg on political questions of the moment, and its primary purpose was to secure a thorough understanding between the French Premier and the Russian Foreign Minister ; the intention of the former being to win over the latter to his point of view. " I wish," cries Poincaré, according to a letter of Isvolsky's of June 20, 1912 [345], " I wish it were already August 10, and I could discuss matters quite openly and in full confidence with M. Sazonov ! " The news of the impending visit had already been given out to the Press, in order to allay the excitement caused by the meeting of the Kaiser and Tsar at Baltic Port ; it appeared in the *Echo de Paris* of June 12.

At the beginning of August, as the event drew near, it was given a great deal of publicity.[1] On August 3 Marcel Hutin stated in an article in the *Echo de Paris* that, as Germany had strengthened her offensive lines on her eastern and western frontiers, Russia had transferred her main mobilization centre to Poland. " It is not impossible that in view of this a revision and extension of the Franco-

[1] F. Gouttenoire de Toury : *Poincaré a-t-il voulu la Guerre ?*

Russian convention may be regarded as essential." On August 6 the same paper published an article containing the following statements :

The object of M. Poincaré's journey to St. Petersburg is supposed to be the strengthening of Franco-Russian co-operation in defence as the basis of the national policy of both countries. . . . The people of the British island Empire must understand the situation, and the Government is pointing the way to it by setting the navy in the forefront of its preoccupations for four or five years. Within this period Great Britain must be ready for a joint defensive with France and Russia.

It may incidentally be pointed out that in the French idiom all German armaments were offensive and those of the Entente defensive ; even at that date Germany's " guilt " was the subject of propaganda.

Meanwhile, Marcel Hutin had gone to Russia as correspondent of the *Echo de Paris* ; on August 5, 1912, he telegraphed to his paper from Eydtkuhnen :

It is true that at Baltic Port the Emperor William was given the news of the naval convention, but it is of the greatest importance that on the initiative of M. Poincaré, supported by the active collaboration of M. Paléologue, Russia has consented to sign an agreement with France under which she will undertake to abstain from discussing any question of European character with Germany without first having consulted and come to an agreement with us.

This agreement was stated to have been signed a fortnight before the meeting at Baltic Port, for a period of three months ; it was now to be renewed by Poincaré. On the following day a correction was published stating that there had been no written agreement but only conversations, in which Great Britain had also taken part. " Under these verbal agreements, none of the three nations of the Triple Entente will begin discussing any international question with another Power without first informing the two friendly Governments." Subsequently Hutin's statements were contradicted by a *démenti* in rather vague terms, but several circumstances seem to indicate that the correspondent of the *Echo de Paris* had certainly been telling tales out of school, and had come very near to the truth.

Now for the journey itself, and what we definitely know about it.

Its public side may be summarized as follows: On August 5, 1912, Poincaré started off from the Gare du Nord, travelling by sea from Dunkirk, avoiding the shorter and more comfortable journey across Germany. On the 9th, at 3 p.m., he reached Kronstadt in the cruiser *Condé*, and was received by the Russian Minister of the Navy and the French ambassador. On the 11th he was granted an audience at Peterhof by the Tsar. Lunch with Kokovtsov followed, the only guest who was not either Russian or French being Buchanan, the British ambassador in St. Petersburg. On August 12 there was a great military parade at Krasnoye Selo. On the 13th Poincaré returned to St. Petersburg, proceeding thence to Moscow for two days, and starting on the 16th on the homeward journey from Kronstadt.

Isvolsky was present throughout.

As to the negotiations carried on, Isvolsky's papers are completely silent. A description of them from Poincaré's pen [1] characteristically reveals nothing of importance. But from a fairly comprehensive report of Sazonov's [401], prepared at their conclusion for the Tsar, we learn a great deal.

First comes the Franco-Russian naval convention :

We took advantage of one of our first meetings to express to one another our satisfaction at the success of the recent negotiations between the Chiefs of the two Naval Staffs. The draft naval convention signed in Paris by Admirals Aubert and Prince Lieven has received the All-highest approval, and I have been most graciously empowered to attach my signature thereto.

The military convention concluded twenty years ago between Russia and France was ratified at the time by a special exchange of notes, and it was decided in agreement with M. Poincaré to follow the same procedure now with the naval convention. Accordingly an exchange of correspondence between Poincaré and myself took place on August 2 and 3,[2] containing the declarations of the two parties that they regard themselves as bound by the naval convention.

---

[1] *Revue de la Semaine*, No. 8, February 25, 1921.   [2] Old style.

The details of the ratification are recorded in a note of the Russian Foreign Ministry, dated August 18 [403] :

In accordance with the arrangement between the Ministers S. D. Sazonov and Poincaré, it was resolved to give the original document concerning the naval agreement the form of an exchange of letters, as was done on the occasion of the military agreement.

Accordingly S. D. Sazonov submitted to His Majesty during a personal audience at Peterhof on August 1 [1] a draft of the letter, which received the approval of the All-highest.

This letter was transmitted to the French embassy on August 2,[1] at the same time as copy No. 2 of the agreement itself, which was in our possession. It had been brought here from Paris by Captain Kartzov in order to receive the signature of the Minister of the Navy, Admiral Grigorovitch.

On the morning of August 3,[1] immediately after his return from Moscow, M. Poincaré on his part handed to S. D. Sazonov the reply.

The first protocol of the conferences of the two Chiefs of Naval Staffs, worked out on the basis of the agreement already mentioned, was submitted to S. D. Sazonov and V. N. Kokovtsov for inspection. At the same time the former expressed his view in a short note on the protocol, while the Prime Minister, to whom I personally handed this document, stated his point of view in a small separate note.

The second point in Sazonov's report [401] is headed " Strategic lines of communication " :

M. Poincaré also spoke of the protocol of the last sitting of the Chiefs of General Staffs, and said that he attached great importance to the realization of the desire expressed therein by the French General Staff for an increase in the efficiency of our railway system leading to our western frontier by the construction of a second track on the lines indicated in the protocol. I replied that I was aware of these desires and that they would probably be taken into consideration as far as possible.

This requires a word of explanation. The protocol mentioned, that of the last sitting of the Chiefs of the French and Russian General Staffs in Paris on July 13, 1912, is known to us. We find in it that in the event of war with Germany and Austria the attempt would be made " entirely to destroy the German forces at all costs."

[1] Old style.

General Joffre, for the French, emphasized the importance " of reducing to a minimum the periods required for mobilization and for the advance of the armies," and demanded accordingly that the Russian single-track railway lines leading to the western frontier should be doubled. It is to this that Poincaré attached great importance.

Very significant is Sazonov's third point ; it contains the following details regarding British-French relations [401] :

British-French relations were the subject of a particularly candid exchange of views between M. Poincaré and myself.

The French Premier mentioned that latterly, under the influence of Germany's aggressive policy towards France, these relations had assumed the character of quite special intimacy, and he confided to me that while no written agreement between France and Great Britain was in existence, the General and Naval Staffs of the two States were nevertheless in close touch with one another, and were uninterruptedly and with entire openness consulting one another on matters of mutual interest. This continual exchange of ideas had led to a verbal agreement between the Governments of France and Great Britain, in which Great Britain had declared her readiness to come to the aid of France with her land and naval forces should France be attacked by Germany. Great Britain had promised to support France on land by a detachment 100,000 strong sent to the Belgian frontier, in order to ward off an invasion of the German army through Belgium, which was expected by the French General Staff.

M. Poincaré begged me urgently to preserve absolute silence about this information, and not to give even the British ground for suspicion that we were informed of it.

When we spoke of the mutual assistance which Great Britain and France contemplated rendering to one another at sea, M. Poincaré touched on the possibility of simultaneous co-operation between the Russian and British naval forces.

Under our naval convention, France has undertaken the obligation to help us by diverting the Austrian fleet in the Mediterranean from us and preventing its penetration into the Black Sea. In Poincaré's view the British naval forces could undertake the same rôle in the Baltic, to which the French fleet is unable to extend its activity. Accordingly, he asked me whether I would not take advantage of my impending journey to England to raise in my conversations with the leaders of British policy the question of joint operation of the Russian and British fleets in the event of a conflict with the Powers of the Triple Alliance.

I replied to M. Poincaré that this question required close consideration.

Here again a word is necessary to complete the picture of the agreements arrived at. It will be remembered that Pichon had already hinted to Isvolsky at military agreements between France and Great Britain, mainly concerning naval co-operation. That these agreements already covered British assistance on land in the sense now revealed by Poincaré is perfectly clear from the minutes of the meeting of the Chiefs of the French and Russian General Staffs on August 31, 1911. According to this document, General Dubail declared " that the French army is concentrated just as quickly as the German, and it is in a position to take the offensive against Germany—with the aid of the British army on its left wing—on the 12th day (after mobilization)." When we add that according to these same minutes " the first big collisions probably take place in Lorraine, Luxemburg, and Belgium between the 15th and 18th days," we have confirmation of Poincaré's statements : the British troops were to be placed in Belgium.

The documents show that Poincaré's suggestion in regard to British-Russian naval co-operation was closely followed. Sazonov writes as follows in a report on his visit to Balmoral in September 1912 [508] :

As a favourable opportunity occurred I felt it useful, in one of my conversations with Grey, to seek information as to what we might expect from Great Britain in the event of a conflict with Germany. What the director of British foreign policy said to me as to this, and King George himself later, I think is very significant. Your Majesty is aware that during M. Poincaré's stay in St. Petersburg last summer he expressed to me a wish that I would clear up the question of the extent to which we might count on the co-operation of the British fleet in the event of such a war. I informed Grey confidentially of the main points of our naval convention with France, and remarked that under the treaty concluded the French fleet would endeavour to safeguard our interests in the southern theatre of war by preventing the Austrian fleet from penetrating into the Black Sea ; and I then asked whether Great Britain for her part could perform the same service for us in the north, by keeping the German squadrons away from our Baltic coasts. Grey declared unhesitatingly that should the anticipated conditions arise Great Britain would make every effort to strike a crippling blow at German naval power. On the question of military operations he said that negotiations had already taken place between the competent authorities concerned, but in these discussions the conclusion had been reached that while the British fleet could easily penetrate into the Baltic, its stay there would be very risky. Assuming Germany to succeed in laying hands on Denmark and closing the exit from the Baltic, the British fleet would be caught in a mousetrap. Accordingly Great Britain would have to confine her operations to the North Sea.

On his own initiative Grey then gave me a confirmation of what I already knew through Poincaré—an agreement exists between France and Great Britain, under which in the event of war with Germany Great Britain has accepted the obligation of bringing assistance to France not only on the sea but on land, by landing troops on the Continent.

The King touched on the same question in one of his conversations with me, and expressed himself even more strongly than his Minister. When I mentioned, letting him see my agitation, that Germany is trying to place her naval forces on a par with Britain's, His Majesty cried that any conflict would have disastrous results not only for the German navy but for Germany's overseas trade, for, he said, " We shall sink every single German merchant ship we shall get hold of." [1]

These words appeared to me to give expression not only to His Majesty's personal feelings but also to the public feeling predominant in Great Britain in regard to Germany.

It is evident from all this how comprehensive were already the war preparations of the Entente Powers. A close network had been placed around the Central Powers. In the North Sea, British and French fleets were to act together. On top of this a British land army of 100,000 men was to join on in Belgium to the left wing of the French army, which had to carry out from there to Lorraine the speediest possible advance against Germany. In the Mediterranean the French fleet recently transferred thither aimed at holding the Austrian naval forces in check, and on the Russian frontier all conceivable measures were to be taken to expedite as far as possible the advance of the troops of the enormous Tsarist empire if the emergency arose. These were, indeed, gigantic plans, covering all Europe, which, as we have just seen, were in important respects developed and promoted by Poincaré's initiative in Russia.

[1] Quoted in English by Sazonov.

Sazonov's report [401] goes on to deal with his conversations with Poincaré on questions of the moment. Once more the familiar thesis reappears that " provided that friendly and confidential relations are preserved between Italy and the Powers of the Triple Alliance, it is to the advantage not only of France, but of Russia and even of Italy herself that she should remain in the Alliance, as a dead weight." The attitude of both parties to the Italo-Turkish war, the Anatolian railways, and other matters of common interest is then defined. The Louis affair is also discussed. Sazonov represents his grievances against Louis, in the version formulated by Isvolsky, and is " unable to conceal " the fact that it would seem of advantage that Louis should be replaced by a more suitable person ; Poincaré is " entirely in agreement." The long report ends with the following description of the French Premier :

Finally, I feel bound to mention that I was very glad of the opportunity to make the acquaintance of M. Poincaré, and to get into personal touch with him ; all the more since our exchange of views left me with the feeling that in him Russia has a true and trustworthy friend, gifted with uncommon statesmanly intelligence and unbending strength of will. In the event of a crisis in international relations it would be very desirable that there should stand at the head of our ally's Government, if not M. Poincaré himself, at all events a personality as resolute as the French Premier, and as entirely unafraid of responsibility.

Thus the purpose of the journey had been completely attained. Louis' removal was a settled matter, and now only a question of time. And the cloud of misunderstandings which had divided Sazonov and Poincaré until now was dispelled. The best evidence of this is Sazonov's enthusiasm over Poincaré. The satisfaction in Paris is easy to understand. On August 14 Sevastopoulo, the Russian chargé d'affaires in Paris, is able to report that M. Paléologue and M. Briand (then acting Foreign Minister) had expressed to him most warmly the thanks of the French Government for the " extraordinary " reception accorded to M. Poincaré by the Tsar and his Government. On August 22, the day

of his return to Paris, Poincaré himself returns thanks
" with emotion." On the 29th Isvolsky writes of his first
meeting with Poincaré on his return, and once more mentions
the satisfaction of official circles in France.

His own feeling of triumph is plainly evident. He himself had done his best to arrange this visit of Poincaré to
Russia, and his meeting with Sazonov. And the result had
been substantially to further the policy which we know,
from his own statements, that he was pursuing.

Nothing could show more clearly the fatal unity of view
between Poincaré and Isvolsky. The Russian sets the ball
rolling with his urgency for a Russo-French naval agreement.
The Frenchman sends it on further with his suggestion of
a similar step between Russia and Great Britain. Both
men were enthusiastic Imperialists, interested only in the
continual expansion of their own countries and brooking
no obstacle to it ; both were, as Sazonov said of Poincaré,
" entirely unafraid of responsibility "—a responsibility
towards their own people and towards Europe. Both, in
the pursuit of their final purpose, were coldly logical,
completely indifferent to the means they adopted, and
astoundingly ruthless. Poincaré, like Isvolsky, already saw
world war as a coming fact ; he too had accustomed himself
to including it as a final possibility in the chain of his
thought, and to guiding his actions by this possibility, not
in the direction of doing all he could to avert it, but in
that of taking every possible step to secure that if it occurred
it should be utilized to the best advantage. We shall soon
see how quickly the peculiar character of these men brought
Europe close to the abyss.

IV

THE FIRST BALKAN WAR

QUITE early there appear from time to time in Isvolsky's papers, like dark cloud shadows, indications of a coming storm in the Balkans. His letter of March 2, 1911 [25], to Sazonov ends with the words : " All this will give you a firm line to take in case we should have to deal in the spring with a Balkan crisis ; this begins to be, if not inevitable, at least possible." Probably " spring " means the spring of the following year. This statement is astonishing, since at the time when it was written the Balkan League had not even come into existence.

When the Tripolitan war broke out, in the autumn of 1911, Isvolsky repeated his mysterious hints, in the form of apprehensions as to the possibility of intervention by the Balkan States. Subsequent events bore out his prophecy so remarkably that it seems necessary to credit him with fairly accurate knowledge of the developments which had occurred, amid great secrecy, in the interim. Negotiations were actually going on, certainly as early as September 1911, for the formation of the Balkan League. On March 13, 1912, the treaty [1] between Serbia and Bulgaria against Turkey was completed. In this treaty the two countries also bound themselves " to support one another with all their forces, in the event of any one of the Great Powers attempting, even temporarily, to annex or to occupy with troops any territory lying in the Balkans and at present under

---

[1] The text of the Serbo-Bulgarian Treaty of 1912, of its secret supplement, and of the subsequent military convention, is given in *Causes of the War*, by M. Bogitchevitch, pp. 100-7. (George Allen & Unwin, 1920.)

Turkish dominion, and in the event of one of the two States regarding this as injurious to its vital interests or as an occasion of war." This provision was clearly directed against Austria-Hungary, who was credited with the intention of reoccupying the Sandjak. This is seen still more clearly from the text of the military convention [1] between the two States which soon followed.

A secret clause [2] added to this treaty provided for arbitration by Russia in regard to the time when war against Turkey should begin, and also in regard to any point of dispute between the two signatory States. Thus Russia not only knew of the whole proceedings, but had in some degree taken the leadership behind the scenes. The contention of her representatives was that this enabled her to intervene should occasion arise and to prevent an armed conflict. But it is a remarkable fact that on March 12, the day before the signing of the treaty, the following order was issued to the Russian army : [3]

In accordance with His Majesty's decision, a telegraphic order for mobilization in the European military commands on account of political complications on the western frontiers is to be interpreted as an order also for the commencement of hostilities against Austria and Germany.

How does this fit the pretext that the aim was to check the outbreak of trouble in the Balkans ? But let us see what more the documents have to tell.

On March 30, 1912 [243], Sazonov informs the ambassadors in London and Paris of the alliance concluded between Serbia and Bulgaria, and requests the latter on some occasion " which he feels to be suitable " to give Poincaré the news verbally, pointing out " with the utmost earnestness . . . that the conclusion of the alliance must be kept absolutely secret."

You may add [continues the telegram] that as a special secret clause binds both parties to ascertain Russia's view before they

[1] *Causes of the War*, by M. Bogitchevitch.   [2] Ibid.
[3] Count Max Montgelas, *The Case for the Central Powers*, p. 54. (London : George Allen & Unwin.)

proceed to active measures, we are of the opinion that this puts into our hands a means of bringing pressure on both parties, and that we have at the same time taken a protective step enabling us to oppose the extension of the influence of a great Power in the Balkans.

In this way Russia secured a leading rôle ; the telegram is also an admission that the move had provided a means of attack in emergency against the Dual Monarchy.

Poincaré does not appear to have paid due regard to the request for secrecy, for on April 6 [248] Sazonov complains in a telegram to Isvolsky that the French Premier has apparently communicated the information to Louis in a cypher message, whereas it " was intended only for his personal information, as the head of an allied Government and in evidence of our trust."

In May, Bulgaria was endeavouring to obtain a loan in Paris, probably with the concealed aim of financing her war preparations. " Despite the benevolent attitude of official circles to the project," the Paris bankers made difficulties, " pointing to the disturbing nature of the general situation " [280]. Sazonov came to the aid of the project with a warning, in a telegram of May 10 [280], that " the attitude of the French might lead Bulgaria to turn once more to Vienna." On the 15th Isvolsky was able to report that the French Minister of Finance agrees in principle to a loan of 180 million francs.

A few weeks later Todorov, the Bulgarian Minister of Finance, came personally to Paris about the loan. Of course he visited Isvolsky, and on June 6, 1912 [317], the latter gives a detailed report of the conversation. He begins by making it clear that he has given " a great deal of support " to Todorov in his negotiations with the French Government, " in accordance with the instructions received," and that " the Bulgarian Minister of Finance has clearly succeeded satisfactorily in getting round the ticklish question of the security for the loan." Then he reports the political information received :

On the day before his departure for Paris Todorov called on me to thank me warmly for the support given him. Then, on his own initiative, he touched on the situation in the Near East and made the following observations, which struck me by their importance and candour :

He is convinced, and this view is shared by the other members of the Bulgarian Government, that a speedy ending of the Italo-Turkish war would not be at all in the interest of Bulgaria. In the end the present struggle should extraordinarily weaken both States, and both are among the Powers which are fundamentally hostile to Slavdom and the Slavic Balkan States. The leaders of all political parties in Bulgaria are of the opinion that a similar state of things will not recur for a long time to come, and Bulgaria would therefore be making an unpardonable mistake if she made no attempt to avail herself of this opportunity to attain her historic aims. From this point of view the Bulgarian Government is against a conference to endeavour to end the Italo-Turkish conflict. A conference will only become necessary when events have further developed and questions have arisen of which the solution is a European concern.

In Todorov's view this attitude of Bulgaria need arouse no uneasiness in Russia. Gueshov's Government is strong enough to be able to wait till a favourable opportunity offers itself. The Bulgarian Government considers its task for the moment to be the preparation of a joint plan of action with the other Balkan States. The alliance with Serbia is the first step in this direction. For the moment every effort must be made to avert Roumanian opposition to Bulgarian action in the south, and Todorov believes that it will be possible to do this at the price of a rectification of the frontier at Silistria.

Conversations are also, he said, in progress at present with Greece, and will most probably lead to an association of the interests of Bulgaria and Greece. The Bulgarian Government is firmly resolved to take no steps which might involve Russia in military measures against her will, but, on the other hand, he said, Russia must allow Bulgaria liberty to make such decisions as may be called for by the course of events and any favourable conditions that may offer, not excluding the possibility of joint action with Italy, who, he said, has already made suggestions in this sense.

Bulgaria admits that Constantinople and the Straits belong to the sphere of Russia's special interests, and bears in mind that we can probably hold aloof so long as these interests are not affected. This would actually be of advantage to Bulgaria, since Russian inaction would prevent Austria from intervening. The general clearing up of the situation would be a European matter, presumably necessitating a congress or conference, at which Russia would be supported not only by France and Great Britain but also by Italy.

This document is noteworthy as containing an actual programme for future developments, which was carried through almost point for point. The adhesion of Greece to Bulgaria and Serbia had already come. And we shall see very shortly how from now onwards Sofia aimed directly at " availing herself " of the Italo-Turkish war " to attain her historic aims," ; that is, to attack Turkey. Of special importance is the fact that St. Petersburg was fully informed ; at the end of the report the prospect is also held out of a visit of Todorov to the Russian capital. It is true that the tale goes that the Bulgarian Premier, Danev, received a " cold douche " from Sazonov when he unfolded similar plans to him. But how much does that count for against the fact that everything actually happened as we have just seen proposed, and that Russia, despite her function of arbitrator, took no effective step to bring the Balkan States to a halt !

An interlude came in June. The King of Bulgaria made a journey to Vienna and Berlin, and at once there were signs of alarm in the Entente camp as to his purposes. Poincaré communicated his concern to Isvolsky, who writes on June 20, 1912 [346] :

" You know," he said to me, " that the French Government was only ready to facilitate the Bulgarian loan in Paris because the Russian Government declared to it that Bulgaria, having arrived at a secret agreement with Serbia, was firmly resolved to place herself on the side of the Entente. Do you not think that in view of the controlling influence which King Ferdinand exerts over Bulgarian policy, and especially foreign policy, we should have evidence in precise form of the King's real intentions before we put important resources at Bulgaria's disposal, and demand from him a guarantee in one form or another that he approves the decision of the Bulgarian Government ? "

But there was no real danger. Bulgaria did not depart from the beaten track. At the beginning of July there are rumblings from afar of the coming storm ; on the 8th [365] Sazonov writes to his representative in Sofia, " go on watching the warlike currents in Bulgaria." He adds, however, a warning that peace between Italy and Turkey is very near, and that the Balkans will then face their powerful opponent, the Porte, alone.   Shortly afterwards, according to a telegram from Isvolsky on July 18, the news of bellicose feeling in Sofia was hastily denied.   Obviously it was still felt to be most important to preserve strict secrecy concerning the coming trouble.

During Poincaré's visit to Russia, however, he was shown the text of the Serbo-Bulgar treaty.   Sazonov makes the following reference to this in his report to the Tsar [401] :

> We had confidentially informed the French Government of the Serbo-Bulgar treaty. M. Poincaré did not conceal from me that he felt some concern at its conclusion. He welcomes the treaty as a factor in increasing the military strength of the Balkan States, but regards it as of an aggressive rather than defensive character, and sees grave danger in this, since complications are possible at any moment in the Balkan peninsula. I remarked that we had drawn the attention of Bulgaria and Serbia to the fact that we were only prepared to recognize the alliance concluded between them as a defensive measure, to preserve the independence and liberty of the two countries against attacks on the part of Austria-Hungary, and that we were by no means prepared to lend a hand in any aggressive plans of theirs.

It will soon be seen how far these words of Sazonov's corresponded to the facts.   Poincaré was hardly back in Paris before the Balkan States began to make out a case for war against Turkey.   On August 18, 1912, Neratov telegraphs that the representatives of Bulgaria and Serbia have asked that at a suitable moment the opportunity should be seized to secure for the Christian population of Turkey the rights just accorded to the Albanians.   The request is, he says, based on the difficult position of the Governments in view of the excitement in their own countries, and among their racial kindred in Turkey, and in the view of the Russian Government it should not be ignored. With the pretext thus found for the Balkan countries' plans of aggression, one blow follows quickly on another.   In a telegram of August 29 [413] Sazonov speaks of the " extraordinarily excited state of Bulgarian public opinion " ; he considers that atrocities are likely to be committed by the

Christian population of Turkey, which feels that Europe is not paying sufficient attention to it. He proposes an exchange of views between the Powers, " so as not to be caught unawares by the events which are already threatening."

Then begins a busy discussion between the Cabinets of the question of intervention by the Great Powers to prevent trouble. But it is already too late. On September 17 [432] Sazonov has to admit that he obtained from a conversation with the Bulgarian ambassador the impression " that the outbreak of hostilities between Bulgaria and Turkey is inevitable unless the Powers are able peacefully to secure Turkish fulfilment of the Bulgarian claims " (in regard to privileges for the Christians). Poincaré now, after consultation with Russia and Great Britain, proposes common action on the part of the five principal European countries ; according to Isvolsky's telegram of September 22 [439], this is to be carried out as follows :

1. The Powers will intervene simultaneously and as soon as possible with the Cabinets at Sofia, Belgrad, Athens, and Cettinje, to advise them to take no action which might be a menace to peace or an infringement of the *status quo* in the Balkan peninsula.

2. Should their advice fail to be followed, the Powers will at once use their joint efforts to localize the conflict and to try to end it. They declare especially to the States which have broken the peace that they must expect no territorial gain in the event of victory.

3. Should the course of events necessitate recourse to energetic measures such as a military or naval demonstration, the Powers will only proceed to this after prior agreement.

4. At the same time as the steps mentioned in Point 1 are taken, the Powers will advise the High Porte to introduce without delay the administrative reforms which the Christian population of the Balkan peninsula is with justice demanding.

St. Petersburg readily agreed to the plan. But its execution was delayed by Sazonov's journey to England, already mentioned. Was this of set purpose or a mere chance ? In any case, it is a suspicious circumstance that, at the moment when the suggestions of the French Premier were being dilatorily dealt with, the acting Russian Foreign Minister requested Isvolsky to inform the Grand Duke Nicholas Nicolayevitch, who in those disturbed days was staying in Paris, of " the views of the Tsar's Government concerning the state of things in the Balkans " (telegram from Neratov, September 22, 1912 [441]), and that, in addition to this, Prince Danilo was suddenly sent by his father, the King of Montenegro, on a journey to this same Grand Duke.

Meanwhile, efforts were being made in Bulgaria to cast on Turkey the blame for the contemplated war of aggression against her, for Isvolsky reports on September 26 [444] :

Gueshov has informed the Bulgarian ambassador in Paris that in Turkey in Europe complete mobilization has already taken place. The Bulgarian Government, which has already taken all steps to dismiss the whole of the troops called up for the manœuvres in Sumla, can only see an open challenge in Turkey's action, and places no trust in the assurance of the Turkish papers that it represents merely the usual manœuvres.

A few hours later Isvolsky has to admit that, according to the French ambassador in Constantinople, the Turkish call to the colours applies only to the Roumelian divisions, and not to the Anatolian Khedives, and that its only purpose is to bring up these troops to normal strength.   Sazonov, however, seconds the Bulgarian diplomat in a telegram from London representing the calling up of the Khedives as an accomplished fact.

Meanwhile, Poincaré continues indefatigably with his work of mediation.   It occurs to him, according to Isvolsky's telegram of September 29 [451],

that if joint intervention by the five Powers in the Balkan capitals and in Constantinople should prove impossible, intervention might be arranged by Russia and Austria, not only because they are the Powers most concerned, but because they might stand in some measure as representative of the two European groups.

This idea also is taken up with the utmost readiness by Russia.   Neratov, in his reply, goes very fully into it, and mentions his conditions—on September 30, the very day on which Bulgaria, Serbia, and Montenegro begin mobilizing against Turkey, as he had, of course, already been fully informed in advance by the Tsar's representatives in those countries. On the same day, moreover, a command was issued to the sixth Russian army corps in Warsaw that " the announcement of mobilization also meant the announcement of war against Germany ! " [1]

By such measures were the efforts to prevent the war accompanied. Russia's double game emerges now more and more undisguisedly from the documents.

On October 2, 1912, Sazonov reached Paris on his way back from England. On this date Neratov telegraphs [460] a report from the military attaché at Sofia that the Bulgarian mobilization will probably be completed on the 7th, and war declared on the 5th. The revealing communication is added [461] that in this event it is expected that the Balkan States will ask Russia to take over the protection of their interests and their nationals in Turkey, but that it is felt that it would be well that Greece should apply to some other Power, for instance, France, " to avoid arousing the suspicion that we have been working at the combination of the four States." A day later it is suggested [462] that the Italian Government, which is beginning to negotiate peace with Turkey, should be advised not to be too accommodating in the matter of an indemnity, as " the smaller the resources of the belligerents, the better are the prospects, if not of avoiding, at least of shortening the war." But as the resources of only one belligerent, Turkey, were to be reduced, the object of the move was clearly to support her aggressors and hasten their victory.

On the same day a telegram [466] from Cettinje announced the intended participation of Montenegro and Greece in the impending struggle. In the view, however, of the Russian ambassador in Constantinople [486], there was still hope that the time for " intervention by the Powers

[1] Montgelas, *The Case for the Central Powers*, p. 56. (London : George Allen & Unwin.)

to avert war is not yet entirely past." In strange contrast with this, the Foreign Ministry in St. Petersburg drew attention on October 4 [470] to " the challenging attitude of the Porte," and sought to attribute to it " the responsibility for the opening of hostilities." A telegram came from Sofia [476] praising the " extraordinary courage and determination of the Bulgarian population and troops." In view of all this it is easy to see with how little conviction Sazonov received and passed to his deputy at home Poincaré's latest proposal of mediation. This ran as follows [484] :

The Powers intimate to the Balkan States and Turkey that—

1. They strongly condemn all measures likely to lead to a breach of the peace.

2. If in spite of everything war should break out between the Porte and the Balkan States, they would permit at the end of it no territorial change in the present *status quo* in the Balkans ; further, on the strength of Article 23 of the Berlin Treaty, they would take in hand, in the interest of the Christian population, the putting into effect of administrative reforms in European Turkey ; needless to say, without in any way injuring the integrity of the territory of the Ottoman Empire. This declaration would, of course, leave the Powers full freedom for further joint examination of the reforms.

In transmitting this Sazonov knew, of course, perfectly well that the whole effort was useless. But he keeps up the fiction of eager love of peace, and when Great Britain objects to Poincaré's formula as imputing too much to Turkey, he reminds the British Cabinet on October 6, 1912 [482], that " it is assuming responsibility for a delay which may have the worst results in the present circumstances." Clearly he is very glad of the opportunity of throwing on London the blame for the failure of the effort at mediation. While discussion is still proceeding over the formula, of which, as we saw, the Russian Foreign Minister is so warm an advocate, Neratov telegraphs [490] the views of the Ministry of the Navy concerning the expected war :

Our fleet is substantially stronger than the Turkish, and ready to sail at any moment. The Minister also considers that the Greek fleet is stronger than the Turkish. He points out that, should our fleet be commissioned to enforce the execution of the declaration contemplated by Russia, and should Turkish ships of war appear off the Bulgarian coast, it would place our fleet at a disadvantage to limit ourselves to a mere protest, and it would be necessary to proceed to action. In this event there would be no need to fear intervention at present by any other Power.—The collision of the two fleets might endanger our hold of Kospoli.

No more need be added. On October 8 Montenegro declared war on Turkey ; on the 17th and 18th Bulgaria, Serbia, and Greece followed. Events developed in the only way that could be expected in face of the documents quoted above.

There is no possible room for doubt as to the double part played by Russia in these fatal weeks. From the first the Balkan League was conceived as an instrument for extending Slav influence in south-east Europe. The Tripolitan war, especially as it dragged on, tempted the allied States to carry out their secret plan of attack against the Porte. There was, perhaps, hesitation in St. Petersburg as to the fitness of the moment chosen. But the more the conviction grew that there could be no drawing back, the more determinedly was secret encouragement offered them, if only not to lose the leadership over them, while outwardly, for the sake of appearances, full support was given to the European Powers in their demands for the maintenance of peace. The necessary preparations were also made for intervention, if any attack were made by Austria on Serbia.

But of this there was little fear ; Vienna was not to be dragged into precipitate action, not least because Berlin urgently deprecated it. In a telegram dated October 3, 1912, Neratov states that two days before the Austro-Hungarian Government, according to news from Italy, declared at Belgrad that the Dual Monarchy would not allow any change in the territorial *status quo* to Serbia's advantage. But on October 5 he quotes [481] a telegram from the Russian military attaché in Vienna according to which the British embassy there had learned that Germany had put " strong pressure on Austria to abstain from aggressive action in the south." Sazonov himself had returned from England via Paris and Berlin, and his own report to the Tsar [508] on his journey is the best of witness. He states that there were fears in Germany of being " involved in a European war " through Germany's commitments to her Ally. For this reason Germany was ready " to localize the Balakn war as far as possible."

According to the same report, there was great anxiety in England, if only on account of India, not to " arouse the discontent of the Mussulman world " in connexion with present events, and, on the other hand, not to let the existing Turkish Government be weakened, lest " the Young Turks, under the leadership of Ferid Pasha, who is regarded as under German influence," should regain power.

Bearing in mind that it was, of course, entirely in Russia's interest that the Balkan States, who were proceeding on lines with which she was in agreement, should not be disturbed by any outside intervention, and especially that there was no need for any spilling of Russian blood, it is easy to understand the evident satisfaction with which Sazonov regarded what had happened. The present aim was to get a smart blow dealt at European Turkey. If all went well, St. Petersburg would have made substantial progress at no cost to itself.

Sazonov was, of course, equally well informed as to the French attitude. In his report on Poincaré's visit he had already dealt with this [401] :

We assured one another of our intention carefully to watch events in the Balkans, and to keep up a continual exchange of views and information ; and I agreed once more with Poincaré that in case of any complications we should at once determine in consultation with one another, according to the actual situation, what attitude we would adopt in order to prevent by diplomatic means any more serious developments.

M. Poincaré felt it his duty to mention that public opinion in France would not permit the French Government to intervene militarily in purely Balkan affairs, unless Germany were involved, and by her own initiative produced a *casus fœderis*. In the latter event we could, needless to say, count on France to fulfil her obligations to us precisely and completely.

On my part I declared to the French Premier our readiness at all times to range ourselves unhesitatingly alongside France in any conditions envisaged in our alliance, but that we should similarly be unable to justify in the face of public opinion in Russia an active participation in military operations occasioned by any sort of colonial, extra-European matters, unless, of course, they affected vital interests of France in Europe.

In the report of his journey Sazonov writes in a similar strain [508] :

The complications in the Balkans give rise to anxiety in France on two counts, which determine the attitude of our Ally to present events :

In the first place there is concern because it is felt that the events in the Balkans might in one way or another bring about intervention by the Powers most interested in that quarter, namely Russia and Austria ; this might involve France in war. It is this fear that led Poincaré to remind us last summer, confidentially and in all friendship, that according to the letter of the treaty of alliance only an attack on Russia by Germany could be ground for the fulfilment by France of her obligations towards us.

In the second place, the French cannot remain indifferent to growing unrest in the Balkan peninsula ; for this must bring them financial losses, since they have sunk considerable capital sums in various enterprises there.

That is why the French Government is so anxious to see a peaceful solution of the conflicts which have sprung up, and is taking the initiative in a number of proposals to this end.

Poincaré's efforts at mediation have already been described. They did not end with the actual outbreak of war. He now, according to Isvolsky's telegram of October 15, 1912 [506], advocated preparation for mediation "immediately the first armed collisions have cooled the ardent spirit of the combatants and their strength begins to be exhausted." There is fresh talk of a conference of the Great Powers, to be preceded by an understanding between the Entente Powers. But M. Poincaré is true to his own nature. The possibility of a world war is kept clearly in view : there are discussions of the way it might develop, and there is even a close consideration at a comparatively early stage of the prospects in it of Russia and France. On September 12, 1912, Isvolsky writes [429] :

Finally, M. Poincaré said to me that the French Government was most earnestly examining the question of all conceivable international eventualities. He was keeping fully in view that some such event as the destruction of Bulgaria by Turkey, or an Austro-Hungarian attack on Serbia, might compel Russia to abandon her passive rôle and have recourse first to diplomatic action and then to military intervention against Turkey or Austria. In accordance with the declarations which we have had from the French Government, we are assured in such an event of the strongest and sincerest diplomatic support from France. But in this phase of events, the Government of the Republic would not be in a position to secure the necessary assent of Parliament or public opinion to any active military measures. Should, however, the conflict with Austria result in armed intervention by Germany, the French Government recognizes this in advance as a *casus fœderis*, and would not hesitate a moment to fulfil the obligations which it has accepted towards Russia. " France," continued M. Poincaré, " is beyond question entirely peaceful in disposition, and neither desires nor seeks a war ; but German intervention against Russia would at once bring about a change in public feeling, and it may be taken as certain that in such an event Parliament and public opinion would entirely support the decision of the Government to give Russia armed support."

M. Poincaré also told me that in view of the critical situation in the Balkans the superior French military authorities are examining with increased closeness all the military eventualities which might occur, and that he knows that well informed and responsible personalities are very optimistic in their judgment of the prospects of Russia and France in the event of a general conflict. Among other things this optimism is based on their estimate of the diversion of forces that the united armies of the Balkan States (excepting Roumania) would effect, by drawing upon themselves the corresponding sections of the Austro-Hungarian forces. A further favourable circumstance for Russia and France would be the mobilization of Italy, who is bound to France both through the African war and by special treaties. As regards the situation in the Mediterranean, the predominance of the French fleet in these waters has been increased by the decision just made to transfer the third French squadron from Brest to Toulon. " This decision," added M. Poincaré, " was taken in agreement with Great Britain, and represents a further development and strengthening of the measures already agreed on between the French and British naval staffs."

Such declarations do indeed go far to reveal the actual standpoint of the man who made them. He is, in the first place, fettered by French public opinion. The French people would refuse to recognize a struggle merely for influence in the Balkans as a *casus belli*. But if the conflagration extends to Germany it may be counted on that it will be possible to bring in France. Here is no peace-at-any-price attitude.

Since, however, there was no present question of a world war, it was important at least to prevent Austria from taking action and reaping any benefit from the Balkan adventure. We noted above, in connexion with Poincaré's first effort at mediation, how he did his best to tie Austria's hands. Once more this aim is evident in his effort to set up a conference.

One of his first cares was, as before, to maintain the solidarity of the Entente as far as possible. Great Britain was the most doubtful member, showing, as we saw, certain sympathies for Turkey. Nothing, therefore, must be allowed to happen to bring a gulf between London on the one side and Paris and St. Petersburg on the other. In this respect Isvolsky's telegram of October 16, 1912 [513], is specially important. According to this Poincaré expressed the fear that the contents of the secret treaties between Bulgaria and the other Balkan States might reach the public. " Should the London Cabinet learn of these treaties from any other source, it may become distrustful of the sincerity of Russia and France, who knew their contents, and an understanding between the three Powers may be rendered more difficult." Isvolsky himself adds " that some of the papers here are beginning already to hint that in the present crisis Russia is playing a double game." It was important, therefore, not to be caught out and so to make the British Government unaccommodating. Accordingly, Sazonov follows Poincaré's advice, and on October 31 requests his ambassador in London to inform the Foreign Office in some detail of the terms of the agreements between Serbia and Bulgaria. The " double game " is continued, however ; Russia's rôle is virtually represented as a passive one, and she is stated to have only learned the wording of the agreements after the event, and to have refrained then from raising objections in order to avoid " deflecting the further development of the policy of the two countries in an undesired direction." [1]

To return to Paris. On October 15, 1912 [507], Isvolsky reports Poincaré's latest proposal for mediation, as follows :

1. The Powers will come to an agreement without delay to enable them to offer their mediation at a suitable opportunity to the High Porte and the Balkan States.

2. If mediation succeeds, an international Conference will assemble in as short a time as possible, to consider and carry into effect the reforms to be introduced in European Turkey.

3. If mediation fails, the conference will nevertheless assemble, in order, when hostilities have come to an end, to take the steps demanded by the concern for general peace and the interest of Europe.

4. In addition, the Powers agree to undertake nothing against the sovereignty of His Majesty the Sultan or against the integrity of the Turkish Empire.

Russia's reply was significant enough. On October 16 [511] Sazonov agrees with Points 1 and 2, but finds the calling of a conference inadvisable, as " during the war it cannot count on the needed authority." He also advises dispensing " for the present " with the reference to the sovereignty of the Sultan. His purpose is clear. He must await the result of the Balkan adventure, and prevent Turkey's aggressors from being robbed of the fruits of victory by a premature intervention of the Powers. Poincaré's suspicions, on the other hand, are of Vienna ; he is afraid, according to a telegram of Isvolsky's of October 16, that the Vienna Government may try to escape from definitely agreeing to joint action with the other Cabinets. This is why he is unable entirely to agree with the objections made by St. Petersburg. On October 17 [515] Isvolsky reports that Poincaré is ready to amend the third point, but insists on the fourth, " as he is convinced that it is the only way of restricting Austria's freedom of action." Thus on

---

[1] Siebert, p. 380.

both sides concealed designs prevent agreement : on one side the effort is to support the Balkan States, and on the other to baulk at the outset any expansionist hopes that the Dual Monarchy might entertain.

But the two points of view grew more easily reconcilable as the probable issue of the war grew clearer. Poincaré was at first pessimistic, while at St. Petersburg there was certainly more confidence. Isvolsky also had no great hopes at first, and advised his Government to take precautions against a defeat of the Balkan peoples. On October 22, 1912 [524], he telegraphs :

When I consider the various possible developments, and dwell on the possibility of a decisive Turkish victory, I am continually reminded that during the abortive negotiations for a military convention Bulgaria mentioned that a possible form of Russian assistance would be the mobilization of the Caucasian military command. It seems to me that the possibility must be kept in view from now onwards that circumstances may require our resort to this effective and comparatively safe method of pressure on Turkey. Taking advantage of the entirely confidential character of my talks with Poincaré, I have mentioned this possibility among other things, taking special care to make it clear that I was speaking for myself only. At the first moment he was clearly startled at the idea, and objected that the move would produce parallel activity on Austria's part, and might result in a strong reaction against Russia in Great Britain and in dissension within the Triple Entente. I replied that should the Slav States suffer a serious defeat Austria would hardly trouble to find an occasion for intervention, and that she would be unlikely to make any movement if complications arose on our Asiatic frontier. Germany is always glad to learn of them. As to Great Britain, it will be to her interest to step in as a mediator between us and Turkey. To-day I was able to satisfy myself that Poincaré regards my idea more calmly and even with some interest. I venture to suggest that should circumstances lead us to decide on mobilizing or concentrating our Caucasian troops, it is essential to inform Poincaré in good time, so that he may work with us in preparing the ground in London.

The line of thought is characteristic of Isvolsky ; he is not deterred by the further danger to European peace involved even by a partial mobilization in Russia. On the following day he pursues it further in a letter [526]. Here again he describes a decisive victory of the Balkan States as " the least probable " eventuality, and urges the usefulness, in view of the possibility of a Turkish victory, of convincing Poincaré " that there is no escape from the necessity of Russia's active intervention in certain circumstances."

However, the pessimists on the Seine were not justified. The Balkan States marched rapidly from success to success, and spirits rose correspondingly in Paris. Isvolsky is able to report this as early as October 28 [532] in telegraphing a public declaration by Poincaré of French loyalty to Russia. " Nothing," he says, " succeeds like success : under the influence of recent events there has been ample evidence of a revulsion of feeling in favour of the Balkan States and of the Russian standpoint."

There is no longer any difference of opinion in regard to the proposed action of the Powers ; agreement is reached on what amounts to a sharp diplomatic blow at Austria under cover of concern for the interests of the Balkan States. On October 29 [534] Sazonov asks for French initiative on the following basis :

1. The declaration of the entire disinterestedness of the Powers in the matter of compensation of any sort as a basis for the mediation between the belligerent parties.
2. Radical reforms over the whole of European Turkey as far as the Adrianople line on the basis already familiar to you, which could be expanded.

Poincaré agrees at once. This was a change entirely in accordance with his views, for the " declaration of entire disinterestedness," accepted by all Cabinets, would rob the Dual Monarchy of any opportunity of adding to its own territory. Isvolsky telegraphs on October 30 [537] that Poincaré has at once approached London to secure its assent. Austria demurs ; according to Sazonov's telegram of November 5 [549], she renounces territorial compensations, but is unable to extend her disinterestedness to the economic sphere. Especially she fears Serbian expansion towards the

Adriatic, which would be liable to injure the commercial interests of the Dual Monarchy.

The attack from Paris on Austria now grows steadily keener. On November 4, 1912 [554], Poincaré sends the following letter to the Russian ambassador :

As I said to you, the mysterious attitude of Austria is exercizing the French Government no less than the Imperial [Russian] Government.

In agreement with the Council of Ministers, I think it prudent to establish at once a general line of procedure in the event of Austria determining to achieve territorial expansion. You have told me that such an eventuality is already provided against in your Racconigi agreements, and that both Italy and Russia have declared their opposition to any territorial expansion of a Great Power in the Balkans. The French Government is also of the opinion that such an enterprise would fling open the door to all sorts of competing ambitions. I should be glad to know whether the Imperial Government is with us in opposing any annexation of Turkish territory by a Great Power, and whether it would be inclined to discuss both with France and Great Britain the means of averting this danger.

Isvolsky realizes at once what this step implies. In his covering note of November 7 [554] he comments as follows :

I come now to Poincaré's proposal in regard to means of preventing Austrian territorial conquests in the Balkans. I regard it as my first duty, in view of mistakes which may still occur in the deciphering of my cipher telegram, to send you herewith the exact text of the communication which M. Poincaré has sent to me on this matter. I telegraphed fully to you the reasons which in my view make it desirable that we should reply to this communication point by point and in writing. This proposal was made after discussion of the matter in the Council of Ministers. It embodies an entirely new French standpoint in regard to the question of Austrian territorial expansion at the cost of the Balkan peninsula. Hitherto France has merely declared to us that local happenings, virtually of purely Balkan interest, could only occasion diplomatic steps on her part and no sort of active intervention ; now, however, she seems to realize that Austrian territorial conquests would affect the general balance of power in Europe, and so France's own interests.

I have not failed to point out to M. Poincaré that his proposal to examine jointly with us and Great Britain the means of averting such territorial conquests, involves also the consideration of the practical consequences of the agreement which he has proposed.

I was able to infer from his reply that he entirely realizes that France may be drawn into military operations. For the moment he is, of course, only proposing the examination of this question, but M. Paléologue has openly admitted in a conversation with me that the contemplated agreement may lead to further active steps. Among other things he said to me that while considering various eventualities with his Chief he had referred to the precedent of 1832. On Austria's occupation of Ferrara in that year France occupied Ancona, and she only withdrew after the Austrian withdrawal from Ferrara. All this seems to me to be worth our most serious attention. We should not let the opportunity go by to settle definitely the new standpoint of the French Government in regard to the possibility of Austro-Hungarian expansion at the cost of the Balkan peninsula. We must prepare the ground for future joint action by Russia, France, and Great Britain should Austria, in the course of further developments, no longer hold to her present declaration of renunciation of territorial compensations.

Isvolsky is clearly triumphant. France has been won over to the support of Russian interests, and probably to joint action against Austrian expansion in the Balkans : a solid gain beyond all that had yet been agreed between the two Powers. Sazonov's reply of November 14, 1912 [566], shows that St. Petersburg also realizes the importance of Poincaré's declarations. Isvolsky is authorized to reply in writing to Poincaré " that Russia is no more able than France to remain passive in face of Austro-Hungarian territorial expansion in the Balkan peninsula " ; and Sazonov notes with satisfaction " that in the view of the Government of the Republic, France could not remain uninterested in such an eventuality."

At the same time, matters were viewed more coolly on the Neva than on the Seine. Sazonov adds the remark that from the news received there is " every hope that Austria, at all events at the present moment, is unlikely to be trying to secure territorial gains." At the same time, Russia is holding Serbia back ; according to Sazonov's telegram of November 11 [562], she has been warned that " there is no intention of entering upon a war with the Powers of the Triple Alliance over the question of a Serbian port on the Adriatic." The policy of St. Petersburg was now as clear as at the beginning of the Balkan campaign : " I wish you luck," she cried fraternally to her victorious protégés, " but don't expect me to move." Their success was to be Russia's, but not their sacrifices. Belgrad, therefore, was told not to go too fast. For the same reason measures had shortly before been taken to bring the advance of the Allies to a stop before they reached Constantinople. On November 4 [546] Sazonov informs Isvolsky of the urgent request of the Turkish ambassador for mediation to prevent the capture of Constantinople ; and Sazonov supports this request. On the 6th [552] he declares that if the Allies occupy the Turkish capital Russia will have to send her fleet there. This move is, of course, dictated by Russia's keen interest in the Straits. Nor was there any desire, as already explained, to complicate the general situation at that stage.

In the face of this attitude of France's ally, what followed in Paris is a striking instance of the ruthless work of Isvolsky and Poincaré. On November 17, 1912 [567], Isvolsky reports that Poincaré has declared his inability to define precisely what France's attitude will be in the event of active Austrian intervention until he knows the views of the Imperial (Russian) Government.

" It is," said Poincaré, " for Russia to take the initiative in a matter in which she is the most closely interested party. France's task is to accord to Russia her most emphatic support. Were the French Government to take the initiative, it would be in danger of forestalling the intentions of its Ally." In order to leave him no doubt whatever as to the degree of our co-operation, I felt it necessary to acquaint him with a passage in M. Sazonov's instructions to the Russian ambassador in Belgrad, in which it is stated that France and Great Britain have declared openly that they have no intention at all of joining issue with the Triple Alliance over the conflict. " Broadly," added M. Poincaré, " it all comes to this : if Russia goes into the war, France will do the same, as we know that in this matter Germany would stand at Austria's back." I asked whether he knew the British standpoint in the matter ; Poincaré replied that according to his information the London Cabinet would confine itself for the moment to promising Russia its full diplomatic support, but that this would not exclude more substantial assistance in case of necessity.

8

This is a document of the greatest importance in the history of the process that led to the world war. Germany has been blamed for allowing Austria a free hand after the Serajevo assassination in her dealings with Serbia, a free hand, that is, in a war which Berlin hoped would be localized. More than eighteen months before this, the French Prime Minister, in saying that " if Russia goes into the war, France will do the same," allowed the Tsarist Empire a much wider measure of unquestioned plenary power, envisaging not a local but a general European conflict. From now onwards St. Petersburg was assured of the intervention of the French army in any struggle for predominance in the Balkans. That is the immense and inestimable significance of Poincaré's statement quoted above. It is not in any way modified by Isvolsky's subsequent statement in his telegram of November 18, 1912 [569], that France would march " if Germany gives Austria armed support against Russia," for Poincaré had already said that he confidently assumed that Germany would do so. The central point remains, that Poincaré is shown to have been ready for a world war in November 1912, at a time when Berlin was exerting every effort to restrain the Dual Monarchy from any action that would endanger peace.

Other happenings at this period show how real was Poincaré's intentness on war. As the telegram quoted showed, he regarded substantial assistance from Great Britain as not inconceivable. He had quite definite grounds for this. For at that moment negotiations were in progress in London on his suggestion for providing a written basis for the intimate relations existing between France and Great Britain. There was an exchange of letters on November 22 and 23, 1912 [1327], between M. Cambon, the French ambassador in London, and Sir Edward Grey, the British Foreign Minister, referring to the joint military discussions. This provided what, as we know, had not existed until then —a written diplomatic agreement.

At the same time, relations with Italy were being cleared

up. On November 20 [573] Isvolsky reports Signor Tittoni, the Italian ambassador in Paris, as saying to the French Premier that in the event of war occurring over the inviolability of Albania, " Italy would be compelled to give armed support to Austria." According to a letter of the same day [574], Poincaré seemed " paralysed " by this declaration. He reminded Tittoni of the Russo-Italian treaty of Racconigi, and of the Franco-Italian convention, and contended that the latter entitled France to count on Italian neutrality in the event of war with Germany and Austria. At Tittoni's reply that the agreement with Austria was of old standing but valid for all that, Poincaré was quite beside himself— further evidence of the extent to which he was filled with the idea of a general collision. To impress Italy, he at once assured Tittoni " that Russia may count at all times on armed support from France if events involve her in war with Germany and Austria." He now [574] suggests to Isvolsky " a mutual exchange of exact information between Russia and France concerning the treaties of the two Powers with Italy " ; this Isvolsky strongly advocates. " Italy's rôle," Isvolsky writes on November 21 [575],

in any general European conflict seems to me to be of very great interest to us. It is really absolutely absurd that the two allied Powers should conceal from one another their treaties with a potential enemy. . . . The declarations made yesterday by the Italian ambassador, if confirmed by the Italian Government, may have very important results on the distribution of troops in the French army. You know that since 1902 France has reduced in an extraordinary degree the proportion of her military forces stationed on the Italian frontier ; if I am not mistaken, by two whole army corps. If it should now prove that France cannot count on Italy's neutrality, this would alter the whole plan of campaign, which is based on this neutrality. The question is so important that, as I have learnt, Poincaré has called an extraordinary Council of Ministers for this morning to discuss it.

On November 28, 1912 [592], Sazonov agrees to the proposed exchange, but desires the following methods to be adopted :

You must give the Premier the information with no one else present, verbally and without handing over anything in writing. Before reading the treaty you will lay stress on our determination to give this information only to M. Poincaré personally ; we count on his promise to preserve absolute silence concerning this matter, not only with the Council of Ministers, but with his most intimate colleagues.

Under these conditions you could read to M. Poincaré the enclosed copy of the treaty concluded at Racconigi, and I venture to beg your high Excellency to send the copy back to me by the next courier, and at the same time to let me have the purport, written down from memory, of the Franco-Italian treaty after you have heard it.

On December 5 [606] Isvolsky reports that this procedure has been followed. All these measures show clearly that towards the end of 1912 Poincaré and Isvolsky regarded the moment for which they had prepared as now arrived. To judge from a telegram of November 25 [584] from the Russian ambassador in Sofia, chauvinists elsewhere had the same feeling. "Moreover," he writes, "my conversations with representatives of *The Times* strengthen my conviction that very many people in England are working at present towards accentuating the complications in Europe to the point of bringing about an armed collision between the Powers of the Triple Entente and Germany and Austria ; they think that conditions are favourable at present for the destruction of the German fleet and of German trade." Thus the clouds drew in from various quarters over Europe.

However this may be, the undermining of peace was proceeding in the most dangerous way in Paris. At first, as we saw, when the issue of the Balkan war was still uncertain, Poincaré referred to public opinion as the obstacle to going all the way with Russia. Isvolsky was faced with the obstacle of the unwillingness above all of the Left-wing groups to see blood shed for Russia's imperialistic aims in the Balkans. Now, however, he secured welcome means of combating these chief opponents of his.

As early as October 23, 1912 [527], he writes to Sazonov that the French Press " is gradually changing its attitude

towards Russia, and its view of events in the Balkan peninsula ; it is steadily going over to the support of Austria and
Turkey." The situation is engaging not only his own
attention but, " as I have been able to satisfy myself, that
of the French Foreign Minister." Isvolsky now recalls
the payments made, with Rouvier's help, through French
banks in 1908 and 1910 to the French Press, and asks for
a sum of 300,000 francs for present needs. He adds :

It is important to do nothing without informing M. Poincaré
and securing his consent, for good results can only be expected
subject to this being done. French statesmen are very adept in
deals of this sort. My conversation with M. Poincaré has convinced me that he is ready to lend us his assistance in this matter,
and to let us know the most suitable plan of distribution of the
subsidies. . . . He expressed to me his liveliest gratitude for my
discussion of the matter with him in all candour, and added that
he would himself have approached me to ask me to do nothing
without prior agreement with him.

Sazonov is not entirely enthusiastic over Isvolsky's plan,
but he discusses it with Kokovtsov, the Russian Premier ;
the latter, not without hesitation, sends Davidov, of the
Russian National Debt Office, to Paris to organize the
proposed action. Davidov receives from Kokovtsov a
letter of introduction to Poincaré, dated October 30, 1912
[539] ; it ends as follows :

I must add that, should you regard direct Russian intervention
in this field as essential, I should fall in with your view, which will
be based on your extensive knowledge and experience in these
matters.

Davidov telegraphs to Kokovtsov on November 11 [564] :

Summary of my discussion with Poincaré and our ambassador.
Both are of the opinion that payments to the Press should be
postponed, but consider it desirable to have ready a credit of
300,000 francs for the purpose of immediate intervention when
embarked on at a later date. That is reasonable, and I agreed
to transmit the proposal to your Excellency. At our request,
Poincaré will sketch with Lenoir to-morrow the plan of the
organization of this service when started. Poincaré also asks me

to receive Perchot and to try to quiet him, as his campaign in the Radical party is becoming troublesome to Poincaré and the Alliance.

Here again, therefore, Isvolsky had attained his purpose. This time the plot against French public opinion had succeeded, undoubtedly because the political head of the Republic, whose advice the Russian Government could not ignore, had himself come to Isvolsky's aid. Funds were at last granted for dealing with Press opposition by means of the " clinking arguments " which he had continually been calling for since the Morocco crisis. The moment for drawing on them came sooner than St. Petersburg expected. As early as December 5 [608] Isvolsky shows the extent of the annoyance caused by the anti-war group in France :

In judging the position taken up by the Poincaré Cabinet in the present crisis it must be borne in mind that within the very party on which the Cabinet depends there is a very influential group which openly calls for " peace at any price." This group, with M. Combes at its head, controls a large number of Press organs, which subject M. Poincaré to severe criticism on account of the line he has taken on various occasions. I gather that similar criticism is to be heard also in the lobbies of the Chamber and the Senate, and the Government has to take serious count of it. . . . In a recent talk with me, Poincaré remarked that opinion in France is strongly pro-peace, and that he has always to keep this in mind. We are, it seems to me, all the more indebted to him for his fixed resolve most loyally to fulfil his duties as an Ally in case of need. While M. Combes and his friends are everywhere declaring in the Parliamentary lobbies that at the critical moment peace or war will depend not on the Government but on them, in reality, if (which God forbid) the crisis comes, the decision will be made by the three strong personalities who stand at the head of the Cabinet—Poincaré, Millerand, and Delcassé. And it is a piece of good fortune for us that we have to deal with these personalities and not with one or another of the opportunist politicians who have succeeded one another in the course of recent years in the Government of France.

Thus it was the " Combists " who would have to be dealt with when the great hour struck. They were the hated supporters of peace.

Very few days later we find Isvolsky convinced that the

crisis for the avoidance of which he had shown such pathetic concern had actually come. On December 9, 1912 [613], he wires concerning Serbian fears of an energetic step on Austria's part in Belgrad, to be accompanied by an armed threat. Immediately after this he sends a second inflammatory telegram :

The French Minister of War has informed Poincaré that, according to the news he has, the Austrian military preparations on the Russian frontier go considerably beyond the corresponding Russian preparations, and that in the event of war this must react to the disadvantage of the military situation of France, since it must permit Germany to bring up a larger number of troops against France. Millerand is asking Poincaré to have this news checked by the French military attaché, as it has reference to November 21 (new style) and is perhaps out of date. Poincaré is telegraphing about this to Georges Louis.

On December 11 [620] he telegraphs, in visibly growing excitement :

To-day I found Poincaré greatly disturbed at the news reaching him from all sides, and from the most reliable sources, of intensive preparations in Austria for war and of impending Austrian action against Serbia. According to this news, the whole of the cavalry forces in Galicia and two corps in Bosnia are fully mobilized, while in ten corps every battalion has been brought up to a strength of 700 men. In face of this situation we, so far as the French General Staff is aware, are continuing to remain completely inactive, and hardly any steps at all have been taken against Austria. This will permit Austria to deal with the Serbs before we have completed our mobilization, and will place us in the dilemma of having either to accept the accomplished fact or to begin a war under exceedingly unfavourable conditions both for us and for France, as Germany will probably seize the opportunity to fall at once on France with all her resources. Instructions urgently requested.

Shortly afterwards [621] he even states that Austria intends " in the immediate future " to issue an ultimatum against Serbia, with terms which that country will be bound to refuse, since they would reduce her to vassalage. The intention, he says, is then to occupy Belgrad, and Vienna will not hesitate even to go to war with Russia.

Alongside these alarmist reports there went increasing

activity behind the scenes.   The 300,000 francs for influencing the Press was, when used, to be divided into three
instalments of 100,000 francs.   It was also agreed that
Lenoir, the French intermediary who was to hand over the
money to the lucky receivers, was to receive his instructions
as to the persons to be influenced from M. Klotz, the French
Minister of Finance, but was to make payment only with
the concurrence of the Russian ambassador and of M.
Raffalovitch, the representative in Paris of the Russian
Ministry of Finance.   On December 3, 1912, Lenoir came to
Raffalovitch and demanded the first instalment.   On the
9th Klotz made urgent representations as to the non-arrival
of the money, of which 25,000 francs had already been paid
out, and on the 12th [625] Davidov agreed to the remit-
tance at all events of the amount already expended.   On the
next day Raffalovitch sent off a telegram entirely in the
agitated tone of Isvolsky's telegrams of this time [628] :

The Russian ambassador in Paris is very pessimistic ; he regards
the situation as serious, and is anticipating a possible occupation
of the capital of Serbia in the event of her refusal to sign the Treaty
of Good Neighbourliness, which amounts to the destruction of the
political liberty of the Kingdom.   The Russian ambassador in
Paris is of the opinion that the remainder of the credit of 75,000
francs should be placed without further bargaining at the disposal
of the Minister of Finance.

Please telegraph me your Excellency's concurrence.   I have to
inform you that Lenoir is away.   The Russian ambassador in Paris
wants 30,000 francs for immediate distribution to persons whose
names are to be known to no one but himself.   Please telegraph
urgently to me and add your personal impression of the situation.

On December 14, 1912, Isvolsky reports [630] :

The French ambassador telegraphs from St. Petersburg that
Colonel de la Guiche [the French military attaché in St. Petersburg]
has been informed in the General Staff, in reply to his inquiry
concerning our military position on the Austrian frontier, that
Austria is only taking defensive measures on the Russian frontier,
that there is no belief on our side in an Austrian attack on Russia,
that we regard an Austrian attack on Serbia as exceedingly unlikely,
and, finally, that even in the event of an attack on Serbia, Russia
could not go to war.   Our War Minister is reported also as having

said to de la Guiche that he is firmly convinced that peace is being maintained, and is thinking of going on December 23 [new style] to Germany and Southern France. Poincaré and the whole Cabinet are greatly disturbed and agitated at this news, as the conviction exists here, as I have already telegraphed, of the warlike character of the Austrian preparations, and it is feared that we shall be taken by surprise and that Germany's attack on France will be facilitated. I have done my utmost to calm Poincaré, and have pointed out to him that two full months ago, at the very beginning of the crisis, we resolved on serious steps to bring our military forces on the Austrian frontier to the utmost degree of preparedness, that no men had since been dismissed from the colours, and so on.

I venture, however, to mention that it would be very desirable to give the French Government, which is seriously reckoning with the possibility of a war, information concerning the military measures which we have adopted, and also concerning our views of events which are more or less possible ; for the present lack of information is certainly producing nervousness here, which is beginning to spread among the public and the Press, and it is becoming more and more difficult for me to keep public opinion favourable to us here. I beg urgently for directions for guidance in detailed discussions with Poincaré.

Thus Paris was actually ready to strike, and only troubled at the apparent absence of similar resolution on the Neva. And in close connexion with the " serious reckoning with the possibility of war," Raffalovitch writes on the following day to his chief, Kokovtsov, Premier and Finance Minister of Russia [633] :

Yesterday I was called on by M. Lenoir, who came to ask whether anything had yet been done with regard to the Press organization with which you are acquainted and which your Excellency and I both view with the same disgust. Our feelings must, however, be suppressed in view of the remarks of M. Poincaré and M. Klotz, which Lenoir conveyed to me.

It seems that your French colleague feels himself embarrassed by the campaign which the Radical Socialists are carrying on ; they are basing their campaign on this declaration : " We shall permit no war arising out of Eastern questions, or in particular the relations between Serbia and Austria."

Raffalovitch is thus fully justified in his later description [649] of these funds as a " war chest." They were expended directly on silencing the voices in France which were opposing participation in bloodshed. Their secret work was already beginning to take effect, for on December 17 Isvolsky is able cheerfully to send the following telegram [636] :

Yesterday, under a resolution of the socialistic Confédération Générale du Travail, a general strike of the French workers was due to take place, to protest against the Balkan war and the possibility of France being drawn into it. The attempt failed completely, both in Paris and the provinces. Only an insignificant number of workers took part in the strike, and there was no disorder anywhere. Poincaré told me that the Government had taken no precautionary measures of any importance, relying on the recent evidence of increasing patriotic feeling and desiring also to avoid giving foreign opinion any reason to suppose that it stood in fear of an anti-militarist movement. Despite this, the number of strikers in, for instance, the State workshops had been less than that of the workmen normally absent on Mondays. In a word, yesterday showed once more that the anti-militarists will have no success.

Everything was, indeed, proceeding as desired. Isvolsky's victory over his opponents in French politics was complete. Only one thing was still lacking—the echo from St. Petersburg. For this there was the utmost impatience on the Seine. On December 18 [639] Isvolsky clearly reflects this impatience in a letter to Sazonov. He complains of the absence of any answer to his telegrams concerning Austrian arming, and continues :

It is still only a short time since the French Government and Press were inclined to suspect us of egging Serbia on, and one was constantly hearing people say that France has no desire to go to war about a Serbian port (*France ne veut pas faire la guerre pour un port Serbe*). Now, however, there is astonishment and unconcealed dismay at our indifference to Austria's mobilization. Anxiety in this regard is finding expression not only in the conversations of French Ministers with me and with our military attaché, but among the general public and in newspapers of very varying political tendency. The French General Staff is so concerned that, as I reported in my telegram No. 445, the War Minister thought fit to draw Poincaré's attention to the fact. Poincaré showed me Millerand's letter, which he had put before a Council of Ministers called specially for this purpose. French astonishment has been anything but dissipated by the telegram from Georges Louis containing the reply of our general staff to General de la

Guiche. I was shown the text of the telegram. According to this, General de la Guiche was told that we not only regard Austria's arming as a purely defensive measure, but that Russia would not strike even in the entirely improbable event of an Austrian attack on Serbia. At this information Poincaré and all the Ministers were utterly astonished.

According to all the news arriving here, Austria is at present on the point of completing the mobilization of ten army corps. Some of these are obviously directed against Russia. This mobilization is a heavy burden for Austria's finances, which are already in a deplorable condition. A critical move by the Austrian Cabinet may therefore be expected any day. Such a move, it is considered here, might involve a Russian defensive move, which in turn would inevitably and automatically drag first Germany and then France into the war. The French Government views this possibility with perfect calmness, aware of its obligations under the Alliance and firmly resolved to act up to them. It has taken all necessary steps ; mobilization on the Eastern frontier has been examined, war material is in readiness, and so on. And at this of all moments France seems to be faced with an entirely different attitude on the part of her Ally, and that in regard to a situation in which it might have been supposed that her Ally is chiefly interested. The conclusion drawn is that either we do not fully appreciate Austria's warlike intentions or for some special reason we have been unwilling at the moment to take France into our confidence. Both suppositions are most prejudicial to us, and despite all my efforts to combat them it is becoming more and more difficult to preserve here a desirable attitude towards us. . . .

To secure this attitude I am at present doing my utmost to influence the Press. In this certain substantial results have been attained, thanks to the timely adoption of the needed measures. As you know, I am taking no direct part in the distribution of subsidies. But this distribution, in which French Ministers (the Ministers of Foreign Affairs and Finances) are concerned, appears to be effectual in every case, and has already produced the needed result. For my part I am taking special pains to influence by personal intervention the most important of the Paris papers, such as the *Temps*, the *Journal des Débats*, the *Echo de Paris*, and so on. On the whole there can be no comparison between the tone of the Paris Press at present and during the 1908–09 crisis. The attitude of the *Temps* is specially noteworthy : four years ago it was remarkable for its violent advocacy of Austria, while at present M. Tardieu is energetically attacking the Austrian policy in its columns. Count Berchtold and the Austrian ambassador in Paris have complained of this several times to M. Poincaré.

In my conversations with French journalists I am trying mainly to get them to see that if, despite the exceedingly reasonable and accommodating attitude shown by Russia, Austria's arming and the demands of Austrian diplomacy result in a European conflict, the war will not have broken out over separate interests of Serbia's or Russia's but over the attempt of Austria, and of Germany at her back, to set up their hegemony in Europe and in the Balkan peninsula.   Thank God, this is becoming realized more and more in French political and military circles and society.   Recently I have no longer had to contend with the view that France might find herself drawn into war over the affairs of other countries, but with the fear that in a matter affecting the position and the prestige of the whole Entente we have been remaining too passive.

Here we have a fairly close contemporary picture of what was then going on in Paris.   Its lines are filled in by a note made on the same day by Ignatyev, the Russian military attaché in Paris, recording a conversation with M. Millerand, the French Minister of War, as follows : [1]

MILLERAND : Well, Colonel, what is your view of the purpose of the Austrian mobilization ?

IGNATYEV : It is difficult to say in advance, but certainly the Austrian preparations against Russia have at present the character of a defensive measure.

MILLERAND : Quite so ; but do you not regard an occupation of Serbia as in itself a direct provocation to war ?

IGNATYEV : I cannot answer that question, but I know that we have no desire to bring about a European war or to take any steps which might start a European conflagration.

MILLERAND : In that case you will have to abandon Serbia to her fate.   That, of course, is your affair ; all we want is that it must be clear that we are not to blame for it ; we are prepared, and that fact must be borne in mind.   But can you not at least say what is the Russian view on the Balkan question generally ?

IGNATYEV : We are still deeply interested in the Slav question, but I need hardly say that history has taught us to think first of the interests of our own State, and not to sacrifice them to abstract ideas.

MILLERAND : But surely you understand, Colonel, that the present is not a question of Albania or the Serbs or Durazzo, but of the hegemony of Austria over the whole Balkan peninsula ? . . . Surely you are doing something on the military side ?

The conversation has a double interest.   In the first place it is fresh evidence that as early as November 1912, France was "ready" for world war.   But it also shows something else : the Russian military attaché was by no

[1] E. Adamov, *Izvestiya* (Moscow), July 29, 1924.

means as eager to take advantage of this readiness as the Russian ambassador, and had accordingly to swallow something like a rebuke from the French Minister of War. Evidently he was better acquainted with the attitude of the Russian governing circles than Isvolsky was.

For matters were on the whole viewed much more calmly in St. Petersburg. There it was still firmly intended to bring the Balkan war to an end without the sacrifice of Russian lives ; and there the alarmist reports of Austrian plans were assessed at their true value. They came mostly from Belgrad, directly or indirectly, and were merely Serbian propaganda aimed at setting Europe afire in order to secure the destruction of the Dual Monarchy. As early as December 10 [613] Sazonov had indicated Russia's attitude. The Serbian ambassador had declared that Austria intended to resort to force in order to subject Serbia to economic and political vassalage. Sazonov replied that Russia was ready to give diplomatic support to Serbia's efforts to gain her freedom, but that in return she must demand that Belgrad should comply with the decisions of the Entente Powers—Russia, France, and Great Britain. " Neither we nor the Powers friendly to Russia can allow the decision as to a European war to be left to the Serbian Government."

The pressure of the Paris politicians towards a general armed conflict did not fit in with this programme, quite apart from their illusions as to aggressive Austrian designs. At the same time, preparations were silently being made for the worst ; there was none of the passiveness which so alarmed MM. Poincaré, Isvolsky, and Millerand, as is shown by the following telegram from Sazonov, dated December 18, 1912 [640], which at last replied to the urgent inquiries from Paris :

The suggestion that Russia has done nothing to maintain her preparedness is not accurate. Some 350,000 reservists have been retained with the colours, some 80 million roubles has been allocated for extraordinary army requirements and for the Baltic fleet, some of the divisions in the Kiev command have been brought closer to the Austrian frontier, and a whole series of further measures have been adopted.—Please note that this information is confidential and that it is desirable that it should be preserved from Press indiscretions. As to the statement heard by General de la Guiche, " that even in the event of an Austrian attack on Serbia, Russia would not go to war," such a statement can hardly have been made by any responsible person, and should the Government really come to any such decision France would learn of it by other means than those on the basis of which the French ambassador considered it necessary to communicate with his Government.

Thus, from the beginning of the Balkan crisis, the Tsarist Empire stood in readiness, prepared, if necessary, for European war. But at that time it desired, if possible, to avoid war, since for the moment the victory of the Balkan States had brought it a sufficient gain in the form of extended influence over the South-Eastern corner of Europe. This gain had first to be consolidated and given the sanction of international agreements ; accordingly the Balkan States were required to observe a certain moderation. For the same reason a conference of the Great Powers was pressed for, to take note of the successes won.

St. Petersburg won its way. Two Conferences were opened in London, one of the Balkan States and one of the ambassadors of the Great Powers ; and the representatives of the Entente countries received precise instructions to support the Russian claims. And the outbreak of the world war was postponed.

But the conclusions to be drawn from the documents quoted are obvious. The development during the autumn months of 1912 represented an important step gained by Isvolsky. France had declared her solidarity with Russia's aspirations in the Balkans. It was now known on the Neva that French armed assistance could be relied on when the time was declared to be ripe for proceeding from the smaller task of turning Turkey out of Europe to the larger one of the destruction of the Austrian bulwark. As we saw, the men in power in Paris were already ready to go as far as this, and to this extent were even ahead of St. Petersburg

for the time being.   But only for the time being.   For
the moment the Tsarist Empire, having made secure the
first phase of its advance, resolved to enter on the second
phase, there was no longer any dividing line between the
St. Petersburg policy and that of Isvolsky and Poincaré,
and then there could hardly be a further pause.   From this
point of view the events described were of fundamental
importance to the fate of Europe.   When France conquered
Morocco, Russia insisted that she was not directly concerned.
But when Russia in turn proceeded to the realization of
Pan-Slav aspirations, France declared that she, too, was
interested in the issue, and regarded herself as bound to
perform the utmost duties of friendship.   This was where
world war first became possible ; for one of the two groups
into which Europe had for years been cloven had now a
positive common purpose of which the attainment was only
to be realized through force.

V

THE SECOND AND THIRD BALKAN WARS

In Isvolsky's letter of October 23, 1912 [526], in which he discusses the various possible issues of the first Balkan war, he mentions the first possibility, a decisive victory of the Balkan States, as eventually the most threatening for the peace of Europe. For

It would at once bring into the foreground in its full historic magnitude the question of the struggle of Slavdom not only with Islam but also with Teutonism. In this case no hope can be placed in any sort of palliative, and preparation must be made for a great, decisive, universal European war.

In the event the victory of the Allied Balkan States over Turkey was as complete as it possibly could be. Isvolsky's judgment of the situation in October 1912 must therefore be borne in mind in considering his attitude at the beginning of 1913. The documents of the period will show whether this man, who since 1911 had kept his gaze steadily fixed on an ultimate European war, was now convinced that he had reached his goal. But first we must turn back a little.

The secret manipulation of the Paris Press, which we have seen Poincaré and Isvolsky plan and prepare and carry out together, did not run entirely to the satisfaction of St. Petersburg. Several documents of December 1912 show that the Russians soon lost their enthusiasm for the cleverness of the French statesmen, so praised at first, in these "deals." Lenoir, it will be remembered, was to operate with the prior approval of Raffalovitch, the Russian financial expert, and Isvolsky, making payment to the editors and journalists indicated by Poincaré. Poincaré had devolved his own task mainly upon Klotz, the Minister of Finance. A first instalment of 100,000 francs had already been taken up. A letter from Kokovtsov, the Russian Premier, to Sazonov, dated November 16, 1912 [635], betrays the dissatisfaction of St. Petersburg with the method of distribution of the fund. Kokovtsov mentions that before the payment of the first instalment Klotz sent for Raffalovitch and expressed his own view in the matter as follows :

> The initiative in the plan came from M. Isvolsky, who consulted M. Poincaré. M. Poincaré adopted the idea in the common interest of the two countries. It has been agreed that we shall direct the distribution and indicate the recipients to Lenoir, as we are in a position to know about them while you are not. We regard it as of importance that we shall know who receives money.

The evident intention of the French statesmen was to keep the whole matter in their own independent control. Raffalovitch writes to Isvolsky on December 24 [648], " Your Excellency has noted that the control is slipping entirely out of our hands," and adds : " You have told me that we were just to let the French Government proceed, as soon as they had placed themselves at our service." This can only mean that Isvolsky approved of Klotz's attitude. Isvolsky says as much himself, for on February 14, 1913 [732], he defends his position, after referring to the letter from Kokovtsov mentioned above, at which he appears to have taken great offence, as follows :

> In point of fact the moment for working on the French Press could not, it seemed to me, have been more favourable. Since the beginning of the Balkan crisis I have taken the greatest pains to secure the support of the most influential of the French papers for our point of view. You must admit that I have had considerable success. Lately, however, in connexion with the Presidential election, a campaign has begun in a certain section of the French Press against the alleged excessive subordination of French foreign policy to Russian interests—a campaign carried on princi-

pally by provincial papers which I was unable directly to influence, but which have great influence on public opinion in France. I said to myself that the French Government, in the person of M. Klotz, knows better than we which papers must be supported, and considering everything I concluded that it would be well not to decline the proposal made by M. Klotz. I put this as my personal view to M. Raffalovitch.

In the course of my talk with M. Raffalovitch I also told him that in recent months I had had occasion to ask for services from all sorts of journalists. With their support I had succeeded in getting the necessary news and paragraphs into the papers, and it would be very useful to me to have at my personal disposal a definite sum, say 30,000 francs, in order to pay them for these services. I only expressed this wish in quite a general way. Consequently I was more or less astonished when I learned that M. Kokovtsov had placed 25,000 francs at my disposal for this purpose. I have not yet touched the money as I am not entirely clear as to how I am to expend it. My impression is that the Prime Minister does not altogether approve of my action in this matter, and I wish therefore to say that I do not at all insist on this sum being placed at my disposal, and that I am ready to pay out of my personal means a few journalists who have done me services.

The injured tone and the offer to dispense with the sum if it is grudged are accompanied still by support of Klotz. Shortly afterwards, on February 26 [745], Raffalovitch reports to Kokovtsov a fresh conversation with the Minister of Finance, which shows the state of affairs still more clearly :

I called on M. Klotz this morning. We touched on the question of Lenoir. I found again the fixed idea that the 100,000 francs paid into the Banque de France for disposal by the Prime Minister and M. Klotz was destined for the joint advantage of the two countries, and represented a first instalment to be followed by two more. Up to now, I was told, Lenoir has expended 40,000 francs. I corrected this and said " 25,000 francs," for I know nothing of the other 15,000. I shall ask Lenoir about this on his return—he has gone again to the Riviera ; for Lenoir knows that we are to be kept informed, and consulted as a matter of form at all events. The Minister seemed to think that the intention was to give us a list of recipients when the 100,000 francs is exhausted and then to proceed to pay out the second instalment.

Thus we are finding ourselves ousted from the control of these subsidy payments, which are apparently being used to prevent counter-manœuvres of other groups to influence the newspapers and Parliamentary correspondents.

The last sentence touches the centre of the whole question. The object in view, as we know, was to silence those who were opposing too close co-operation with Russia as a danger to peace ; but the French statesmen were combining this purpose with another, a matter of internal politics, which they regarded as part of the same purpose : the combating of their own opponents in the Radical camp. This was why they were so keen to have the whole management of the matter in their hands. This was not understood in Russia, but Isvolsky knew all about it, and was supporting his friends in Paris. He knew from experience the close connexion in France between the foreign situation and home politics, how the one determined the course of the other, how closely connected the victory of the so-called " moderates," the Right wing, over the Left was with that of Russia's schemes in world politics. Thus it was, in his view, entirely in Russia's interest to allow the Press fund which she had provided to be used by MM. Klotz and Poincaré against their own opponents.

There is a classic example of this interaction of the struggle for power of the French Right wing and of Russian Pan-slavism : the Perchot case. It is of some historic importance, and what our documents have to tell about it deserves careful attention. The first reference to it is in Isvolsky's telegram of November 5, 1912 [348] :

In view of the campaign opened by the *Radical*, M. Perchot's paper, against Poincaré's policy and indirectly against Russia, I feel it my duty once more to invite your serious attention to the matter ; I telegraphed to you about it in my No. 300.

Six days later there follows a further telegram [561] :

I venture once more to call your most serious attention to the Perchot case. The campaign which he has begun, not only in the Press but in Parliamentary circles, is growing from day to day, and is causing great anxiety to Poincaré, who is urgently asking for it to be submitted to a fair arbitration court, as legal proceedings will be bound to be long drawn out. To agree in principle to arbitration would be enough to quiet Perchot. Poincaré spoke to-day to Davidov,[1] who has telegraphed to Kokovtsov.

[1] Director of the Russian National Debt Office.

The substance of Davidov's telegram (November 11 [564]) was given in Chapter IV.   Its last sentence is :

Poincaré also asks me to receive Perchot and to try to quiet him, as his campaign in the Radical party is becoming troublesome for Poincaré and for the Alliance.

On November 21 [575] Isvolsky returns to the matter in a letter to Sazonov, which contains the following warning passage :

Do not forget that Poincaré has to battle with very influential elements in his own party, who are very hostile to Russia and are openly proclaiming that France must in no case be drawn into war over the Balkan affair.   From this point of view I greatly regret that nothing has yet been done in the Perchot affair, which is a permanent source of grave anxiety for Poincaré.

Perchot was owner-editor of the *Radical*, the importance of which lay in its number of readers among the Deputies. The paper was carrying on a bitter campaign against the Prime Minister, declaring that his policy was a danger to peace.   Perchot was now to be " quieted " ; that is, converted by financial means, like other representatives of the extreme Left wing in the Press.   As a specially hot opponent it was proposed to deal with him by extraordinary methods ; these were indicated in Isvolsky's reference to a fair arbitration court in his second telegram.   A fresh telegram of January 3, 1913 [662], shows that bribery on a big scale was proposed :

Poincaré asked me to draw your attention again to the Perchot affair, which continues to be a source of anxiety to him.   He says that the arrangement with the Russian banks mentioned in Perchot's letter to V. N. Kokovtsov is at present under consideration in the Finance Ministry, and that he hopes that you will make a point of working for a satisfactory settlement.   I learn from an entirely trustworthy source that it is very important to Poincaré that the affair shall be disposed of by January 4 [old style], the date of the Presidential election, for Perchot can do a great deal of harm in this election.   I am of opinion that it is greatly to our interest to give Poincaré's candidature this assistance.

In this connexion it is interesting to observe the anxiety with which Isvolsky follows French internal politics in the first weeks of 1913, and his immense concern to see Poincaré elected President of the Republic. The decision was to be made on January 17. On the 12th [674] he telegraphs to Sazonov that Millerand has unexpectedly withdrawn his candidature ; the step is described as the result of " a political intrigue of the Radical Socialists against Poincaré's candidature." On the 16th [686] he writes in the greatest excitement, " To-morrow the election for the Presidency takes place. Should Poincaré fail—which God forbid !— it will be a disaster for us, for it will be the beginning of an era of Combes and the rest." A Combes era would, as we know, have brought to power the friends of peace, so that Isvolsky's anxiety is only too intelligible. If Poincaré, who had made such far-reaching concessions to Russia's aspirations, were to disappear, all Isvolsky's successes would be brought to naught.

Isvolsky had certainly rendered great service to the new President. But we shall soon see that the return was by no means inadequate.

On January 20 Sevastopoulo telegraphs from Paris as chargé d'affaires, Isvolsky being ill, that Poincaré has expressed himself as " deeply touched " by the large number of congratulatory telegrams sent to him from Russia, and declared that his election implies approval of a close agreement with Russia. On January 22 [694] M. Jonnart, Poincaré's successor as Foreign Minister, declares that he will continue his predecessor's policy, and on the 25th [695] he declares that he is a long-convinced adherent of the Franco-Russian alliance, and " will always be ready to give full support to the political, economic, and other interests of Russia." On January 28 Isvolsky, now back at work, has his first meeting with Poincaré's successor at the Quai d'Orsay, and it proves that Jonnart is in fact true to the spirit which has ruled there. The Young Turks had come to the helm, and refused the British demand for the cession of Adrianople to Bulgaria. Russia was considering energetic pressure on the Porte, which in view of the strained general situation must have led to further complications. Jonnart says [699] : " France is ready to fulfil all her obligations towards Russia, but the French Government has to reckon with Parliament and public opinion, and to keep both perfectly clear at all times as to matters which might draw France into war." This is a repetition of the familiar note of the year before, and we also learn at once where it originated. On January 29, 1913 [705], Isvolsky telegraphs :

I have just had a long talk with Poincaré. He told me that in his capacity of President of the Republic it would be perfectly possible for him directly to influence France's foreign policy. He will not fail to take advantage of this during his seven years of office to assure the permanence of a policy based on close harmony with Russia. He also expressed the hope that he would continue to see me often, and asked me to go direct to him in every case in which I felt this desirable. In regard to current affairs he spoke in much the same vein as Jonnart yesterday. As he put it, it is of the greatest importance to the French Government to have the opportunity of preparing French public opinion in advance for participation in any war which might break out over the Balkan question. This is why the French Government asks us not to take any separate action which might result in such a war without a prior understanding with France.

Thus Paris was still ready for war the moment Russia struck, but needed due notice in order to prepare public opinion. On the next day Isvolsky gives a full account of the statements of Jonnart and Poincaré [711] :

As to the statements made to me first by M. Jonnart and then by M. Poincaré, they are essentially in entire agreement, as you were able to see from my telegrams, and beyond doubt they are not merely a casual expression of opinion but a careful definition of the point of view adopted by the French Government as a whole. From my long talks with the two statesmen I have come to the following conclusions : The French Government is firmly resolved to fulfil all its obligations towards us as our Ally, and admits quite coolly, and with its eyes open, that it is possible that the ultimate issue of the present complications may involve it in the necessity of taking part in a general war. The point at which France will be compelled to draw the sword is precisely defined by the Franco-Russian military agreement, and in this regard the French Ministers show no doubts or hesitations. On the other hand, the French Government is bound to take account of the feeling of Parliament and of the public; to both of these, the events now taking place in the Balkan peninsula are in some degree an unfamiliar subject; they are, moreover, only of indirect importance to the vital interests of France. Under present conditions, and in view of the existing system of alliances and agreements, any isolated action in Balkan affairs on the part of one Power or another may very quickly lead to a general European war. The French Government fully realizes and recognizes the special situation of the Russian Government, which has to take account of nationalist feeling and of all-powerful historic traditions; the French Government is making no attempt to rob Russia of her freedom of action or to throw doubt on her moral obligations towards the Balkan States. Russia is therefore assured by France not only of armed assistance in the event defined in the Franco-Russian agreement, but also of the most decided and energetic support of all measures adopted by the Russian Government in the interest of those States. But precisely in order that France may be able at any moment to extend to Russia her friendly help as an Ally in the fullest degree, the French Government earnestly asks us to take no steps on our own account without a prior exchange of views with France, our Ally; for only on this condition can the French Government successfully prepare public opinion in France for the necessity of participating in a war.

Under such conditions it is easy to understand Isvolsky's satisfaction with the new order of things on the Seine. In the same letter he enumerates its advantages:

Poincaré's election to the highest post in the Republic means a decided victory of the moderate political groups over extreme Radicalism, which has always shown itself hostile to Russia and to the Franco-Russian Alliance. Poincaré's energetic, resolute, and unbending character is a sufficient guarantee that in his capacity of President of the Republic he will not be content, like M. Fallières, with a merely passive and, if one may be allowed the expression, decorative rôle; he will at every moment be exerting his whole influence on French policy, especially foreign policy. Both the wording of the Constitution and the practical development of the mechanism of the State have given much greater scope for the influence of the President of the Republic than is generally assumed: he cannot allow a Cabinet to remain in power when it has only a minority behind it, but it always depends on him to determine the composition of the Cabinet and to choose a Foreign Minister who is entirely reliable from his point of view. We are therefore, for the period of his seven years' term of office, perfectly safe against the appearance of such persons as MM. Caillaux, Cruppi, Monis, and so on, at the head of the French Government or of the diplomatic administration. It also depends on his choice whether he will personally preside over the Council of Ministers, before which, as you are aware, in times of grave foreign complications all details of current diplomatic negotiations are placed, without exception, for discussion.

It had been well worth while to assist Poincaré's election by softening his opponents with money ; now it might be hoped that French co-operation with Russia was assured for seven years to come : no small gain, from Isvolsky's standpoint. But it was not enough to maintain the course : the speed was increased. To begin with, a great personal satisfaction fell to Isvolsky's share, no doubt as a direct recognition of his good services : on February 17, 1913 [734], he is able to report that " the French Government has decided on various grounds, and especially on account of his poor health, to recall Georges Louis." So ended the intrigue against the French ambassador in St. Petersburg, with a victory for Isvolsky.

But of more fundamental political importance was the selection of Louis' successor. This was none other than Delcassé, well known for his anti-German bias. Considering that the Paris Press gave the news on the same day as Poincaré's first message from the Élysée, it may well be understood what an impression it must make in those excited times. The following is the comment of the Belgian ambassador in Paris, Baron Guillaume : [1] " Was the coincidence intentional ? Apparently it was ; in any case it excited a great deal of remark and exerted a depressing influence on the Bourse." He adds later :

Many political leaders had been afraid of this election, fearing that it might have the appearance of an anti-German demonstration. Must the selection of the new ambassador in St. Petersburg be interpreted in this sense ? I do not think so ; but I think that M. Poincaré, as a Lorrainer, took pleasure in proclaiming from the first day of his high office his endeavour to show firmness and to hold up his country's flag. It is here, in the disturbed times through which Europe is passing, that the danger lies of M. Poincaré's presence at the Élysée. Under his Premiership the militarist and rather chauvinist instincts of the French people were awakened, and in this change his hand was evident.

[1] *Belgische Aktenstücke*, 1905-1914 (published by the German Foreign Office), p. 116.

Had the writer had any idea of what was happening at the same time behind the scenes, his anxieties would have been considerably greater, and he would have had no hesitation as to the anti-German character of the proceedings. For the documents reveal that Delcassé was not to represent his country with her ally in the ordinary way, but was entrusted with a quite definite mission, for which " anti-German " is a very mild term. In his telegram of February 17, already referred to [734], Isvolsky writes of Delcassé as follows :

Jonnart has also asked me to transmit to you the request to obtain the all-highest approval of the appointment of M. Delcassé as ambassador in St. Petersburg. He added the following information : The French Government has been moved to this choice mainly by the circumstance that in the eyes of leading French circles and of public opinion M. Delcassé is regarded, in the present exceedingly grave international situation, which may call for the application of the Franco-Russian Alliance, as a personality of quite special authority, a sort of personification of the Alliance. From this point of view it is very important that when appointed ambassador M. Delcassé shall be able to retain his mandate as Deputy. The legal obstacle to this, arising from the principle that Deputies may only be entrusted with temporary commissions, is purely formal in character and can be overcome by periodical renewals of the decree by the President, for which precedents exist. I venture to add on my own account that M. Delcassé, whose past political career is familiar to you, is entirely devoted to the idea of the very closest association between Russia and France, and, as one of the most influential parliamentarians in France, may play, if the critical moment should come, a decisive part in overcoming any hesitation on the part of the Government, which is always exposed to pressure from various quarters. I know that it is desired here to proceed as quickly as possible with Delcassé's appointment.

It emerges clearly from Isvolsky's remarks that Delcassé is to be a second guarantee alongside Poincaré for France's preparedness at any time for war.   A letter of March 13 [762] reveals a little more :

As you are aware, M. Delcassé is specially competent not only in questions of foreign politics but in all that concerns military and especially naval matters. Our military attaché has learned that he is specially commissioned to persuade our military administration of the necessity of increasing the number of our strategic lines, in order to enable our army to be more rapidly concentrated on the western frontier. M. Delcassé is so well informed on this matter and is so familiar with the views of the French General Staff that he can discuss the question quite independently with our military authorities. He is also empowered to offer Russia all the financial assistance required, in the form of railway loans.

This throws valuable light on what was going on. Before going further into that matter we must devote some attention to events in France during roughly the same period.

It is quite evident that since Poincaré's return from Russia a great deal of importance had been attached to the revival of the Russo-French comradeship in arms. In September 1912, as already mentioned, the Grand Duke Nicholas Nicolayevitch, later Commander-in-Chief of the Russian Army, was on a visit to France. He had come to attend the manœuvres at Nancy, in the immediate neighbourhood of the Alsace-Lorraine frontier. He described his impressions in an enthusiastic telegram to Nicholas II. At the beginning of 1913 General Suchomlinov, the Russian Minister of War, went at the Tsar's desire to Paris [657]. On January 12 he was received by Poincaré [673], and also had a long talk with the Chief of the French General Staff. A few weeks later there were conversations with British naval experts. On February 27 Isvolsky reports [747] his own audience with the new President of the Republic, to whom, by the Tsar's command, he handed the order of St. Andrew, and from whom he received the following confidential information concerning relations with Great Britain :

Great Britain is not bound to France by any definite political obligations, but the tone and the character of the assurances which the French Government is receiving from the London Cabinet permit the French Government to count on British armed support for France, in the existing political situation, in the event of a conflict with Germany. The plans of Franco-British co-operation at sea are worked out down to the smallest details. The First Lord of the Admiralty, Mr. Winston Churchill, who is staying at present in the South of France, is to visit Toulon in a few days, and to consult the French naval staff when he passes through Paris.

Thus there is busy preparation in order to be perfectly

ready in the event of " the critical moment " arriving. The French Government also took a further step of the greatest military importance : it resolved on the introduction of three years' military service in France. The ostensible reason was the recent increase of the German army, though that was to be carried out only gradually. But it is a peculiar fact that the moment the German measures became known the three years' bill was introduced in a completed form. At all events, the Press agitation over Berlin's new measures provided very welcome arguments for quickly pushing on the French plans. Isvolsky's letter of February 27 [748] contains the characteristic remark that " the German Government has once more, just as at the time of the Agadir incident, given the most violent impulse to the growth of nationalism and the military spirit in France." He adds later : " The view is even being expressed by responsible persons that Germany is compelled to take account of the military and political weakening of the Triple Alliance resulting from the diversion of an important section of the Austrian army from our (the Russian) frontiers by the Balkan States " ; thus plainly admitting that Berlin was merely filling up a gap in the defences of the Central Powers caused by recent events, so that no real occasion had arisen for a French counter-measure. In point of fact the introduction of three years' service gave the Franco-Russian military forces an enormous numerical preponderance over the united German and Austrian forces.[1] This was, of course, not only known, but intended, however cleverly it might, as so often, be represented as a forced measure of defence.

In this matter again Poincaré took the lead. Isvolsky writes on March 13 [760] :

The regulation issued on January 20, 1912, at the instance of the Poincaré Government, determining the composition of the Supreme War Council and the method of convening it, gives the President of the Republic for the first time the right to convene the War

[1] Montgelas, *The Case for the Central Powers*, pp. 105 sqq. (London : George Allen & Unwin.)

Council, under his own chairmanship, when he deems it necessary. On these occasions the Prime Minister takes part in the meetings of the Supreme War Council. During the first days of March the War Council examined and adopted the bill for universal three years' military service, with no provision for special exemptions, and the President of the Republic then resolved to make use of the new power given to him before introducing the bill into Parliament, and called together the Supreme War Council in the Élysée on March 4. He asked the opinion of each general separately, so that light was thrown from every side on the question of the defence of the country. In the evening an official communication was issued that the War Council had come to the conclusion that in the interest of the defence of the country it was absolutely essential to increase the numerical strength of the army ; it had examined the various existing means of attaining this end, namely, the extension of the period of liability to service beyond the existing limit, the monthly calling up of reservists, a 27- or 30-month period of service, and had unanimously found them insufficient ; with the same unanimity it had approved the obligation to three years' service, which must apply on absolutely equal terms to all and must admit of no privileges for anyone. On the following morning the Council of Ministers adopted the definite text of the bill, and it resolved on the same day to introduce it in the Chamber of Deputies and to make it a question of confidence. I have the honour to enclose the text of the bill and its preamble.

Thus was the adoption of the law pushed forward and the great move made a national affair. Isvolsky continues :

In view of the steadily growing popularity of M. Poincaré and his entire agreement with the Government, which is quietly and deliberately pursuing the national aim, the President's altogether unusual step in coming forward as the supreme head of the army in a question so important to France has made the greatest impression on all classes of the French people.

Further reference will be made to the significance of this important innovation for France. It was directly connected with the dispatch of Delcassé to Russia. On March 20, 1913 [776], Poincaré wrote to the Tsar recommending Delcassé, and adding :

When I had the happiness last year of being received by Your Majesty at Peterhof, I drew your exalted attention to the advantages which, in the view of our General Staffs, would be secured by the acceleration of the construction of certain railways on the western frontier of the Empire.

The effect of the great military effort which the French Government intends to make for the maintenance of the balance of the European military forces is that corresponding measures, as to the necessity of which the General Staffs of the two allied parties have agreed, are at present of special urgency. M. Delcassé will keep Your Majesty and Your Government informed on these important questions, as on all other questions which affect the working of the Alliance and may enable us to pursue the maintenance of peace with greater confidence.

The intended " great military effort " was, of course, the introduction of three years' service. Delcassé's task was to use this to spur on the Russian Government to " corresponding measures," the nature of which is not difficult to discover. Poincaré writes that " the General Staffs of the two allied parties " have agreed as to their necessity. As we know from the protocol of July 14, 1912 [368], the French representatives were then demanding an extension of the Russian railways leading to the western frontier. We read also in Isvolsky's letter of March 13, 1913 [762], that Delcassé was to discuss this with the Russian military authorities and to offer railway loans. But later documents go to show that this was not all. The armament increases were so definitely related to the coming struggle of France and Russia with the Central Powers that the war aims of the two Allies were already beginning to be defined. In the autumn of 1914,[1] after the outbreak of the world war, Isvolsky sent several telegrams to his Government from Bordeaux, then the seat of the French Government, in which he discusses war aims on the strength of talks with Delcassé. On October 13, 1914, he mentions as France's aims the restoration of Alsace-Lorraine, some colonial demands, and, as the principal aim, " the destruction of the German Empire and the weakening as far as possible of the military and political power of Prussia." In a further telegram of the same date we read :

Delcassé then referred to the negotiations which took place in St. Petersburg in 1913, and earnestly asked me to draw your attention to the fact that the demands and aspirations of France

[1] See Appendix IV, p. 247.

remain unaltered, with the addition only of the necessary destruction of the political and economic power of Germany.

These words prove that Delcassé's was a war mission in the true sense of the word. He was not only to urge Russia to great military efforts but to agree upon her reward, which obviously was to be won by arms. A phrase of Isvolsky's was quoted at the beginning of this chapter, in which he described the struggle of Slavdom with Teutonism as rendered inevitable by the successful end of the Balkan war. The facts just mentioned show that his words were not merely the casual expression of a momentary idea, but the expression of the guiding principle followed by himself and Poincaré. Had it lain with these two men, Europe would have been already at the brink of the abyss.

Involuntarily one asks, What, then, deferred the issue ? The answer is clear : the course of events upset their calculations for the time being. The decisive victory of the Balkan States, which, as we saw, was to be the prior condition of the great general conflict, was cut short and turned to something very like failure.

As already mentioned, in the London negotiations the Young Turks' Government refused to give up Adrianople. The result was the outbreak on February 3, 1913, of the second Balkan war. The new victories of the Allied States over the Crescent at first provided encouragement for the sinister designs just described. But they contained the seed of disaster for the victors, and it became necessary for those designs to be deferred. Over their enormous booty the Balkan States fell into discord.

Our documents give various interesting glimpses of the reaction of this briefly sketched development on the atmosphere in Paris.

Let us first watch the months during which all was going well. The year 1913 begins with the continuation of Poincaré's strong opposition to Austria-Hungary. Negotiations were proceeding in London over the delimitation of the frontiers of the State of Albania, then in the making. The

Dual Monarchy demanded the incorporation of Scutari in the new State. On January 2 [658] Isvolsky telegraphs that it has been learnt at the Quai d'Orsay that Russia agrees to this, but that the Quai d'Orsay is unable to do so : " Poincaré told me that he was rather astonished at the news, and could not but fear the impression that further concessions to Austria would make in France and elsewhere." On the 6th [666], in telegraphing to Sazonov, he again mentions this attitude :

From my talk with Poincaré I gained the impression that he regrets your decision to enter into negotiations over the Albanian question before Austria has begun to demobilize, and that he is very little inclined to make further concessions to Austria.

Mistrust of Vienna was clearly stronger in Paris than in St. Petersburg ; sudden Austrian action against Serbia was still expected. On January 22 [692] Sevastopoulo reports that Paléologue, then head of the political section at the Quai d'Orsay, has learnt from a very secret but entirely reliable source that Serbia too is in fear of a separate move by Austria. On February 2 [719] the news comes from St. Petersburg that the Emperor Francis Joseph intends to send Prince Gottlieb zu Hohenlohe with an autograph letter to the Tsar " in order to make clear the principles by which Austrian policy is being guided in the present crisis." Despite this plain effort to clear the air, Jonnart once more, on February 10 [726], expresses grave fears concerning the plans of Vienna. Even when news came of Austrian dismissals from the colours in Galicia and of a telegram from Archduke Ferdinand to the Tsar denying all warlike intentions, Paris continued to be sceptical [749, 752]. Montenegro's siege of Scutari brought a fresh aggravation of the situation, being obviously directed against the Dual Monarchy, and at once the French Government expressed its old fear of independent Austrian action [774]. To prevent this the Entente Cabinets considered making a naval demonstration in Montenegrin waters. Russia [785] proposed the sending of British and French

ships, not desiring herself to take part for fear of the effect
on Montenegrin opinion ; for a similar reason, M. Pichon
[812], the successor of M. Jonnart as Foreign Minister of
France, agreed to his own country's co-operation only if
she were " expressly authorized by Russia." The King
of Montenegro was encouraged to persevere by secret
information of the Russian and French attitude, and did
not allow the naval demonstration, when it actually took
place, to deter him from taking Scutari on April 22, 1913.
His action was an open defiance of the Dual Monarchy,
and was generally so felt. The Ambassadors' Conference
in London demanded that Scutari should be handed over
to the Powers, but even this was of no avail. Definite steps
were then taken in Vienna to retrieve this moral defeat.
According to Isvolsky's telegram of April 25 [852], the
Austrian ambassador declared to Pichon, " in the name of
his Government, that in the view of the Vienna Cabinet
joint measures of compulsion must now be resorted to
against Montenegro ; should the Powers decline to join in
a general action, Austria would be compelled to proceed
alone." True to the method hitherto adopted, Pichon had
already, in agreement with Sazonov, expressed the view that
joint pressure should be put on Montenegro to induce her
to evacuate Scutari, and that to make this easier for King
Nicholas he should be accorded financial assistance. But
this time again, when faced with the crisis, Sazonov replies,
on April 26 [854], that for Russia it is " impossible, in view
of popular feeling, to take part in measures of compulsion
against Montenegro, or even to empower France to act in
Russia's name." On this Pichon also, on April 28 [857],
refuses to join in, taking refuge behind the fact that French
public opinion will not permit active measures to be taken
without Russian co-operation. He adds, however, that as
Great Britain will also refuse there is obviously a danger
that Austria will be given a free hand. On the next day
[859] he is already considering the possibility of separate
action by the Dual Monarchy, which would receive support

from Germany and Italy, and asking that the French
Government may be informed what attitude Russia will
adopt in this event.

But M. Pichon was mistaken ; Austria was not being
urged forward but emphatically discouraged by Germany.
On May 1 [864], Isvolsky reports :

Pichon told me to-day that according to all the news he has
the Italian Government is most urgently advising Austria to
abstain from active steps against Montenegro. Should the Vienna
Cabinet decide on action, Italy will take no part in it, but will
merely occupy one or two points on the Albanian coast, probably
Valona and Durazzo. The Vienna Cabinet is aware of this, and it
will probably have a moderating effect on it. Pichon has reason
also to believe that the Rome Cabinet has once more confidentially
informed the Austrian Government that, should Austria be drawn
by single-handed action into a war, Italy will not regard herself
as bound by her Treaty of Alliance to support Austria, but will
stand aside. This last news is confirmed among others by the
strictly secret authority which I have already had occasion to
name to you.

The " strictly secret authority," who appears again and
again during these weeks in Isvolsky's papers, placed
France in a position to receive information concerning
important events within the Triple Alliance, and on the
strength of this information Isvolsky gives on May 8, 1913
[876], a full description of the events mentioned in the
foregoing telegram :

As soon as there began to be talk of Austrian separate action
against Montenegro, the Rome Cabinet made the strongest and most
serious effort to restrain the Vienna Cabinet from any such step.
When, however, the Austro-Hungarian Government declared in
London that it was firmly resolved forcibly to compel the evacuation
of Scutari, either jointly with the other Powers or, if they refused,
on its own account, the Italian Government replied that it would
take no part in such action against Montenegro, but would take
action on its own account in Albania. In consequence of this
declaration there were busy discussions between Austria, Italy,
and Germany, which at one moment were even of an acrimonious
character. The Vienna Cabinet did its very utmost to obviate
an Italian landing in Albania, and to this end it offered to help
Italy to acquire some island in the Ægean, for instance Rhodes.

Italy still showed her absolute intention to take parallel action in Albania if Austria took action against Montenegro, and the Vienna Cabinet then decided to come to an agreement with Italy on this basis. Germany, who was concerned above all to maintain close agreement between the Triple Alliance Powers, very warmly supported the idea of such an agreement.

It was thus due to the intervention of Germany and Italy that Austria once more refrained from the action foreshadowed. She waited patiently until the King of Montenegro, tempted by the financial assistance promised by France and Russia and by certain territorial concessions [868], finally, on May 3, placed Scutari at the disposal of the Powers, who occupied it on the 14th.

In the same letter [876] Isvolsky refers to the attitude of France. He quotes Pichon as saying :

The part played by the French Government has always consisted in giving undeviating support, of the most loyal and emphatic character, to France's Ally. The refusal of the Paris Cabinet to take part in any measure of compulsion against Montenegro without Russia's co-operation or at least authorization, is attributable not only to the pressure of public opinion, but above all to the fear of taking up an attitude of opposition to Russia, or even one which might be so construed.

The course of events has shown us how little this policy was calculated to maintain peace.

Still more questionable was the part played by official circles in Paris in another question which brought Europe near to war early in 1913—that of the conflict between Roumania and Bulgaria.

On January 2, 1913 [659], Isvolsky telegraphs to Benckendorff concerning a conversation between Poincaré and Take Jonescu, the Roumanian Minister, then staying in Paris. He quotes Jonescu as saying that

If Bulgaria refused to meet Roumania's desires in regard to the cession of Silistria and the rectification of the Dobrudja frontier, the Roumanian Government would not content itself with half measures, such as the occupation of Silistria as a pledge, or the like. It would mobilize and declare war.

Accordingly Jonescu asked that the Entente Powers should put pressure on Bulgaria to induce her to give way. Poincaré characteristically asked what attitude Roumania would take up if the existing crisis led to a general war, and Jonescu replied :

Sympathy for Russia was increasing in Roumania in the existing circumstances ; but should a collision occur between Austria and Russia, with the Balkan States on Russia's side, Roumania's existing obligations would render it impossible for her to remain neutral ; she would be compelled to give armed assistance to Austria.

Poincaré at once proposed to Russia that the desired pressure should only be put on Bulgaria if Roumania would give positive guarantees to the Entente that in the event of a " general war " she would remain neutral. As will shortly be shown, there were Russian commitments to Bulgaria which made it impossible for St. Petersburg to agree to this proposal. Paris, knowing nothing of these, continued to press its proposal, until it was learnt, according to Sevastopoulo's telegram of January 15 [677] to Sazonov, that Roumania had turned to Italy. On the following day Sevastopoulo telegraphs [680] that Paléologue has knowledge—once more from the " secret source "—of the existence of the most intimate relations between Bucarest and Vienna, so that it is now, in Paléologue's view, " too late to hope to detach Roumania from the Triple Alliance." A fresh request, from the Roumanian ambassador, M. Lehovari, for diplomatic assistance from the Triple Entente was accordingly received very coldly [685] at the Quai d'Orsay. It was in vain that Take Jonescu shortly afterwards [688] threw out the suggestion of a great alliance of all the Balkan States, including Turkey, which should assure peace and Russia's predominant influence in the Balkans for a long time to come. From now onwards Roumania was given the cold shoulder in Paris, as there was no alienating her from the Central Powers.

Meanwhile her relations with Bulgaria grew more and

more strained. In his telegram of January 28, 1913 [700], Sazonov expresses the fear " that Roumania may issue an ultimatum or take active measures against Bulgaria," which would entail the gravest possible consequences—consequences which must on no account be allowed to come. Accordingly he is for strong pressure from the Entente Powers on both parties. The obvious agitation of the Russian Government contrasts strangely with the French indifference recorded above, but it is explained by Sazonov's telegram of January 29 [706] to Benckendorff, which also went to Paris :

Inform Grey in entire confidence of the following : In 1902, when it was discovered that a military agreement existed between Austria and Roumania, Russia and Bulgaria concluded an agreement under which Bulgaria undertook to come to our assistance in the event of war with one of the Powers of the Triple Alliance, and in return for this we guaranteed to Bulgaria the integrity of her territory. This agreement has since bound Bulgaria, entirely to our advantage. We had been asked only what political and psychological considerations would have made it impossible for us to refuse even in the absence of an agreement. Now, however, that Roumania has adopted a threatening attitude, we have felt it our duty to give a friendly warning through our ambassador in Bucarest, and of this too you may inform Grey in entire confidence. For our part we should be very glad if the London and Paris Cabinets would also put pressure on Bucarest.

This statement, which came as a surprise to Russia's political friends, at once clears up the position. Russia was bound by the convention of 1902 [1] to come to the aid of Bulgaria if attacked. If Roumania carried out her threat, Russia would thus be drawn in. Under the circumstances this was not at all to the interest of Russia—what had she to gain from drawing the sword for Bulgaria ? She was therefore trying to prevent the treaty from becoming operative. British and French diplomatic support was sought ; and in another telegram of January 29 [707],

[1] See Appendix I, p. 217. The text of the subsequent Russo-Bulgarian military convention of December 1909 is given in *Causes of the War*, by M. Bogitchevitch. (George Allen & Unwin, 1920.)

Sazonov instructed Russia's representative in Bucarest to give the Roumanian Foreign Minister "urgent, friendly, and grave advice" that his Government "should observe a wise moderation in its demands," as it would be impossible for Russia "to permit the forcible annexation of a part of the territory of Bulgaria."

It is quite clear that if Roumania had maintained her resolute attitude she could successfully have ignored this threat, as Montenegro had done with Austria at Scutari. But there would then have been no preventing a disastrous extension of the Balkan conflagration. The French Foreign Minister realized the gravity of the situation at once when Isvolsky informed him of the existence of the Russo-Bulgar Convention. Isvolsky telegraphs on January 30 [708] that Jonnart was "exceedingly agitated," and emphatically declared that France had known nothing about Russia's commitment to Bulgaria. Isvolsky replied that "Russia's withdrawal from this commitment would mean the complete destruction of her position in the Near East, and from the beginning of the present crisis it has been impossible for anyone in Europe to suppose that Russia would permit any territorial injury to the Balkan States which she had set up." To this Jonnart replied that a Russian move to protect Bulgaria might result in a general war "over—Silistria."

Evidently offended at these reproaches, Isvolsky went to Poincaré and discussed the matter with him. Unfortunately we have no record of this conversation, but a telegram which preceded the one describing Jonnart's attitude (this was numbered 41) must have given great satisfaction, to judge from its echo from St. Petersburg; Sazonov writes [712] :

Your telegram No. 40 received. Would you very kindly take the first favourable opportunity to express to Poincaré the very lively satisfaction with which we have learnt of the intention which he expressed to you of continuing to influence French policy in the direction of alignment with ours? Being ourselves convinced supporters of agreement with France, we are sincerely anxious to keep in constant touch with the directors of her policy on all questions of interest to both Allies, and have no intention of taking any step which might entail the operation of obligations under the Alliance without prior agreement with the Paris Cabinet. The sympathy and respect which Poincaré has inspired in Russia for his personality have found clear expression in the satisfaction which Russian public opinion has shown at his election to the Presidency of the Republic. We are firmly convinced that the hopes placed in him here as the means of a further consolidation of Franco-Russian friendship will prove thoroughly justified, and from this standpoint we specially welcome the declarations which he has made to you.

Thus, while Jonnart was startled and drew back at the prospect of grave European complications, Poincaré was ready to support Russia, though this involved possible armed intervention in the Bulgaro-Roumanian conflict. All that was asked was, as before, that St. Petersburg should not bring into operation " the obligations under the Alliance " " without prior agreement with the Paris Cabinet." This was no more than a repetition of Poincaré's well-known view, but its application to a case actually impending shows plainly that the view was by no means purely theoretical.

In this crisis a resort to force was once more avoided by the drawing back of the party belonging to the Triple Alliance. On February 2, 1913 [720], Sazonov telegraphs that the representations in Bucarest have had a " beneficent effect " on the Roumanian Government, which " is clearly inclined to give way and promises to do everything to secure a peaceful settlement of the dispute with Bulgaria." This relieved the tension in the first phase of the development which we are describing.

In any case, the two instances here quoted—that of the attitude towards Austria and that of the Roumanian affair— show that the diplomatic venturesomeness of the beginning of 1913 was fully in accordance with the military measures which we have described. Paris was undismayed by the spectre of European war. The same impression was given by the French attitude at the Ambassador s'

Conference in London. Benckendorff writes in a report of February 25 [1] : [1]

To begin with France. If it was agreed (I shall return to this) that the British support was to be simply and purely diplomatic, without prejudice to what might eventually happen, France at all events formulated no such reservation. This was beyond doubt, and the fact must be kept clearly in mind ; for all his prudent and moderate (though never ambiguous) attitude during the sittings, M. Cambon in reality always inclined towards my view, even in preference to his own first idea. Indeed, when I recall the substance of his conversations with me, and go briefly over the words exchanged, and add to these considerations Poincaré's attitude, I get the feeling, almost the conviction, that of all the Powers France is the only one which, not to say wants war, at all events would see it without great regret. In any case, nothing showed me that France is actively contributing to work in the direction of a compromise. Well—compromise is peace ; beyond compromise lies war.

And farther on :

The situation seems to me, so far as I have been able to observe it, to be that all the Powers are working sincerely for the main-tenance of peace. But of all of them France is the one which would accept war with the greatest comparative equanimity.

To use a familiar expression, France is " on her hind legs again." Rightly or wrongly, she has complete trust in her army ; the old ferment of exasperation is once more at work, and France might very well believe that the circumstances are more favourable to-day than they are ever likely to be in the future. I do not want to prolong this report by considering whether they are actually so. But France may very well be rightly estimating the situation from her own point of view.

Isvolsky's papers amply confirm this judgment. They justify us, moreover, in holding that Poincaré's course was laid directly for an early armed conflict.

But as already mentioned, the turn of events in the Bal-kans had made some change of course and some trimming of sail necessary. For Russia especially the second Balkan war was a source of grave anxiety. Bulgaria, above all, in her insatiable thirst for power, took an undesired

[1] German Foreign Office White Book concerning responsibility for the war, pp. 156 sqq.

direction : she was soon threatening Constantinople again. On March 28, 1913, the Russian ambassador in Sofia telegraphs that there is reason to fear that the Bulgarian army will break through the Tchataldja line, and adds [795] :

> Success in this would bring the Bulgarian troops marching into Constantinople. Are we ready, whatever happens, to face the possibility of having to send our fleet there with a sufficient landing party at the first sign ?   I venture to express once more the conviction which I have repeatedly expressed during the war, that in the last resort nothing but our plain threat and actual readiness to occupy Constantinople and the Bosphorus will succeed either in preventing Austria from expansion in the Balkan peninsula or in inducing Great Britain to conclude a definite and formal treaty with us to cover the eventuality of a clash between the Great Powers.   The ovations in the Duma have made the greatest impression here, both on the Bulgarians and on the diplomatic corps.   The conviction is gaining ground here that the Imperial [Russian] Government will under certain conditions be unable to maintain neutrality.   Instructions are requested.

In view of this advice it is significant that a report of Sazonov's dated December 8, 1913 [1157], reveals that a landing in Constantinople was very seriously contemplated in Russia, but the plan had to be abandoned owing to insuperable military difficulties.   Consequently all efforts were now directed to bringing the second Balkan war to an end.

Three weeks before the threat to Constantinople, the Turkish ambassador in London had, according to Isvolsky's telegram of March 2, 1913 [750], declared that " the Ottoman Government accepts the mediation of the Powers for the restoration of peace."   The Balkan States accepted mediation only with reluctance.   Sazonov telegraphs on March 5 [754] that the Bulgarians claimed the Enos-Ergene-Midia line as their frontier.   Greece replied evasively. Serbia's main demand was for an indemnity.   Telegrams of March 8 and 10 [755, 758] show that mediation was beginning to seem hopeless.   A British suggestion followed, for the Great Powers to put pressure on the Allied Balkan States by refusing them financial assistance [759, 768].   The French

Foreign Minister agreed, but Sazonov did so only condi-
tionally [768]. Only when the threat came to Constantinople did he push forward the work of peace-making with
full energy, and indeed with extreme haste. On March 27
[789] he wires : " In view of the fall of Adrianople and of
the serious danger involved in a continuance of military
operations, it is desirable that Turkey should without
loss of time give her assent to the frontier line indicated
by Bulgaria." As regards an indemnity for the Balkan
States, a way out was found by entrusting a special commission [801] with the task of fixing its amount. This
concession was also due to Russia's fear of a Bulgarian
advance on Constantinople, as is clear from Sazonov's
telegram of March 31 [807] to Benckendorff :

> The explanation of the necessity of agreeing in principle to a war
> indemnity lies in the serious situation which would arise if the
> Bulgars were to march into Constantinople. It would be difficult
> to secure their withdrawal then from the shore of the Sea of
> Marmora without resort to compulsion. And if the Bulgars were
> to reach this Sea, there would be so little security for the fate of
> Constantinople and the free passage of shipping through the Straits
> that it would be absolutely necessary for us to have effective
> guarantees, without which the freedom of our export trade on the
> Black Sea would be dependent on the will of Bulgaria. Thus the
> whole course which the Balkan crisis has pursued so far might
> undergo an important change, and, of course, it is not impossible
> that extremely serious complications might arise.[1]

In the end the belligerents signed an armistice agreement
on April 16, 1913, and the acute danger for Russia passed.
    The financial commission decided on was to meet in Paris.
It thus fell within the sphere of Isvolsky's activities, and he
gives details of it which are of general interest. On May 22
[890], five days before the expected assembling of the
commission, he discusses its purpose and prospects. At
the very outset he opposes the " decision come to, on
Germany's initiative, to allow the delegates of the belligerents only consultative status." On the 24th [893] he

---

[1] Compare also, *Ministère des Affaires Étrangères : Documents Diplo-
matiques, les Affaires Balcaniques*, 1912-1914, Tome II, Nos. 193 and 220.
Paris, Imprimerie Nationale.

reports Grey's objection, though only a half-hearted one ; Sazonov telegraphs on the same day [892] that if Germany carries her proposal the whole commission can only be allowed a deliberative character, without the power to make binding resolutions.   So from the first moment Russia endeavoured to make impossible an issue of the negotiations prejudicial to her protégés.   Isvolsky had other objections to make.   He fears [890] that " the position of the Russian delegates will certainly be very difficult," as they will be " to a great degree isolated " as advocates for the Balkan States.   He shows in detail that there are strong currents of opinion, especially in financial circles, which are interested in Turkey and will accordingly come to her support.   His complaints then lead on in the familiar way to a proposal that the Balkan States shall undertake extensive bribery of the French Press.

Of importance to the main argument is Isvolsky's expressed anticipation of a difference between Paris and St. Petersburg over the financial treatment of the Ottoman Empire ; and it will soon be seen that the second phase, less favourable for Poincaré, of the Balkan troubles, had already come.   To be able to judge its effect on the attitude of the French Government, it is necessary to recall what had been going on.   The Balkan Allies fell out with one another over the booty they had seized.   First signs of their disunion appeared quickly.   Sazonov telegraphs as early as April 6 [823] that he has had to warn Greece against " mischievous steps against Bulgaria," and on the same day Benckendorff is instructed [824] to draw Grey's attention to the fact that " the relations between Bulgaria and Serbia have become dangerously strained."   The tension between these two countries has so increased by May 11 that France is asked [878] to declare to Sofia and Belgrad that she will only grant credits when they have signed the peace preliminaries.   To end the Greco-Bulgar quarrel, St. Petersburg proposes arbitration by the Entente Powers, but Isvolsky telegraphs on May 26 [898] that the French

Government feels unable to support this ; Russia in turn [900] rejects the counter proposal of arbitration by all the Great Powers.

Meanwhile Bulgaria's attitude grows more and more provocatory. On June 3 [905] Isvolsky mentions that Sofia has refused offers of armed help from Bucarest, having no intention of making concessions to Roumania. Shortly after this Russia takes steps independently to avert the threatened clash. Nicholas II, in a personal telegram [909] to the Kings of Bulgaria and Serbia, reminds them of their earlier undertaking to submit their differences to Russia for settlement. The replies are satisfactory, and on June 13 [913] Sazonov is able to state that the Russian Government is inviting the Prime Ministers of the Balkan States to St. Petersburg, " where all questions at issue, and the means of their settlement, are to be examined, and a definite course adopted." This appeared satisfactorily to have disposed of the trouble, and Sazonov was already [931] preparing for the proposed negotiations, when Bulgaria, fearing to be caught in a vice between her opponents, suddenly struck out on June 29, 1913, and so let loose the third Balkan war. Roumania and Turkey now turned against her, and she was soon outnumbered and helpless in the face of her enemies.

The situation had at once changed. The Balkan Alliance was in ruins, and the co-operation of the peoples of southeastern Europe under Russia's guardianship had suffered a grave interruption. In the face of this disastrous development, St. Petersburg no longer regarded itself as bound by the old agreement to protect Bulgaria's territorial integrity, and tried only to save what could be saved, moving heaven and earth to bring the bloodshed among the Allies to a speedy end.

A special difficulty arose through the success of the Porte in recovering Adrianople. The idea re-emerged in Russia of winning the Straits by a *coup*. As already mentioned, for military reasons the idea of a direct blow at the Bosphorus

and the Dardanelles had been rejected; the question
of proceeding through Asia Minor was now considered.
This is indicated by the raising of the Armenian question.
According to a telegram of July 11 [951] from the Russian
ambassador in Constantinople, reforms in Armenia were
demanded from Turkey—probably to provide a pretext for
action—reforms which, says the ambassador, were not
calculated " to prevent the dissolution of the Ottoman
Empire." Isvolsky's telegram of July 25, 1913 [970],
is still clearer :

> As regards the possibility of separate action on our part against
> Turkey, in Pichon's view this would entail the gravest risks to
> European peace : it would necessarily result in counter-measures
> being taken not only by Austria, who would avail herself of the
> opportunity to put pressure on Serbia, but by Germany, who is
> not abandoning her rôle of protector of Turkey, and is unlikely,
> therefore, to remain passive in face of *the events in Asia Minor*. . . .
> There is nothing of which Pichon is so much afraid as independent
> action on our part *in Asia Minor*, as this might end in the collapse
> of the Turkish Empire and raise the question of the partition of
> Turkey in Asia, for which Europe is not ready.

The difference between Paris and St. Petersburg over this
matter grew pretty acute. According to a second telegram
of July 25 [971], Isvolsky told the French Foreign Minister
that his reply " may give a very painful impression in
St. Petersburg, especially at a moment when the honour and
the historic traditions of Russia are at stake." He even
regarded it as not impossible that Germany might take up
an attitude of opposition, " in order to accomplish the dream
of Emperor William, the destruction of the Triple Entente."
On the following day Pichon was less unyielding, but suggested reference to Berlin, probably in order to shift the
appearance of hostility to the Russian plans from himself
to Germany. He added [973] that he would prefer " action
in Turkey in Europe, either directly against Constantinople
or by a landing at some point on the Black Sea coast."
Did he know that for the reasons already mentioned
this was virtually impossible, and was this his reason for

advising it ? One thing is clear : France was then opposed to measures of compulsion against Turkey, not desiring her downfall, and the strange situation arose of a diplomatic approach between Austria and Russia, both Powers following [973] " the same aim, the prevention of the collapse of Bulgaria." Isvolsky's telegram of July 28 [977] throws further light on the situation :

Pichon read to me a telegram from Berlin, in which J. Cambon reports the following :

1. Jagow has asked the Austrian Government what would be its attitude towards Russian separate action against Turkey, should it occur. The reply was that Austria would not prevent it, but reserved the right to take corresponding measures for the protection of Bulgaria. J. Cambon adds that this obviously refers to the Sandjak.

2. The same question was asked from London, and Jagow replied that Germany would raise no objection to Russian action, provided that it were confined to European Turkey and of limited duration, and that the Powers were informed in advance by Russia.

It is obvious what were the real reasons for the French attitude. They were precisely as indicated in Isvolsky's letter, already quoted, on the prospects of the financial conference in Paris to settle the indemnity to be received by the Balkan States. He wrote that powerful French banking groups were closely interested in deals with the Porte. The documents now reveal to us an astonishing fact, but one which fully bears out Isvolsky's statement.

While Russia was taking up a threatening attitude towards Turkey, and insisting that in order to induce her to give way over Adrianople she should at all events be refused all financial assistance, negotiations were being carried on in Paris with Turkish representatives with no other end than the granting of financial assistance. The first indication of this comes in Sazonov's telegram of August 1 [981], mentioning news of assistance, " not official," from Paris banking circles, and adding :

It would be well to call the most serious attention of the French Government to the fact that so fundamental a divergence between us and our Ally in regard to a matter which threatens to entail grave complications cannot be permitted.

Briefly, the conversations were concerned with Turkish railway lines which were to be turned over to French capitalists, and with payments to the Porte by the tobacco *régie*.

On August 4, 1913 [987], Sazonov telegraphs :

A very painful impression has been created here by the news that France is about to sign the treaties with Turkey.

We think it would be well that you should speak about this to Pichon in a friendly way, but seriously. Latterly it has been getting more and more difficult for us to meet the questions and apprehensions of the representatives of the Press and of business ; they are noticing the continual divergences of view between ourselves and our Ally in questions which are of much greater importance to us than to him.

The disagreement continues, and becomes very embarrassing to Isvolsky. On August 9 [998] he telegraphs, almost in despair :

I am taking every opportunity to prepare Pichon for the probability that we shall be compelled very shortly to resort to measures of compulsion against Turkey to secure the evacuation of Adrianople. I venture urgently to ask for the earliest possible news of the nature of the measures which we propose to adopt. Business circles here, and especially the very influential financial circles, are altogether weary of this long continued crisis, and any fresh complication would have a very bad reception here. The newspapers of all parties are continually expressing opposition to any revision of the Treaty of Bucarest, and recalling that we have ourselves opposed the incorporation of Adrianople in Bulgaria, and that we have declared that those responsible for the fratricidal war would have to bear their own burden. As the French Government is very greatly dependent on public opinion, all this must be borne in mind.

On August 11 [1000] Sazonov replies that Russia is endeavouring " in the matter of pressure upon Turkey to evacuate Adrianople, to avoid, in accordance with the desire of France and the other Powers, the necessity of active intervention," but requests—maintaining his former standpoint—that France and Great Britain " shall declare openly that so long as Adrianople is not evacuated Turkey will be refused all financial facilities." Pichon's evasions in regard to the payments of the tobacco *régie* (he contended that in this matter the Republic had not had a controlling vote) are dismissed by Isvolsky on August 12 [1001] as based " on an incomprehensible mistake."

Again and again Isvolsky tries to find a way out of the difficulty as desired by his Government, but without success, as is shown by his telegram of August 12 [1002] :

Opinion here on the Adrianople question is causing me more and more anxiety. In my conversations with Ministers, politicians, and journalists I am declaring most emphatically that this question affects our historic traditions, and that if at such a moment we should fail to secure sufficient support and sympathy from France, our Ally, the effect on the future of the Alliance might be of the worst. The Government clearly understands this, and assures us that we may count on our Ally, but at the same time Ministers do not conceal from me that all sections of the population are tired out by the long-drawn-out crisis, that financial circles are thirsting for more settled conditions, and that it is very possible that in the event of fresh complications public opinion would not support the Government.

As ill-luck would have it, another difference had arisen at the same time in the Entente camp over the Kavalla question. Greece and Bulgaria were both demanding Kavalla. As early as July 12, 1913 [955], Russia declared her inability to support the Greek claims, " which would be objected to by Austria and her allies." On August 1 [982] Sazonov informed Benckendorff that Athens was reluctantly prepared to give way. On the 3rd Demidov, the Russian ambassador at Athens, reports that his French colleague has stated that in his Government's view Kavalla must fall to Greece. On this Sazonov states, on August 4 [986], the grounds of his contention " that Kavalla must remain Bulgarian." They are of some importance to what follows, and must therefore be quoted :

1. This port is not at all necessary economically to Greece, who already possesses Salonika and the Gulf of Orfano ; for Bulgaria it is indispensable, as the only port on the Ægean Sea which is

capable of development.   The Powers have already promised the
Bulgarians the island of Thasos, the possession of which renders
essential the possession of Kavalla, as otherwise the neighbourhood
of the port and the island must necessarily produce friction.

2. We are prepared to agree to the naval strengthening of Greece ;
the Powers of the Triple Entente desire to make use of her services.
But we have no desire at all to assist Greece in gaining disproportionate influence in the direction of the Dardanelles, and we
consider that Kavalla and Thasos in Bulgarian hands could play
the useful part of a protective barrier against this.

3. The Austrian intention of giving up Kavalla to the Bulgarians
would place us in a delicate position if we failed to support this
just claim.   This also makes our attitude plain in the eyes of the
Greeks ; our attitude is not due in the slighest to ill-feeling
towards them.

For these reasons Sazonov was unable to understand the
French attitude, and he requested Isvolsky to convert
Pichon to his view [986].   " Point out to him," he writes,
" the bad impression that will be created in public opinion
in Russia by the fact of our opposition in this matter, and in
that of the financing of Turkey, not to our usual opponents,
but to France."   Here again, however, Isvolsky's representations were in vain, and in the end Paris won and
Kavalla went to Greece.   For the second time Russia had
failed to get her way through objections raised by her Ally.

How is it that such a breach could arise ?   As regards
the Turkish issue, the extracts already given from Isvolsky's
papers afford sufficient explanation.   As regards Kavalla
he writes on August 12 [1006] :

The [French] Government must have had a weighty reason for
its decision to cross the plans of its Ally.   In my opinion the reason
is to be sought in the fact that the question at issue was not purely
a Balkan but a Mediterranean question, and one regarded here
as of fundamental importance.   You are aware, both from my
reports and from those of our chargé d'affaires at Rome, that
serious tension has arisen lately between France and Italy owing
to the attitude of the Italian Government in the question of the
Ægean islands.   Pichon has expressed to me a very strong suspicion that Italy is secretly aiming at retaining one or more of
these islands (which she occupied during the Tripolitan war).   It
is held here that this would disturb the balance of power in the
eastern part of the Mediterranean, and Pichon has declared to me

several times over and with the utmost emphasis that neither France nor Great Britain can permit this, and that the French Government intends to oppose any such plan " with all its resources " —in other words, even by war. M. Pichon has had reason to believe that the Marquis di San Giuliano, when staying at Kiel, persuaded the Emperor William to amend the agreements of the Triple Alliance to the extent of assuring to Italy one or more islands in the Ægean Sea. The action of the Italian Government in opposing Greece in the Kavalla question was connected here with these plans and intrigues, and has accordingly been met with particularly strong opposition. You are, of course, familiar with all the details of the obstinate struggle between the French and Italian ambassadors during the London Ambassadors' Conference, a struggle which was only brought to an end by a candid exchange of views between Pichon and Tittoni, about which I telegraphed to you. M. Pichon, in his talk with the Italian ambassador, described to him with some vigour the standpoint of the Italian Government in regard to the balance of power in the Mediterranean, and asked him whether any change had taken place in this regard in the agreements between the Triple Alliance. As you are aware already, M. Tittoni replied in the name of his Government that the agreements mentioned remained unaltered, and that Italy intended to continue to fulfil with complete loyalty the agreement concluded with France. This statement went far to relieve Pichon, and since this occasion there has been a noticeable diminution in the bitterness of the controversy between the French and Italian Press. Nevertheless, M. Pichon said to me to-day that even now he is not entirely convinced of the sincerity of the Italian Government, and he thinks that the resolution adopted to-day at the London Ambassadors' Conference concerning the islands may play into the hands of Italy if she continues to try to maintain her hold of Rhodes and Stampalia.

These remarks are undoubtedly thoroughly justified, and need no comment. In the Mediterranean, French and Russian interests did not run parallel, and hence the friction produced by the third Balkan war with its strife over the division of the booty. Isvolsky's letter deals less fully with the Adrianople question, and only repeats what we have heard already :

In my telegrams I have told you of the apprehensions and anxieties which the Adrianople question is causing me. The crisis has lasted eleven months, and has inflicted great economic injury on European markets ; everyone here, as elsewhere, has become very weary of it, and financial circles are loud in their demand for peace and demanding that decisions shall be come to which take account of Turkey's capacity for payment. Nor are pro-Turkish tendencies confined to the business world : as you are aware, the bureaux of the Foreign Ministry are thoroughly infected. Djavid Bey, who is staying here, is in constant touch with the Press here, declaring, despite the bareness of the Turkish exchequer, that he has the disposal of large sums for influencing journalists. Under these circumstances, and in view of the extent of the dependence of the French Government on public opinion, it is to be feared that we cannot count on sufficient support in Paris in regard to Adrianople, and that if one or two Powers, for instance Germany and England, declare in favour of accepting the *fait accompli*, this attitude will find more or less open support here. Some of the important papers are recalling that when the crisis first broke out we ourselves declared against the cession of Adrianople to Bulgaria, and that before the second Balkan war began we declared that those who began it, that is, in this case, Bulgaria, must bear the responsibility for their actions. In view of the foregoing I have made every effort to make clear both to the French Minister and the Press that if in this question, which touches our honour and our historic traditions, France does not give us adequate support, the effect on the future of the Franco-Russian Alliance may be of the worst. As I have telegraphed to you, Pichon declared to me quite definitely that in regard to Adrianople we may count on the fullest support from France, our Ally, but at the same time he does not conceal from me that he himself fears opposition from public opinion in France, and especially that he sees no practical way of securing evacuation by peaceful means.

Isvolsky might have cut this tale short if he had simply admitted that France disagreed with Russia because the complete destruction of the Turkish Empire, entailing operations against Turkey in Asia, would have meant for the Republic the loss of irreplaceable financial assets. Paris knew that England agreed with the French standpoint, as Grey had several times emphatically insisted in public statements that Turkey must retain her Asiatic territory.

But there is a further consideration which explains the attitude of the dominant circles in Paris. Isvolsky makes no mention of it, but in the general development which we are observing it is of the first importance. It has several times been mentioned that the warlike efforts in Paris which were being made with such intensity at the beginning of 1913 were in some degree interrupted by the later Balkan troubles. At first, it will be remembered, the French Government was thoroughly aware that the situation might drive France into war, and it envisaged this possibility undisturbed. Its attitude at the London Conference was such that Benckendorff, in the note of February 25 from which extracts have been quoted, goes as far as to say that war might break out on account of interests which were " more French than Russian." Now, finally, Russia's proposed advance through Turkey in Asia arouses obvious distaste. Are the financial interests of the Republic sufficient explanation of this ? They are not ; here, as in the case of Kavalla, we must look for deeper causes, and we shall soon discover them if we take every factor into account.

After the victory of the Balkan States at the end of 1912 it was expected in Paris, as we saw, that Austria-Hungary would attack Serbia. This meant general European war, in which Germany would necessarily be involved, and such a war was what was desired by men of the stamp of Poincaré. It deserved Benckendorff's description ; it lay more in France's than in Russia's interest. The situation was quite changed in the period which we have just been considering ; had Russia begun her advance through Asia Minor for the conquest of the Dardanelles, the great conflict would have been avoided. We saw that Great Britain had made her objection unmistakably clear. Russia would have attained her own ambition while France would have been unable to seize the occasion to gratify her lust of revenge against Germany ; apart from this, a cleavage would have arisen between Great Britain and Russia which would have destroyed the Entente. These were the ultimate considerations which determined France's attitude. For those forces on the Seine which, like Poincaré, had inscribed on their banner the destruction of the hereditary enemy Germany, the general struggle between Entente and Central Powers was the one and only way of proceeding ; hence it was bound to be not at all to their taste for their Slav ally to find a solution of his own problem which avoided the general struggle.   This is why we heard Poincaré repeatedly declaring that France would fulfil her obligations if Germany were drawn into the war.   And this is why a certain nervousness always made its appearance in Paris if there were prospects of Russia taking " arbitrary " action.   Only if the conflict were general would it be to the taste of the Republic.

Did St. Petersburg realize the moral of the experience it had just had ?   The Straits were its goal—of this, in view of the events of 1913, there can no longer be the slightest doubt.   The direct road to the Bosphorus was first tried, and abandoned as impracticable.   Then the *detour* through Asia Minor was attempted, but at this Russia's own Allies cried Halt !   Was it not logically inevitable that a third way should now be sought, and found along a route which would no longer be encumbered with obstacles but, as had so unmistakably been promised, would be followed with energetic assistance from, at all events, France ?

Once more we will let the documents speak.   The next chapter will give us the answer to the question.

VI

TOWARDS THE WORLD WAR

In a letter sent on August 14, 1913 [1010], to Sazonov, Isvolsky describes the attitude of the French Government during the third Balkan war, and estimates the outcome of the political events of recent months from Russia's point of view. His remarks are noteworthy as showing how well the war of aggression against Turkey in Europe fell in with the Tsarist aims. Apart from that, they introduce us to the position which emerged as the Balkan unrest gradually died down. Isvolsky is unable to understand the dissatisfaction in St. Petersburg with the Peace of Bucarest, and the desire for a revision of its terms. On the contrary, he writes, it seems to him that the turn of events was exceedingly advantageous to Russia :

However distressing the second Balkan war may have been from a purely human and sentimental point of view, it relieved us of the very troublesome obligation of arranging the partition of Macedonia among the Allies. This was a quite impossible task, and would have destroyed our good relations with all the Balkan States at a stroke. I have in my time had many long discussions with Balkan politicians, and have always had the conviction that a peaceful partition was impossible. What the Bulgars were after can be seen very clearly from the enclosed map, which was officially sent out by Bulgaria shortly before the outbreak of the Second Balkan war. It is worth noting that on this map Albania extends to the Ægean—distinct evidence of Austrian co-operation. In conversations with me Danev [1] made very similar claims, and he told our pressmen and politicians quite openly that, if Russia did not help Bulgaria to establish these claims, they would be realized with the help of Austria : that definite promises had been given by Austria to this effect. I think there can be no doubt that

[1] The Bulgarian Prime Minister.

Bulgaria has been in close touch with Vienna from the beginning of the crisis. If Austria had not been wrong in her calculations and Bulgaria had been victorious in the second war, the result would in my opinion have been extremely dangerous and injurious to us, for, as the map shows, a Greater Bulgaria would naturally have been valueless as a bulwark of equilibrium in the Balkans ; the way would merely have been paved for more far-reaching Bulgarian plans in the direction of Constantinople, and Bulgaria would probably have become a member of an Austro-Bulgarian coalition directed against us.

After these very characteristic opening remarks, which show clearly enough, as usual, Isvolsky's rooted hostility to the Dual Monarchy, he continues, in still plainer language :

I have always regarded as your political masterpiece, and I do so still, your weaning of Roumania from Austria. It was always my dream, but I could never see how to bring it about. It was Roumania's intervention that defeated the Austro-Bulgarian plans, and I see no reason why we should specially regret this. If any question had arisen of partitioning Bulgaria, we should, of course, have had to oppose it. As a matter of fact, Bulgaria's loss owing to the treacherous manœuvres of Danev and Company has been comparatively insignificant. Her vital interests have not suffered, only her extravagant ambitions. In my opinion the Kavalla question is only of secondary importance. It is being said that the Peace of Bucarest will not last long, and will lead to a new war over Macedonia ; if, however, Bulgaria's plans had succeeded, Serbia and Greece would, without question, have planned revenge in a few years' time. It does not seem to me to be reasonable to suppose that Bulgaria's gratitude and the maintenance of our influence in Sofia are to be assured by returning Kavalla to the Bulgars. It must be made clear to them that they have lost Kavalla and everything else primarily because those in power in Bulgaria turned a deaf ear to the disinterested advice of Russia, and listened to the fatal promptings of Austria. I am convinced that this simple truth will be easily apprehended by the shrewd Bulgarian people, and that it will not be Russia who will lose their respect, but Ferdinand and his advisers, over whom there is no reason why we should grieve.

As regards the question of the revision of the Bucarest Treaty, here again what has happened is entirely a matter for congratulation. The Treaty does not injure the interests of Russia, but of Austria, who has done everything to weaken Serbia, even to the extent of letting loose a fratricidal war, and has been presented, as a result, with a Serbian kingdom grown powerful and strengthened both morally and physically. To insist on revision is to give

Austria the occasion and the means of working to upset this result, and possibly to win back all that she has lost. At the present moment, Austria is entirely isolated both morally and politically, and even Germany is turning away from the impossible Austrian policy. At such a moment, are we actually to help Austria, and so to destroy at a stroke all that I have accomplished ? Common action with Austria in the Balkans has never brought us good fortune ; this I know from my own bitter experience.

It must be admitted that, in the main, this correctly describes the situation. The issue of the Balkan wars had brought Russia great advantages, while the position of Austria-Hungary had apparently been threatened, especially, as Isvolsky maliciously notes, by the advance of Serbia, whose dreams of further expansion could only be satisfied at Austria's expense. Isvolsky's reference to his " own bitter experience " at the time of the Bosnian crisis contains an implied warning to Sazonov, who, as will be remembered, had been working a good deal with Vienna in regard to Bulgaria.

The main thing, in view fo later developments, to note is that the net result to Russia of the issue of the Balkan wars was an important extension of her sphere of influence. The ultimate object of her ambition, however, the Straits, she had, in spite of several attempts, failed to attain. The question which we must ask ourselves is : How did all this influence Russia's subsequent attitude ? Did she now give up the attempt, or were other means being devised for the conquest of the Dardanelles ?

Let us try first to see what we can learn from the events then happening in Paris.

The first fact is that, even before the outbreak of the third Balkan war, strong pressure was once more being exerted in France for the introduction of the three years' term of service with the colours. On June 12, 1913,[1] the Belgian ambassador in Paris reported that the French Government was confident of obtaining the assent of the Chamber.

[1] *Belgische Aktenstücke*, p. 124.

At about the same time M. Klotz, the Finance Minister, asked for the payment of the second instalment of 100,000 francs out of the secret fund for influencing the Press. According to a letter of June 17 [920] from Kokovtsov to Sazonov, Klotz mentioned " the possibility of a campaign against the new military law." This reveals the connexion of the two activities, and we can once more watch the French Government trying to use Russian money for its own ends, on the ground that Russian interests benefit simultaneously. As before, Kokovtsov does not share this view ; he complains [920] that the money is being expended " for the needs of the French Government and not of the Russian," and he asks Sazonov's opinion. Sazonov in turn, on July 1 [941], asks Isvolsky's opinion. On July 7 [948] Sazonov is able to send this reply to the Prime Minister :

According to the view of Comptroller Isvolsky, the request of M. Klotz appears admissible on the condition that the newspapers receiving subventions from the above fund devote their advocacy mainly to our interests in, for instance, the Balkans, also giving support to the policy of the French Cabinet and the passage of the French law for three years' compulsory service with the colours.

If our conditions are complied with, I should personally consider it possible to approve a present grant of 100,000 francs to the French Press as desired by M. Klotz. In this case, Privy Councillor Raffalovitch should impress on M. Lenoir the conditions under which the payment is made.

On July 15 [956] Kokovtsov agrees to the proposal, and directs that 100,000 francs shall be remitted to Lenoir's account. According, however, to a letter from Raffalovitch, dated July 16 [958], M. Klotz is very indignant at the Russian demand for " semi-official support in Balkan affairs," and twelve days later [979] Raffalovitch actually states that 80,000 francs out of the newly provided second instalment had already been distributed, so that there could no longer be any question of carrying out the conditions mentioned by St. Petersburg.

The introduction of three years' military service was, as

we know, one of the measures, dating from early in 1913, which aimed at the material strengthening of the Franco-Russian military forces. Undeterred by its diplomatic reactions, it was now pushed through, and it is instructive to hear what the Belgian observer already mentioned, Baron Guillaume, tells his Government about its probable consequences :

Thus it is now certain that the new French legislation will contain provisions which the country is unlikely to be able to bear for long. The burdens of the new law will be so heavy for the general population, the expenditure involved will be so huge, that the country will soon protest, and France will then be faced with the alternative of either renouncing the unendurable or very shortly going to war. It will be a heavy responsibility for those who have brought the nation to this pass. They are followed in a sort of stupor, an interesting but deplorable dementia. . . . The propaganda in favour of the law for three years' military service, aiming at producing a resurrection of chauvinism, was brilliantly prepared and carried through ; it began with the demand for the election of M. Poincaré as President of the Republic ; it is still going on, regardless of the risks which it is provoking ; there is great uneasiness in the country.

The conclusion of Delcassé's negotiations on military questions with St. Petersburg was undoubtedly connected with the final introduction of this great increase in the French army. The fact that the two movements were contemporaneous is evidence enough of this.

On June 27, 1913 [936], Kokovtsov, in his capacity of Russian Minister of Finance, addresses a letter to Sazonov which begins with the following information :

The Chairman of the Paris Stock Exchange, M. de Verneuil, has told me that while in St. Petersburg he is commissioned to communicate to us the standpoint of the French Government in regard to the floating in France of Russian Government loans, guaranteed by the State. This he has defined to me as follows :

" I have been authorized to tell you that the French Government is ready to allow Russia to obtain in the Paris market every year from 400 to 500 million francs in the form of a State loan, or of a loan guaranteed by the State, for the realization of a national programme of railway construction, subject to two conditions :

" 1. That the construction of the strategic lines planned out in collaboration with the French General Staff is begun at once ;

" 2. That the effective peace strength of the Russian army is considerably increased."

It will be remembered that Delcassé was commissioned to see that the strategic railways leading to the western frontier of Russia, for which the French General Staff was pressing, were laid down, and to offer financial assistance from France. Now the demand comes for a substantial increase in the Russian army. The statement quoted above sketches the proposed form of the mutual undertaking which had been agreed on. Kokovtsov is very gratified at the prospect of the important sums mentioned, and considers that the network of strategic railways on the western frontier can be completed without delay. He considers, however, that it is important to secure certain alleviations in the taxation of the loans in France.

On June 30 [938] Sazonov requests Isvolsky to obtain official confirmation from the French Government of De Verneuil's statements. Isvolsky transmits the request to the Quai d'Orsay in a note dated July 2, and on August 24 confirmation is sent through the French embassy in St. Petersburg to Sazonov, who in turn informs Kokovtsov on the following day [1030].

On September 6 [1043] the latter replies to the Foreign Minister with some counter-proposals. As regards the military demands, he writes :

To prevent the possibility of any future misunderstandings, I feel bound to draw Your Excellency's attention to the fact that the proposal of the French Government, which is coupled with decidedly difficult material conditions, would be burdensome for us, if, for example, the French Government's desire for the raising of the peace strength of our army had not already been borne in mind in the reorganization of our forces, quite apart from any financial operation on the Paris market. I should also point out that the French Government's proposal concerning the construction of strategic railways in Russia can on no account be taken as meaning that certain lines serving military purposes must be constructed, but only that, as regards our railway system, steps should be taken which correspond to our new needs of transport in connexion with the altered distribution of our army, and which serve in other respects to adapt the technical equipment of the lines to the altered conditions of transport. Measures of this latter kind are being carried through by us on a very considerable scale, and in the budget of our railway administration credits are constantly being taken up which are intended for the strategic development of our railways ; in particular, the budget of 1914 allocates a very substantial sum for the increase of our rolling-stock to provide for the eventuality of a general mobilization.

As regards the particular lines of railway, and especially lines of considerable length, particularly in the western districts of Russia, I have received no concrete proposals of any sort either from the War Office or from the Chief of the General Staff. In the conversation which I had with the Chief of the French General Staff, General Joffre, when he was here recently, I explained to him in detail that our defence requirements are amply provided for by the work on our railway system which has recently been completed or is on the point of being carried out. On that occasion no objections of principle were made to me by General Joffre, and personally I received the impression that the French Government did not intend to put forward any definite demands in this respect.

Kokovtsov thus tries to water down the French stipulations by treating the French money as not simply for strategic railways, but also for the general improvement of transport. The Russian Foreign Office hesitates, however, to pass his remarks on to Paris. M. Schilling writes on September 15 [1048] to Sazonov, who was then away on a holiday .

Bearing in mind Poincaré's negotiation with you last year, his letter to the Tsar, and Delcassé's later request, it seems unlikely that the French will be satisfied with the reply proposed by V. N. Kokovtsov.

Up to the present we have not received the minutes of the discussions between General Zhilinsky and General Joffre, so that, curiously enough, we do not yet know what agreement about the railways has been come to between the two Chiefs of General Staff this year. As regards the lines discussed last year, our Chief of General Staff, as you will remember, concurred in the desirability of two of those proposed by the French, and objected only to the third, the Baltic line. Before Zhilinsky's return (middle of September) it will hardly be possible for us to discuss this question. After he returns, and we have cleared up this point, we must consider the matter in a conference between the Finance Minister, the Foreign Minister, the War Minister, and the Minister of Transport, and then give the French a definite answer whether we accept their conditions or not. To play with words in dealing with allies, telling them that we accept their conditions, but in quite a different sense to that in which they put them forward, appears to me extremely dangerous to our mutual relationship, since it will only engender distrust of us.

Schilling therefore proposes a preliminary, somewhat indefinitely worded reply to the French Government, with no mention of Kokovtsov's objections. The minutes of the conference between the Chiefs of the French and Russian General Staffs in August 1913 [1040] show that Joffre once more demanded certain railway lines " connecting Eastern Russia with the Warsaw area," in order to provide for more rapid concentration of the Russian army against Germany.

The next mention of the loan question comes in a fresh letter from Schilling to Sazonov dated October 1, 1913 [1071] ; the French chargé d'affaires, Doulcet, he writes, has advised Russia to wait before replying, since a provisional answer " would be unlikely to satisfy the French Government." The nervousness of the Foreign Office, however, gives evident annoyance to Kokovtsov ; on October 4 [1074] he sends to Sazonov from his train, on arrival at Poltava station, some particularly blunt and plain-spoken lines. His handling of the affair has been conducted, he says, under " precise instructions from His Majesty," and he adds :

It is impossible for us to say beforehand whether we shall obtain legislative sanction for the construction of any particular line, or shall find contractors who will be prepared to construct the line, just when it suits the French. I have therefore asked His Majesty's approval for our answer to be given a sufficiently elastic form to save us from getting into difficulties later on. My standpoint has been acknowledged to be quite correct, and it seems to me that a slight amendment in this sense is all that is necessary. I should be glad if you would insert in the reply drawn up at Kiev a clause to the following effect, at the point where reference is made to the comprehensive measures of our Government for the development and completion of our railway system :

" Among the measures of this nature are important works for the laying of a second track where necessary, the development of junctions, and the construction of new lines of considerable length, which will, among other things, serve important strategic functions in facilitating the concentration of our army on the western frontier."

Finally, Kokovtsov declares that M. Doulcet knows nothing whatever and that no particular significance need be attached to what he says.

On October 11 [1086], Neratov telegraphs that Kokovtsov's instructions have been carried out, and the French embassy in St. Petersburg is being given a somewhat " elastic " reply.

In November Kokovtsov himself comes to Paris, in order to hasten matters to a conclusion by direct negotiations. In a very long report to the Tsar on December 13 [1169] he describes, amongst many other things, his discussions concerning the railway loans, and expresses himself as well satisfied with the results achieved. The interest of his remarks lies in the arguments with which he endeavours to win over the French to his proposal for the general development of the Russian system of communications :

To get rid, therefore, of the French Government's concern with our strategic lines, I have proposed a more general formula, recognizing the necessity of strengthening, improving, and extending the Russian railway system as required by the economic as well as the strategic needs of the country. In support of this formula, I have used two groups of arguments :

(1) Quite independently of our discussions about fresh loans, the Russian Government is at present expending large sums on its railway system ; in the 1914 Budget more than 66 million roubles were provided solely for the purchase of rolling-stock, including the so-called reserves for mobilization.

(2) When a State decides to raise the peace strength of its army by 366,000 men, increasing the yearly contingent of recruits by nearly 100,000, and when it approves a special vote for this purpose of more than 500 million roubles, with at least 100 million roubles annually, in addition to the sums already being expended, such a State must naturally take thought at the same time for its railways. If it were to disregard this aspect in strengthening its army, and

to fail to develop its railways correspondingly, all its plans for strengthening the army would be futile. An enlarged army can only be concentrated and forwarded to its destination by means of a correspondingly developed railway system. My reasonings were, I believe, recognized by the other side as quite convincing, and the formula proposed by me has met with no objections.

In spite of this attractive picture of the increase of the Russian army, Kokovtsov's point of view was not accepted without qualification. Sazonov telegraphs on December 16 [1177] the final proposal of the French Foreign Office following on the discussions ; its main points are :

(1) The Imperial [Russian] Government may take up annually on the Paris market in the course of five successive years a maximum sum of 500 millions, in the form of State loans or State-guaranteed loans for the carrying out of a programme of railway construction.

(2) The railway works recognized as necessary by the Chiefs of the French and Russian General Staffs in the course of their deliberations in August 1913 shall be begun as soon as possible, so as to be finished within four years ; the cost will be met, at the option of the Imperial Government, either out of the yield of the loans or out of the surplus on the Russian budget.

This did not go as far as Kokovtsov had wanted, and Sazonov adds that Kokovtsov had objections to Point (2), but was willing to waive these in order to avoid delay.

On December 30, 1913 [1191], M. Doumergue, who had become Foreign Minister, informs Isvolsky " that all objections on the part of the French Parliament to the railway loan have finally been withdrawn, and that the said loan can be raised at any time convenient to Russia." Thus this matter also had been brought to a successful issue.

This comprehensive financing of the construction of the Russian strategic railways meant increased Russian dependence on France, and this dependence extended into a sphere which was of great significance for the general determination of policy. We saw in the preceding chapter how France's rulers objected to independent Tsarist action in regard to the Straits, fearing that their Slav ally might attain his object without at the same time co-operating in the realization of the specific French ambitions, which were directed primarily against Germany. The arrangements initiated by Delcassé aimed at preventing this, by forcing the Russian war preparations into the direction desired by Paris, against, that is, the Central Powers. Thus a new poisoning of the atmosphere was added to the introduction of the three years' service in France, which, in the opinion of the Belgian ambassador, tended to drive the French people into war to escape from the pressure of the burden laid upon them. The character of the railway loans impressed on Russia also this impulse towards collision with Germany and Austria, especially the former.

The enhanced danger to peace would, however, only become acute if in St. Petersburg this impulse towards world war awoke to conscious will ; that is, if Russian policy deliberately took the path along which men like Poincaré, Delcassé, and Isvolsky were trying to attract it. Are there any indications of this happening ? Once more, let us see what the documents reveal.

The diplomatic collaboration between Paris and St. Petersburg after the Balkan wars aimed principally at gaining the greatest possible control over the Balkan nations. The surest means to this was financial influence, for the Balkan States were exhausted by their long struggle and needed money above all things for their recovery. Here France, the whole world's banker, could perform the most useful services. And we find that all the Balkan countries turned to Paris for financial assistance.

About the first to arrive was Montenegro. At the beginning of October 1913 [1077], the Cettinje Government was begging urgently for the payment of the foreshadowed advance on account of a loan, with fervent declarations of its constant loyalty to the Triple Entente. The King of Montenegro was suspected, however, of having dealings with Vienna, and France showed a cold shoulder to the proposal. Not until December, when Russia recommended [1172] a loan of 40 million francs, did the French Foreign

Minister declare [1190] that he was prepared to grant the sum in question.

In October there were also negotiations about a loan for Roumania. But to Isvolsky's great regret they fell through, probably because the French banks were unwilling to grant the full amount asked for. On October 6 [1076], Isvolsky telegraphed that the Roumanian Minister of Finance, then in Paris, had suddenly broken off negotiations, which were approaching settlement, and had come to terms with the Disconto-Gesellschaft of Berlin instead. In a letter of October 9 [1082] the case is dealt with in greater detail : " for some years " the French Government " had disapproved the quotation of new Roumanian loans on the Paris Exchange, so long as Roumania felt politically drawn towards Austria and the Triple Alliance " ; but now, " in consequence of the new political situation which has arisen in recent months, it has changed its original attitude." However, to the disgust of the Paris Government, the matter came to nothing ; the responsibility for this was ascribed by some to the banks, and by others to the "arbitrary " head of the National Debt Office in the Ministry of Finance.

Somewhat changeable was the relationship to Greece, which country we saw France championing so vigorously in the Kavalla affair. In September 1913 relations grew rather strained between Paris and Athens, because the King of the Hellenes had ventured, when in Potsdam on a tour of the European capitals, to make a very Teutophile speech. Sevastopoulos writes on September 25 [1052], that the King had a very cold reception in Paris on this account. Both the population and the Government of the Republic made clear to him their disapproval of his attitude, and Poincaré's address of welcome, which consisted mainly of a review of the " unchangeable friendship of France for Greece," was " entirely approved " by the Press " as a well-merited lesson." Early in 1914, however, there came a turn for the better ; Isvolsky telegraphed on January 13, 1914, that Venizelos had visited Paris and had been promised a loan, which, according to Isvolsky's letter of January 28 [1245], was to amount to 500 million francs.

Both France and Russia exerted themselves to extend their financial influence in Turkey. In the case of France these endeavours were of course of old date, and we have already noted them several times. Russian annoyance at French finanical support of the Porte flamed out more and more frequently. Finally, it was stated in Paris that there were indications of an inclination of the Young Turks " to draw nearer to the Entente Powers " [1242], and that this inclination must be supported by alleviating the financial need of the Ottoman Empire. The Turkish negotiator, Djavid Bey, applied for a loan, insisting, in order to secure it, that there had been " a change of feeling in leading circles " in his country [1247]. When rumours arose that the United States of America proposed to come to the assistance of the " Sick Man " at the Golden Horn, Gulkevitch, the Russian chargé d'affaires at Constantinople, urged [1252] the removal of the Russian veto against a French loan to Turkey. Shortly afterwards Russia too began to look for opportunities of Turkish business. Gulkevitch wired from Constantinople on February 7 [1260] the advice to found an independent Russian institute, " which by carrying out financial and economic operations could serve our ends, and could pave the way for the firm establishment of our influence in the parts of Asia Minor adjoining our frontier." A little later the admission of a Russian delegate into the council of administration of the Ottoman Debt was discussed.

These, however, were comparatively small matters. Both Russia and France were much more concerned about the two remaining Balkan countries, Serbia and Bulgaria.

Serbia seems to have been quite the darling of the two Powers. As early as August 16, 1913 [1016], Isvolsky telegraphed that a French financial group intended to grant Serbia at once " not an advance, but a loan of 100 million francs," as temporary assistance until a larger loan could

12

be arranged. Some weeks later there came an acute conflict between Austria and Serbia, Serbia having occupied
some villages on the farther side of the Albanian frontier as
fixed in London, ostensibly as a precaution against Albanian
raids. Russia regarded the step as justified, but hoped
that Belgrad would show prudence [1059]. Italy and
Austria suggested joint representations by the Powers at
Belgrad to secure the observance of the London decisions,
but this was objected to by St. Petersburg [1066], on the
ground that Serbia's action was due to " her need for self-
defence against the attacks of a State whose neutrality has
been guaranteed by the Powers ; the latter should, therefore, give Serbia certain guarantees against Albania."
As, however, Vienna insisted on the protest being made,
France, according to Isvolsky's telegram of October 18
[1093], advised the Serbian Minister, Vesnitch, then in
Paris, that Serbia should " begin at once to evacuate the
territory occupied in Albania."

In order [Isvolsky adds] to make this step easier for Serbia, the
French Government has decided in principle no longer to hold
back the Serbian loan. A formula is being sought which will
enable it to conclude the loan in spite of its decision to grant no
further loans to the Balkan States until the conclusion of the
labours of the Finance Commission. Pichon would like also to
take this opportunity to arrive at a settlement of the Serbian
railway question by redemption or internationalization.

The preferential treatment is very evident when it is
borne in mind that France's financial position at that time,
according to Kokovtsov, was anything but specially good.

As regards the railway question mentioned at the end
of the telegram, here again a dispute between Serbia and
Austria was threatening. Isvolsky writes on October 23
[1101] that it concerns the railways " in the parts of Macedonia newly acquired by Serbia." Austria is endeavouring
" to ensure the freedom of her commercial relations with
the port of Salonika," and to this end desires that the lines
affected " shall remain in the hands of the Company which

owns them at present ; most of its shares, as is well known, have been bought up by Austria." In order to prevent a conflict and to settle the matter in advance in Serbia's favour, Pichon, the French Foreign Minister, proposes to internationalize these lines. In Vienna, to judge from Isvolsky's letter of December 6 [1155], the idea is readily accepted, to the " great satisfaction " of Paris. Isvolsky, always on the alert, expresses the fear " that this friendly action towards France many be the beginning of a series of manœuvres designed to open the Paris money market to Austrian securities." He regards it, moreover, as extremely undesirable " that the French should be left alone with the Austrians to settle questions which are so important for Serbia and Greece," and considers that Russian representatives must also be included in the financial organizations " in which the designed internationalization may find expression," as that would provide " the means of watching operations and of putting pressure on the French financiers."

All this merely shows the French and Russian eagerness to acquire financial and political influence in Serbia. Everything possible is done to hasten the granting of the loan. Isvolsky wires on November 18 [1125] that it is to be issued immediately after the first instalment of the great Russian railway loan. On January 4, 1914 [1209], he wires that it is to be issued on the 12th, and will amount to 250 million francs.

A report from Sazonov to the Tsar at the end of a journey undertaken in the autumn of 1913 throws interesting light on the history of the diplomatic preliminaries to this transaction. He writes on November 6 [1114] :

My stay in Paris coincided with fresh Austro-Serbian tension arising from the occupation by Serbian troops of several strategic points in Albanian territory. Fearing that Austria-Hungary might succumb to the temptation to secure an easy diplomatic success in this sphere, Pichon and I advised the Serbian ambassador to inform his Government that it would be preferable in this case to yield to the friendly representations of Russia and France rather than await threats from Austria. M. Vesnitch fully shared our view, and at once telegraphed to Belgrad in this sense, but the Vienna Cabinet did not give the Serbian Government time to take the steps contemplated and sent, on the following day, a very curt ultimatum.

I was a witness of the entire disapproval with which the French Government and people viewed this step of Austria's, and I utilized this favourable moment for Serbia to persuade Pichon to show his recognition of the discretion displayed by that country. I pointed out that France herself was interested in an increase in Serbia's strength, for in the event of grave international conflicts Serbia would of necessity stand on the side of France, being in the nature of things an enemy of Germany's most important ally. M. Pichon promised me that he would exert his influence in favour of the early placing of the Serbian loan on the Paris Bourse.

Here, then, we have financial support of Serbia recommended on the ground that that country will fight on the side of France and Russia in a war against the Central Powers. After what we already know, it is no surprise that an argument of this kind at once made the desired impression on the French Foreign Minister. Were concessions beginning to be made in Russia also to the menacing impulse to world war ?

Various other documents relative to Serbia make this more than probable. We will merely adduce two, both of which have been of common knowledge for some time. The first is a passage in a letter from Sazonov, dated May 6, 1913, to the Russian ambassador at Belgrad :

Serbia has passed only through the first stage of her historical career. To reach her goal she must endure another frightful struggle, in which her very existence will be staked. . . . Serbia's Promised Land lies in the territory of the present Austria-Hungary, and not in that for which she is now striving, with the Bulgarians barring the way. In these circumstances it is of vital importance to Serbia to maintain the alliance with Bulgaria, and on the other hand by patient and tenacious effort to bring herself up to the necessary standard of preparedness for the contest which is inevitably coming. Time is working for Serbia and for the destruction of her enemies, who already show plain signs of dissolution.[1]

[1] *Deutschland Schuldig ?* German Foreign Office White Book, p. 99.

A week later the Serbian ambassador in St. Petersburg reported to his Government :

> Sazonov told me again that we must work for the future, as we shall get a great deal of territory from Austria-Hungary. I replied that we shall gladly give Monastir (Bitolin) to the Bulgarians if we can get Bosnia and other Austrian provinces.[1]

In the light of these utterances, Sazonov's statement to the Tsar, that in a war with the Central Powers Serbia would take side against them, acquires, of course, much greater weight. For we are justified now in concluding that Russia purposed setting the principal victor in the Balkan wars directly against the Dual Monarchy, and that she thus had quite definite plans in the direction of a general resort to arms.

How did this come about ? A brief investigation of Russia's relations with Bulgaria in the months after the Peace of Bucarest will help to show. Bulgaria caused as much anxiety to Russia as Serbia brought her satisfaction. The disastrous conclusion of the third Balkan war brought bitter disappointment in Sofia, where the most extravagant ambitions had been entertained. Resentment at the *débâcle* turned partly against the great Slav brother, who was reproached with having deserted his ally of 1902 in the hour of need. From Isvolsky's letter of November 6, 1913 [1116], reporting a " candid and thoroughgoing discussion " with Gennadiev, the Bulgarian Foreign Minister, it appears that there was then an inclination in leading political circles in Bulgaria to swing round to the side of the Central Powers. Gennadiev denied this, and argued that his country must first recover itself, and later " as the vanguard of Russia " help the latter " to conquer Constantinople and the Straits " ; but an event nevertheless soon occurred which caused great uneasiness in St. Petersburg. At the end of this letter Isvolsky states that " at the present moment the most urgent and vital question for

---

[1] Bogitchevitch, *Causes of the War* (George Allen & Unwin), pp. 99, 100.

any Bulgarian Government is the question of finance, in other words of the conclusion of a loan."

In my view [continues Isvolsky] we must proceed very cautiously in this matter, and neither hasten its settlement nor delay it too much. Any opposition on our part would at once be known in Sofia and could only increase the feeling there against Russia. On the other hand, the matter will unavoidably hang fire of itself, since no foreign loans can be arranged here until after the issue of the great French loan (a milliard or a milliard and a half of francs) which is needed to balance the budget, and the various Balkan loans cannot be arranged before the end of the labours of the international Finance Commission. Thus the big Bulgarian loan cannot in any case be arranged before the New Year; at the moment there can only be a question of the postponement of the repayment of the advances which have been made by the bankers against Treasury bills, and we could scarcely have any reason for interfering with this.

In this case, however, the familiar tactics of retaining the Balkan States as faithful vassals by judicious play with financial promises failed. On November 20, 1913 [1131], Sazonov reported fresh signs

that the present Cabinet at Sofia officially makes a show of desiring to retain Russia's confidence, but is in reality carrying on an organized campaign of calumny against us, and endeavouring to enter into the closest possible political relationships with Austria.

The suggestion is therefore made, in order to injure the Radoslavov Government, that the French should not grant any loan to Bulgaria during its period of office. In reply, Isvolsky telegraphs on November 25 [1137] that Pichon has told him that negotiations for a Bulgarian loan " have not even been begun," but that when the time approaches for a decision " the French Government will most certainly give no authorization until we (Russia) have been consulted and our full concurrence obtained."

Suddenly, in the spring of 1914, the news comes from Savinsky, the Russian ambassador at Sofia (April 22, [1322]), that " negotiations are being carried on in Berlin for a Bulgarian loan of some 250 million francs "; Savinsky adds:

It is a matter of life and death for the Radoslavov Cabinet to obtain the loan within a month, and it has accordingly agreed to all the conditions of the Berlin banks, though they were hard.

There begins at once behind the scenes a busy intrigue to hinder as far as possible, at the last moment, what was doubtless looked upon as serious mischief. Two days later [1324] Savinsky wires that he and the French ambassador are exerting themselves to demonstrate to the King of Bulgaria and to public opinion " the ruinous character of the financial policy of the present Ministry, both from the economic and the political point of view." In his opinion " every effort must be made to frustrate the plans of Radoslavov and Tontchev." France immediately [1325] takes a helping hand, the Foreign Minister, Doumergue, giving the French banks " categorical orders to place no support at Bulgaria's disposal in respect of any Bulgarian loan issued in Germany." Shortly afterwards [1328] French and Russian efforts are made to persuade Bulgaria to negotiate a loan in France ; in this way also the obnoxious Radoslavov Ministry may be brought down. On May 12, 1914 [1335], Savinsky telegraphs that he has pointed out to Dobrovitch at Sofia

that the moment the King decides to dismiss the present Government, France, with Russia's cordial approval, will either grant Bulgaria a loan under more favourable conditions or at least an advance before the conclusion of the loan.

On the following day [1336] Savinsky, filled with the desire " to prevent the increase of Austro-German influence here," recommends, after sounding his French colleague and the representatives of the French banks, that " as a last resort "

We might bring to the knowledge of the King that Russia, though she has no confidence in the present Government, is always concerned for Bulgaria and her political and financial independence, and now makes him the following proposal : France will be induced to supply the King personally with the advance of some 100 millions which the country requires, without making the hard conditions which are now under discussion in Berlin. At the same time there

must be a declaration that, until a loan is concluded, France and
Russia renounce the repayment of the 75 millions and 45 millions
of Treasury Bills outstanding for military supplies.

On May 18 [1342] Isvolsky reports :

In the view of the French Government, it is as much to the
interest of France as of Russia not to allow Bulgaria to come under
the financial and consequently the political influence of Germany
and Austria. The French Government is therefore prepared to
accept the plans put forward by our ambassador at Sofia. It is
admitted that a compromise can be found in the formation of a
Malinov-Gennadiev Coalition Cabinet. The immediate grant of
an advance will make it impossible for a loan to be concluded
elsewhere. The grant of the loan can then be made dependent
on the trend of political events. If Russia agrees and withdraws
her veto, the French Government believes that it can induce the
French banks to grant Bulgaria an advance of 80 to 90 million
francs, and also not to insist on the repayment of the 75 millions
of Treasury Bills. The loan could take place towards the end of
the year.

According to a further telegram from Paris on May 22
[1346], the French Government was prepared, at the
renewed instance of Savinsky, to approach the banks about
an advance of 90 million francs. Difficulties arose, however,
about this [1348], and through the stubbornness of the
French financiers a serious delay occurred. While efforts
were still being made to arrive at some result, the Quai
d'Orsay proposed, for reasons of diplomacy, to abstain for
the time being from asking the King to dismiss the Radoslavov Ministry ; and, according to Isvolsky's telegram of
May 30 [1354], it recommended the following very characteristic communication to the King by the mouth of the
Russian ambassador at Sofia :

Your Majesty is aware that the Bulgarian Government—as is
learnt from private sources—has not considered it necessary to
turn to the French Government in order to employ the resources
of the Paris market in satisfying Bulgaria's financial needs. The
Bulgarian Government has applied to the German banks, and an
agreement, on very burdensome conditions for Bulgaria, is about
to be concluded. Such an agreement threatens to prejudice the
economic and even in some degree the political independence of

the country for a considerable time. The Russian and French Governments, animated by the desire of giving Bulgaria proof of their disinterested friendship, have applied to the Paris and St. Petersburg banks, to ascertain whether the resources required for immediate needs could be placed at the disposal of the Bulgarian Government, until in, perhaps, a few months' time more favourable circumstances permit of the conclusion of a definite loan. The Russian and French banks have, in their reply to this inquiry, declared their readiness to advance some 60 million francs at once. They also agree that the repayment of the Treasury Bills shall be put off until the loan is concluded. I am commissioned to make this communication to Your Majesty, showing the interest which Russia and France take in Bulgaria. My Government hopes that Your Majesty will appreciate the significance of this step.

Immediately afterwards [1355] Isvolsky telegraphs that it is hoped in Paris that this statement will give the King an opportunity " to take steps for a change of Ministry," for the following reason :

So long as we limit ourselves to an advance and the loan is not concluded, Russia and France will have the opportunity of exercising controlling influence over the course of Bulgarian politics. As regards the ultimate demand for an undertaking from the King to nominate another Cabinet, we should be able to formulate this later, when Bulgaria, having accepted a considerable advance, will no longer be able, financially speaking, to free herself ; and we should only need to do so if the King by the end of the year, i.e. when the conclusion of the loan becomes due, should not have found a favourable opportunity to hand over the Government to other Ministers. Margerie adds that more drastic procedure at the present moment would offend the King and produce the opposite of the desired result.

This, then, was the nature of the " disinterested " friendship which it was proposed to offer to Bulgaria.

Savinsky, who was at the centre of operations and was mainly concerned to secure prompt action, showed no enthusiasm over the finesse of the Quai d'Orsay. He wired on June 2 [1356] that he was opposed to the Paris plan and demanded urgently to be told whether the French banks were prepared to pay. Only two days later [1358] he gave up hope of success in preventing the signature of the loan in Berlin, and made preparations for a campaign to induce

the Bulgarian Sobranje to reject it. For this also he
requested French support.

Meanwhile the negotiations of the Bulgars in the German
capital came to a standstill [1360, 1361], and were even
broken off for a time. Savinsky's hopes of a fall of the
Radoslavov Cabinet at once increased, and he advised
[1363] a generous gesture from Russia, to make it possible
for Bulgaria " at last to approach " her. On June 11
[1365] he learned " that at the instance of Tarnovsky and
Berchtold the negotiations in Berlin have recommenced
after pressure on the banks by the German Government,"
and he pressed again for the consent of the Paris banks
to be procured. It was at last obtained ; on June 19, 1914
[1369], Isvolsky telegraphed that a group of financiers
was prepared to grant at once a Bulgarian loan of 200 million
francs. The last news contained in the documents is a
statement of Radoslavov's reported on June 30 [1374] by
Savinsky, " that after the murder of the Archduke (of
Austria) there is little prospect of concluding the loan in
Berlin." It was also considered necessary that the Russian
State Bank should take part in the loan, so that Russia
could not be reproached with only being concerned to wreck
the negotiations in Berlin, without being willing to pay
out anything herself.

What is important to our inquiry is the clear evidence
that St. Petersburg and Paris were, in the period here
dealt with, struggling vigorously and even passionately
over Bulgaria. This cannot be explained merely by the
fear of losing a formerly devoted adherent ; much graver
matters must have been at stake, and we shall see at once
that this was so.

Little material has at yet come to light concerning the
policy of St. Petersburg immediately before the war. But
we already possess a few isolated but very significant
documents. There are, first, the various reports of Sazonov
to the Tsar from which several extracts have already been
quoted. It must, of course, not be forgotten that their

tone is adapted to the addressee. Nicholas II was a weak character, difficult to move to energetic decisions, but otherwise responsive to adroit handling. When his Foreign Minister writes to him, one can watch the cautious administration of judiciously adjusted doses of advice, carefully made palatable, to bring him to the point desired by degrees and without frightening him. Sazonov's report of December 8, 1913 [1157], is very characteristic in this sense; it also gives us an unusually deep insight into Sazonov's own thoughts. It deals with the question of the attitude which should be taken up by the Russian Foreign Office towards the new political conditions resulting from the events in the Balkan Peninsula. Sazonov first touches in very general terms on " the possibility of the final dissolution of the Ottoman Empire," already awaited, it is true, for two centuries; but the Empire is, he says, now so weakened that it " could no longer ward off a vigorous blow from without."

Our doubts of the continued vitality of Turkey bring again to the fore the historic question of the Straits and of their political and economic importance to us. . . . Can we permit any other country to obtain entire control of the passage through the Straits ? To ask the question is to answer it—" No." To give up the Straits to a powerful State would be equivalent to placing the whole economic development of Southern Russia at the mercy of that State.

This is supported by particulars from the Finance Ministry, from which it appears that the temporary closing of the Straits in 1912 inflicted on Russian export trade a loss of 100 million roubles. As to the political significance of the mastery of the Straits, " The State which has possession of the Straits will have in its hands the key not only to the Black Sea and the Mediterranean, but to the penetration of Asia Minor and the overlordship of the Balkan countries." Sazonov proceeds then to deal with the significance of Bulgaria to Russia :

At the beginning of the Balkan war Bulgaria had some success for a time, and her ambitious army leaders dreamed of taking

Constantinople and setting up a Bulgarian overlordship over the Balkan countries. Bulgaria's boundless pretensions united her recent Allies against her ; Roumania joined them, and the war ended in Bulgaria's defeat. But it can hardly be supposed that she will reconcile herself to this ; is she not more likely to seek an opportunity to recover her losses ? The old dream of hegemony and of the conquest of the Straits may return. Fortune is fickle, and Turkey is incapable of learning from experience. No one can tell the day or the hour when Bulgaria will pounce on Turkey in one of those wild attacks of which the Bulgars are capable. This might bring final disaster to the Ottoman Empire.

Let us bear this passage in mind, and not break the thread of Sazonov's argument. After this long and significant prelude on Bulgaria's aspirations, the Russian Foreign Minister proceeds at length to an open statement of Russia's own designs. He recalls the re-establishment of the Black Sea Fleet " by the late Tsar Alexander III, and the commencement of steamer traffic on the Black Sea. Both undertakings are bound up with the idea of Russian power, and with the possibility of safeguarding our interests in the Straits." Then he allows himself to be carried away to the following admissions :

Hundreds of millions have been spent on this task, and on the upkeep of the army in the Odessa command, which will operate with our fleet. It is well known that as early as 1895, at the time of the Armenian massacres, the question of the temporary occupation of Constantinople by our troops was discussed, with the knowledge and consent of Great Britain, then our most dangerous rival. We had to give up this plan owing to insufficient means of transport and to defects in our mobilization on land.

Eighteen years have passed since then. We are still spending hundreds of millions, and are still not a step nearer to our goal. Warships are built and large sums spent every year on the upkeep of our merchant fleet. Yet when the moment comes in which it might be desirable to proceed to an important landing operation of some sort or other, the Government shrinks from it because it is almost entirely impossible to carry out.

When last year there was a question of a possible advance of our armies on Constantinople, we discovered that in two months we could take over no more than two army corps in small transports, and that the preparations for mobilizing the transport vessels and for moving the land army would take so long that it would have been impossible for the operation to have the effect of a surprise attack. In other words, the enterprise proved simply impracticable, quite apart from the fact that the numerical strength of the expeditionary force would have been disproportionate to the tasks before it.

Russia, he says, must therefore make comprehensive preparations to place herself in a position to advance on Constantinople as soon as it becomes necessary. Four main proposals are made :

1. To reduce the time required for the mobilization of an expeditionary corps of adequate strength ;
2. To lay down the necessary lines of communication for mobilization ;
3. To bring up the Black Sea Fleet to preponderance over the Ottoman Fleet, so that it may be able, in combination with the army, to force the Straits, in order to effect a temporary or, if necessary, permanent occupation ;
4. To increase our means of transport up to the strength required for our landing operation.

In the observations which follow, the design of gaining influence over Asia Minor finds vigorous expression. Here and there Sazonov pauses in his description of the aggressive efforts recommended to interpolate an assurance of the advantage to Russia of the maintenance of the *status quo*. But that does not diminish the strong impression that the conquest of the Dardanelles has been thought out to the last detail. Bearing in mind what happened in 1913, this is not surprising or particularly new.

The last part of this communication, however, contains certain passages which go far beyond what has so far been revealed of Sazonov's policy :

Moreover, I must repeat that the question of the Straits can hardly be advanced a step except through European complications. To judge from present conditions, these complications would find us in alliance with France and possibly, but not quite certainly, with Great Britain, or at least with the latter as a benevolent neutral. In the event of European complications, we should be able to count in the Balkans on Serbia and perhaps also on Roumania. This makes clear the task of our diplomacy, which consists in creating favourable conditions for as close a *rapprochement* with Roumania as possible. This policy must be pursued uninterruptedly, cautiously, and openmindedly. Roumania's position among the Balkan countries recalls in many respects that of Italy in Europe. Both Powers suffer from megalomania, and as they are not strong enough to realize their plans openly, they have to content themselves with an opportunist policy, constantly watching to see on which side the power lies, and going over to that side.

In a provisional estimate of forces it would be dangerous to rely on such vacillating elements, but imprudent to leave them entirely out of account.

There are two main factors in the uncertainty of the present position in the Balkans. The first is the unrest among the nationalities of Austria-Hungary, which is noticeably growing, owing to the success of the Serbs and Roumanians and the impression made by these successes on their fellow-countrymen within the frontiers of the Habsburg monarchy. The second is the impossibility of Bulgaria accepting the painful consequences of the Peace of Bucarest.

These two States may either unite in a common purpose, the alteration of the map of the Balkans, or find themselves in opposite camps if Bulgaria can hope to get Macedonia by other means. However hard it may be for Serbia and Bulgaria to come together, they can only continue to strive for their national ideal if they are in alliance. As enemies the two States will paralyse one another. Serbia can only realize her high ideal of the union of the whole Serb people if Bulgaria not only does not oppose it but lends assistance, her reward being the restoration of her lost Macedonian territory. Nevertheless, there can be no doubt that for either of these hypotheses to become actuality Russia must also strive for the realization of her historic aims, and act in common with these countries. Alone, the Balkan States are inevitably doomed to conflicts among themselves, which can only be avoided by Russia's presence and active guidance.

This passage is an admission of enormous import. The kernel lies in the first clause, with the declaration that " the question of the Straits can hardly be advanced a step except *through European complications.*" The further reflections sketch a sort of programme for this advance. The passage establishes Sazonov's conversion to the idea of world war. Thus at the end of 1913 the Russian Foreign Minister had, as regards the attainment of the specifically Russian aims, completed that fateful change of course which Poincaré on behalf of France had resolutely made as long ago as the end of 1912, when he was ready to attack Austria and Germany. The inclination of the political leaders of the French Republic towards world war now found an echo in the conviction of this powerful Russian statesman that his country too could not advance except along that road. It was this that sealed the doom of Europe. For the moment the Great Power in the West and the Great Power in the East, both secretly intent on aggression, began to put pressure on the Central Powers, world war had become unavoidable, and only a question of time.

Why Sazonov came over to this view is evident from the events already described. He was simply convinced by the force of the facts with which he had to square his direction of Russian policy. He went through much the same development as Isvolsky had done during his time as Foreign Minister. Isvolsky had at first tried to settle the question of the Straits by diplomatic means, and, when this failed, adopted what in my first chapter I called " the great solution," that just described by Sazonov. Sazonov at first sought the solution through a military *coup* in connexion with the Balkan wars, but this proved impracticable. The plan of an advance through Asia Minor fell through owing to the opposition of Great Britain, and the disfavour which this enabled France to express— a repetition of Isvolsky's experience in 1909. There remained only the path " through European complications " which Sazonov describes in such amazing detail in his report to the Tsar. France is counted on with confidence. Serbia is assigned the part of the battering-ram against Austria-Hungary, and Bulgaria is of such importance because if she goes over to the Dual Monarchy it will considerably increase the difficulty of the " great solution," whilst as the friend of Serbia she represents a significant plus in the calculations of the Russian Foreign Minister. These political considerations fully explain the financial operations mentioned above. They too were links in the chain which was being forged ever more closely about the Central Powers, until the hour approached when it could be drawn together to suffocate them.

In fact, towards the end of 1913, the world war was born in the heads of the statesmen with whom lay the decision in our Continent. All that happens afterwards only adds to the proof of this.

Turkey had the intention of making the German General Liman von Sanders Commander-in-Chief over her land forces, in order to reconstruct her army. Russia at once protested energetically. On November 26, 1913 [1140], Isvolsky wires that Pichon, the French Foreign Minister, shares Sazonov's view " that it is out of the question to give German officers the command over the troops in Constantinople. . . . France cannot permit Germans to command in Smyrna and Beyrout." On December 3 [1148], he reports a " proposal by Grey for an identic communication from Russia, Great Britain, and France to the Porte in the matter of the German officers." The three Entente Powers had thus found themselves in agreement on this matter, although it appears from a telegram from Benckendorff on December 9 [1158] that London was advising caution, " to avoid a *cul-de-sac* and leave a line of retreat for the German Government." It was, of course, inadvisable for Great Britain to adopt too stiff an attitude, since the Turkish fleet was commanded by a British admiral and Germany could quote this as a parallel case to that of Liman von Sanders. In France, Russian action is once more feared which " might lead to the break-up of Asiatic Turkey " [1179], but it is nevertheless declared " that the Government of the Republic is firmly resolved to support all steps taken by the Tsar's Government " [1192]. M. Bompard, the French ambassador in Constantinople, even gives the advice [1198] that permission should be obtained for a Russian ironclad to enter the Bosphorus and then to declare that " it would only leave after an alteration of the agreement with General Liman and his officers." Poincaré again shows himself the most resolute ; from his words Isvolsky concludes (January 5, 1914 [1212]) that France is " calmly resolved in existing circumstances not to evade

the obligations which her alliance with us imposes on her."
Ten days later [1227] Isvolsky reports that in conversation
with him Poincaré repeated several times, "We shall
support you." The dispute was eventually settled by
Germany and Turkey giving way.

What is particularly interesting is that a special secret
conference was held in Russia on December 31, 1913,
with the Prime Minister, Kokovtsov, in the chair, Sazonov
also being present ; at this conference the possibility of
the use of force against Turkey in connexion with the Liman
von Sanders affair was discussed, and Sazonov particularly
emphasized "that the measures of compulsion against
Turkey were contemplated only in the closest co-operation
with Great Britain and France." [1] Thus he hinted once
more at adherence to the "great solution"; Kokovtsov
spoke energetically against war.

On February 8, 1914, there met, this time with Sazonov
himself in the chair, a fresh conference with the heads of
the Russian army and navy, in which preparations for
conquest of the Straits were discussed on the basis of the
report of December 8, 1913, to the Tsar. Two passages
may be quoted from the minutes, confirming what has
already been adduced :

Replying to the question whether . . . we could count on
support from Serbia, S. D. Sazonov said that it could not be assumed
that our operations against the Straits could take place without a
general European war, and that it was to be assumed that under
such circumstances Serbia would direct all her forces against
Austria-Hungary.

With reference to what the Foreign Minister had said concerning
the general situation in which a decision of the question of the
Straits might be expected, the Chief of the General Staff expressed
his conviction that the struggle for Constantinople would hardly
be possible without a general European war. [2]

Thus the military leaders of Russia associated themselves
with the menacing attitude of Sazonov, and decided, on his
initiative, on a series of measures to put Russia in a position
to advance on Constantinople at the appropriate moment.

[1] See Appendix II, p. 219.   [2] See Appendix III, p. 230.

It should also be noted that the Tsar entered on the minutes of the conference the remark, " I entirely approve the decisions of the conference." Thus he too had come round to the point of view of the Foreign Minister.

Other evidence shows that, in consonance with the policy initiated by Sazonov, activity in St. Petersburg was greatly increased. The reforms in Armenia were demanded from Turkey and enforced, and on the founding of the Bank of Salonika the demand was made that " preponderating influence, if not complete independence, in the Armenian department shall be conceded " to the representative of Russia. Endeavours were also made to secure further extensions of influence in Asia Minor by concessions for railway construction. At the same time the purely military preparations were accelerated as much as possible. Sazonov transmits on January 8, 1914 [1217], a request from Kokovtsov to the French Government for the first instalment of the railway loan to be increased to 600 millions, and in a very secret telegram of the same day [1218] he explains this proposal by the necessity " of giving a part of the orders for the artillery department to the French factories, since the Russian factories are not in a position to execute them by the date fixed."

The Russian determination to cut a path by means of European complications to the realization of Russian interests is, however, shown above all by a step taken during these months, the true significance of which can only be understood in connexion with what has already been adduced—namely, Russia's approach to intimacy with Great Britain.

In his report to the Tsar, Sazonov lays stress on the fact that a general collision will find Russia " in alliance with France, and possibly, but not quite certainly, also with Great Britain." At the special secret conference on December 31, 1913, he argues :

In reality a Russian initiative supported only by France would not appear particularly dangerous to Germany. The two States would hardly be in a position to deal Germany a mortal blow, even in the event of military successes, which can never be predicted. A struggle, on the other hand, in which Great Britain participated might be disastrous to Germany, who clearly realizes that if Great Britain were drawn in, the result might be social disturbances of a catastrophic nature within her frontiers in less than six weeks. Great Britain is dangerous to Germany, and in the consciousness of this is to be found the explanation of the hatred with which the Germans are filled in the face of Great Britain's growing power. In view of this it is essential that before taking any decisive steps the Tsar's Government shall assure itself of the support of the London Cabinet, whose active sympathy does not seem, in the Minister's view, to be certain.

It is unnecessary to point out how exactly all this agrees with what has already been noted, and how entirely it confirms the contention that Great Britain was the ultimate obstacle to the march on Constantinople. A way out was now to be secured and the last and most important stone laid in the preparation of " the great solution."

Hitherto it had always been Paris that made overtures to Great Britain ; now the initiative came from St. Petersburg, though by way of Paris. Isvolsky reports on March 18, 1914 [1297], that M. Paléologue, Delcassé's successor as French ambassador on the Neva, has told him that

In the course of the conversation with which His Majesty graciously honoured him after the handing over of his credentials, His Majesty had been pleased to touch on the question of the rôle of Great Britain in the Triple Alliance, and on the fact that it was desirable to bring to the notice of the London Cabinet the necessity of undertaking more definite and binding obligations towards Russia.

The Tsar's desire corresponded of course entirely with the views of Isvolsky, who had for years been working for the rounding off of the Entente, and he hastens to emphasize in this letter that " British-French relations are at present defined by two documents, the military and naval agreement (the agreements between the two general staffs and naval staffs) and the political agreement (Grey-Cambon correspondence). After some discussion of these agreements Isvolsky concludes :

I took advantage of my last meetings with M. Doumergue and with the President of the Republic to touch on the question of Russo-British relations. Both of them have full information of what His Majesty was pleased to say to M. Paléologue. M. Doumergue said to me that he entirely agreed that after the recent experience during the Balkan crisis, and in view also of the harmonicus and united action of the Triple Alliance Powers, it would be very desirable to induce Great Britain to undertake more definite obligations towards us. He added that the impending arrival of Sir Edward Grey, who is accompanying King George here, will give him the opportunity personally to touch on this question in the conversations with the British Minister. M. Poincaré expressed himself in the same sense, and said that he intended to draw the attention of King George to the same question. The British King and Queen are due to arrive on April 8/21. If, therefore, you should be of the opinion that in this matter MM. Doumergue and Poincaré might be able to exert a useful influence on the London Cabinet, I would beg you to provide me in good time with indications as to your views on this question. It seems to me personally that the impending discussions between the leaders of French and British foreign policy might afford a very good opportunity for ascertaining how far the London Cabinet is prepared to go along the road of a closer agreement with Russia, but that the question of the form and the content of such an agreement must be discussed directly between ourselves and the Englishmen.

The proposals of Doumergue and Isvolsky were adopted. On April 2, 1914 [1310], Sazonov writes that he agrees

that it would be useful if MM. Poincaré and Doumergue availed themselves of the personal meeting with King George and his Ministers to mention confidentially to them that a closer agreement between Russia and Great Britain would be welcomed in France also as a happy event which is equally desirable for all three partners in the existing Triple Entente.

Isvolsky replies on April 9 [1313] :

M. Doumergue confirmed to me definitely his intention of expressing, at the impending meeting with Sir Edward Grey, his view of the desirability of such an agreement. He considers that it will be very easy to find convincing arguments for this view, since it is obvious that as France has special military and naval agreements with Russia and with Great Britain, this system must be harmonized and completed by a corresponding agreement between Russia and Great Britain. M. Doumergue is of the opinion that the Russo-British agreement should take the form of a naval convention, and the occasion would perhaps call for technical discussions between all three naval staffs.

The Tsar's keen interest in the matter is evident from a secret telegram sent by Paléologue to Doumergue on April 18 [1319] :

I learn from a *private* and reliable source [" private " is twice underlined in blue pencil] that the meeting between the Tsar and his Foreign Minister before the departure for the Crimea was devoted to a very thorough discussion of the question of the British-Russian Alliance. [In the margin here there is a note of interrogation, made with an ordinary lead pencil.] During the discussion of the more or less closely threatening collision between Russia and Germany, His Majesty considered also the possibility of the resumption of hostilities between Greece and Turkey. In this event the Ottoman Government will close the Straits. Russia would be unable to remain indifferent to this step, with the injury it must entail on Russia's commerce and her prestige.

His Majesty is reported to have said : " In order to open the Straits I should resort to force."

The Tsar's attitude shows how completely he had adopted his Foreign Minister's standpoint.

On April 29, 1914 [1327], Isvolsky describes the negotiations between Grey and the French political leaders on the occasion of the King's visit to Paris. They took, unexpectedly, a very favourable course :

When the discussion of the various questions of current politics on the order of the day had come to an end, M. Doumergue came to the question of Russo-British relations, and made to Sir Edward Grey the representations which he and I had agreed on. He brought into the field two main arguments in favour of a closer Russo-British agreement :

1. The German efforts to detach us from the Triple Entente, as a weak and unreliable political combination, and

2. The opportunity afforded by the conclusion of a naval convention between us and Great Britain of releasing part of the British naval forces, not only as regards active operations in the Baltic and North Sea, but also in the Mediterranean.

[M. Doumergue mentioned to Sir Edward Grey, among other things, that in two years' time we should have a strong Dreadnought squadron in the Baltic.]

Sir Edward Grey replied to M. Doumergue that he was personally entirely in sympathy with the ideas which he had expressed and was quite ready to conclude an agreement with Russia in the form of that in existence between Great Britain and France. But he did not conceal from M. Doumergue that there were, not only in the Government party but even among the members of the Cabinet, persons who were prejudiced against Russia and very little inclined to any further approach to her. However, he expressed the hope that he would be able to bring over Mr. Asquith and the other members of the Government to his view. He suggested the following procedure : First the two Cabinets—London and Paris—should, after mutual agreement, communicate to the St. Petersburg Cabinet all existing agreements between Great Britain and France, namely : (1) The land and sea conventions worked out by the general and naval staffs, which, as you are aware, have something of a conditional character ; and (2) the political agreement, which is in the form of an exchange of letters between Sir Edward Grey and the French ambassador in London. In these letters it is stated that if in the course of events Great Britain and France should decide on joint active operations, they "would take into consideration" the conventions mentioned. In making this communication to us, the London and Paris Cabinets could ask us what was our attitude towards the subjects on which it touches, and this would give us the opportunity to enter into a discussion with Great Britain in regard to the conclusion of a corresponding Russo-British agreement. Sir Edward Grey's idea is that only a naval convention could be concluded between us and Great Britain, and not a land convention, since all the British land forces are already distributed in advance and they obviously could not co-operate with the Russian forces. He added that on his return to London he would at once submit the above plan to Mr. Asquith and his other colleagues for examination. M. Doumergue asked him if he did not think it would be desirable not to give the agreement between Russia and Great Britain the form of a parallel agreement but that of a single three-party agreement ; Sir Edward Grey replied that he did not personally exclude this alternative, but it could only be considered later, in connexion with the technical elaboration of the contemplated Russo-British agreement.

All three of the persons who had taken part in the discussion —MM. Doumergue, Cambon, and de Margerie—told me that they had been astonished by Sir Edward Grey's clearly and decidedly expressed willingness to proceed towards a closer *rapprochement* with Russia. They were convinced that his reservations in regard to Mr. Asquith and the other members of the Cabinet are only of a formal character. If he were not certain already of their agreement he would not have made such concrete proposals.

From the foregoing, it seems to me, it may be concluded that the question touched on in your letter of March 20 has been fairly launched. MM. Poincaré and Doumergue promised me that M. Cambon would devote his best attention to realizing the plan foreshadowed by Sir Edward Grey. While our ambassador in London, Count Benckendorff, was here, I gave him full details of the matter. He also is of the opinion that there is every reason for confidence that the matter will continue to proceed satisfactorily.

To this very revealing communication there are appended copies of the letters exchanged by Grey and Cambon in November 1912.

On May 12, 1914 [1334], Count Benckendorff reports a conversation with the British Foreign Minister :

> On this occasion Grey spoke with a warmth unusual for him, showing that he has a solid basis for his conclusions. It is evident what led him to send for me to make such a communication. He wanted to let me know that a new phase of still closer approach to France was beginning. This intention was still more evident to me when he went straight on to remark that I had no doubt been informed of the discussion which he had had with Doumergue about Russia. He told me that in Paris, away from his colleagues, it had been impossible for him to do more than express his own personal agreement with the plan that the Governments of Great Britain and France should inform the Russian Government of all the existing military agreements between Great Britain and France. To-day, he said, he was able to tell me that immediately after his return to London he had discussed this with the Prime Minister, and that the latter had agreed with his view and had had no objections to offer to the proposed plan ; the whole matter was, however, too important for a decision to be taken without the concurrence of the Cabinet Council.

According to a telegram on May 15 from Doumergue to Paléologue, the British-French agreements were now communicated to the Russian diplomats, and on the following day [1340] Benckendorff reports that the British Cabinet has approved Grey's attitude in the matter. He proceeds to describe Grey's views as to the execution of the work begun :

> On receiving authority from his Government, Cambon would inform me of the Notes exchanged, and at the same time Sir Edward would send me the text for transmission to the Russian Government. While the agreements with France covering the event of war were primarily concerned with the co-operation of the armies, any agreements with Russia must, in Sir Edward's view, from the nature of things have reference to the navies. The negotiations should accordingly be carried on between the Russian and British naval staffs. The negotiations with France had taken place in London ; the French military and naval attachés in London had gone over to Paris as necessary when further instructions were needed. Finally Prince Louis of Battenberg had gone quite unofficially to Paris to initial the agreements.

Cambon's view was that after the Notes had been communicated it would be necessary to determine the further procedure to be adopted. He told me that in Sir Edward Grey's view precisely the same procedure could be followed as with France : our naval attaché in London should be empowered to enter into negotiations with the British naval staff after he had received instructions from St. Petersburg ; for even repeated journeys of the naval attaché would be unlikely to arouse public curiosity, while the arrival of senior Russian naval officers in London would be sure to become known and give rise to undesired comment.

Writing on May 18 [1343] in a very optimistic tone, Benckendorff advises that the conclusion of a formal alliance with Great Britain should not be attempted, since it would be a very difficult matter for any British Cabinet for reasons of internal politics. Moreover, the lesson of the past was that it was unnecessary :

Looking back at the various phases of the Entente, it is undeniable that at moments of danger Great Britain has never hesitated to place herself at the side of France ; the same applies to Russia whenever British and Russian interests have been simultaneously affected, and this despite the difficulty of bringing the policy of the two countries into line on all the questions cropping up from day to day, and despite the reasons (which it would take too long to discuss here) which have prevented the Entente between Russia and Great Britain from striking root as deeply as that between France and Great Britain.

From a later letter of Benckendorff, dated May 23 [1349], we learn that a discussion took place on the previous day between Grey, Cambon, and himself, in the course of which Grey stated " that the British Cabinet had approved the reply which he had given to Doumergue in Paris in his own name." In this connexion the next step proposed is " that the Russian military attaché in London shall be empowered to get into touch with the British naval staff." Action is taken accordingly ; on May 28 [1353] Sazonov writes to Benckendorff :

We are exceedingly gratified at the readiness of the British Government to begin without delay the negotiations for the conclusion of an agreement between Russia and Great Britain concerning the joint operations of our naval forces in the event of joint military action. Apart from the desirability of such an agreement from a specially military point of view, we attach great importance to it from general political considerations. We see in the conclusion of such an agreement an important step towards associating Great Britain more closely with the Franco-Russian Alliance, and an effective means of strengthening the recognition of the common interests of Great Britain and Russia, which, we are convinced, will be of great advantage in all questions affecting British and Russian interests. I have pointed out to our Ministry of the Navy and especially to our naval attaché in London the great political importance of the impending negotiations, which the latter will have to carry on with the British naval staff. We regard the proposal made by the British Government as to the form in which the agreement is to be drawn up as entirely suitable, and Captain Volkov is empowered to enter into negotiation with the British Government. The principles to be kept in mind during the coming negotiations were the subject of a conference with the Chief of Naval Staff on May 13/26.

An enclosure to the letter reports the results arrived at at this conference ; special stress is laid on the necessity of co-operation between the British and Russian fleets in the North Sea and Baltic and in the Mediterranean. On June 11 [1364] Benckendorff mentions Captain Volkov's return from St. Petersburg with his instructions ; Grey, he says, is at once informing the First Lord of the Admiralty. With this the technical negotiations for the preparation of the naval convention began.

It is noteworthy that Russia pressed for the negotiations to be expedited. On June 15 [1371] Sazonov writes to Benckendorff :

At the present moment it seems to me essential to conclude the contemplated naval convention as quickly as possible. It is important that this agreement shall not be delayed, and His Majesty has been pleased to express this view to the British ambassador in my presence. I should mention finally that Sir George Buchanan was received in special audience yesterday by the Tsar and handed him an autograph letter from King George. This letter is written in a very friendly style, and expresses His Majesty's hope that the relations between Russia and Great Britain will suffer no disturbance in connexion with the Persian questions.

The documents reveal pretty completely the preliminary history of the proposed treaty, but do not reveal whether it was finally completed and signed.   Probably it was rendered needless by the outbreak of the world war.   For the historian of the period immediately preceding the war it is amply enough to record that in his new course Sazonov met with very ready co-operation in London.

It is instructive also to observe that St. Petersburg was careful to leave Great Britain in the dark as to the real aims which it was pursuing, as it had, as we have seen, no assurance that these would receive British assent.   In the enclosure to Sazonov's letter of May 28, 1914 [1353], there is this significant sentence (referring to the technical negotiations for the naval convention) :

If, in the discussion of the situation in the Mediterranean, conversation should turn to the Straits (Bosphorus and Dardanelles), political questions should not be touched on, but only temporary operations in the Straits foreshadowed as one of our strategic measures in the event of war.

The actual Tsarist aims must be concealed, to avoid arousing British opposition.   On the other hand, strong pressure was exerted to secure co-operation from the British fleet in the Mediterranean, as the preceding paragraph of the enclosure shows :

The situation in the Mediterranean closely affects our interests, as, if the Austrian and Italian fleets win the upper hand in this sea, it will become possible for the Austrian fleet to launch an attack in the Black Sea, which would be a very dangerous blow for us. From our point of view, therefore, it is exceedingly important that in the Mediterranean an assured preponderance of the Entente naval forces over the Austrian and Italian navies should be maintained.   The naval forces of Austria and Italy are together stronger than those of France, and it is therefore desirable that Great Britain should ensure the preponderance of the Entente Powers by leaving the necessary number of ships in the Mediterranean, at all events so long as the development of our fleet does not enable us to take over this task.   It would be desirable also that Great Britain should agree that our ships may use British ports in the Eastern Mediterranean as a base, in the same way as the French naval convention permits us to make use of the French ports in the Western Mediterranean.

It is entirely in consonance with Russian policy as it has

here been revealed, when we find close attention paid from
the beginning of 1913 to the attitude of Italy. The last
news given in the documents concerning the relations
between Italy and the Entente was of rather serious tension
between Paris and Rome over the question of the Ægean
Isles. Sazonov's report of November 6, 1913 [1114], to
the Tsar on his journey to Paris and Berlin mentions an
improvement in this respect :

> M. Poincaré gave me, in strict confidence, information which is
> worthy of special note concerning the new turn in Franco-Italian
> relations. It appears that after a certain estrangement which
> became noticeable last year between the two Latin neighbour
> States, the desire for a *rapprochement* with the powerful Republic
> has now been evinced in Italy. The French Minister of Foreign
> Affairs attributes this change of front to Italy's growing mistrust
> of her Austrian Ally, whose interests in the Adriatic Sea conflict
> with her own, and also to the impression created in Rome by the
> fresh *rapprochement* between France and Spain. This acquired
> special significance through the presence of a British warship at
> the French naval review at Cartagena.
>
> The French Government, Pichon told me, welcomes this change
> of feeling in Italy and is prepared to examine Mediterranean
> questions in collaboration with the Italian diplomatists in order,
> if all goes well, to arrive at an agreement on this subject. On the
> allied question of the future destiny of the islands in the Ægean
> Sea, France is in agreement with Great Britain, and will not permit
> any of the Great Powers to seize a single one of the islands.

On November 18 [1126], however, the Russian chargé
d'affaires in Rome writes of a fresh crisis in Franco-Italian
relations, and on the same subject Isvolsky writes on the
20th [1132] :

> M. Pichon did not conceal from me that the French ambassador
> at the Quirinal, M. Barrère, who recently arrived here, was sum-
> moned by him in order to discuss the situation which has been
> created between France and Italy and to determine France's further
> policy towards her Latin neighbour. I know that at the Quai
> d'Orsay the question was seriously considered whether the moment
> has not come for emphatically demanding from Italy an answer
> to the question whether the terms of the Triple Alliance treaty in
> its latest form are reconcilable with the existing separate agreements
> between France and Italy. I have reason for believing that
> though M. Barrère does not regard as out of the question a sudden

turning of Italy towards the Triple Alliance (he points out among
other things that lately the supporters of friendship with France
have all, to the last one, been removed from the Consulta and
replaced by persons devoted to Germany and Austria), he is nevertheless advising the French Government to take the matter calmly.
Barrère prophesies the early fall of the present Italian Cabinet and
its replacement by a Government less ready to bow to the promptings
of Berlin and Vienna.

Thus there were fresh fears that Rome was falling away
towards the Central Powers ; an eager discussion now began
on this question.   Krupensky, the Russian ambassador in
Rome, writes on November 26 [1141] opposing Pichon's
pessimistic views, mentioning especially that both the
Marquis di San Giuliano, the Foreign Minister, and Signor
Giolitti, the Prime Minister, have given him the most
definite assurances that the Triple Alliance Treaty " has
been renewed with no change whatever ; not a comma has
been altered in it, and all reports to the contrary are entirely
baseless."   Isvolsky opposes to this, in his letter of December 4 [1152], the authority of the " secret source " already
frequently referred to, from which Paris draws its information concerning the internal affairs of the Triple Alliance.
On January 1, 1914 [1197], Isvolsky reveals the source :

The Foreign Ministry here has the key to the Italian cypher
and is able to take note not only of the telegrams sent to the
Italian ambassador in Paris, but of those exchanged between Rome
and its ambassadors in Berlin and Vienna.

By such means the Quai d'Orsay kept watch over its
Mediterranean rival.   Isvolsky adds that the false information received by Krupensky at the Quirinal " only shows
the   great   insincerity   and   untruthfulness   of   Italian
diplomacy."

Shortly afterwards the question of the islands again
attained importance.   On January 5 [1213] Isvolsky
telegraphs that Poincaré is convinced that Italy is moving
heaven and earth to discover a pretext for declining to
evacuate the Dodecanese.   On the 13th [1225] he wires
that Venizelos has learnt while in Rome that Italy has no

intention of retaining a single one of the islands of the
Dodecanese or as much as a single rock, but that she will
demand certain compensations. She is prepared to see
them partitioned between Greece and Turkey. Negotiations then proceeded between the Cabinets, but were pro-
longed by disunity among the Powers. The details are not
of great importance to us ; but a letter of April 21, 1914
[1321], from Krupensky must be noted ; it shows plainly
that Franco-Italian relations had improved. Krupensky
writes that the Italian Foreign Minister, San Giuliano,
" anxious to restore the confidential relations between
France and Italy, is doing all that lies in his power to attain
this end."

While London and Rome were thus working hard to provide the most favourable conditions for the success of the
Russian plans along the road to world war on which Sazonov
had entered, Isvolsky was watching in Paris with close
attention, and not without lively anxiety, the development
of internal politics in France. In view of the latest turn
which the policy of St. Petersburg had taken, it was of
special importance that France should remain the absolutely
reliable basis of all the calculations of the Tsarist empire in
regard to a general conflict.

In the latter months of 1913 the Radicals and Radical
Socialists in France began to show fresh activity. At a
Congress in Paris in October, most of the speakers complained
bitterly of the decay of discipline in the ranks of the party,
and Camille Pelletan proposed an electoral pact with the
United Socialist party in order to put up a joint fight against
the parties of the Right. " The revision of the three years'
service law " was adopted as a special plank in the programme. The Barthou Ministry was also charged with
reactionary tendencies, and the President was charged with
attempting to pursue a personal policy and endangering
the prestige of Parliamentary institutions. This was the
first sign of a revolt of the Left.

On December 2 came the fall of the Barthou Cabinet.

M. Caillaux led the Opposition, and criticized the attitude
of the Government in the matter of the proposed French loan.
Isvolsky writes on December 4 [1153] that this loan was
coupled with the putting into execution of the three years'
law, and that he fears the return of his hated " Combism."
A Ministry depending on the parties farthest to the Left
did in fact come into power, with Doumergue as Premier
and Foreign Minister and Caillaux in charge of Finance.
But in practice it proved by no means so bad as Isvolsky
had feared. As soon as he took office the new Premier
declared that he would " maintain and conscientiously
put into execution " the three years' service law, and that
in foreign affairs he would " continue the policy of close
and hearty co-operation with Russia " [1180]. Isvolsky at
once expresses his satisfaction [1181] ; he believes that the
new men, " having arrived unexpectedly in power, have
had at once to abandon most of their radical demands,"
and he adds that in the questions of interest to Russia they
are following exactly the same policy as their predecessors.
Now it became thoroughly clear how injuriously Poincaré's
influence was affecting developments in France. With the
whole strength of his personality he had driven this development into the channel desired by him, and there was now
no going back for his opponents. Isvolsky's contentment
accordingly continues. On January 1, 1914 [1198], he
writes to Sazonov :

    During the few weeks that the present Government has held
office there has, it seems to me, been ample evidence that the
Cabinet of MM. Doumergue and Caillaux, however harmful from
the point of view of internal politics in France, deserves no reproach
from us so far as our immediate interests are concerned.

The controlling hand of Poincaré behind the scenes
became evident again at the beginning of January 1914,
when Delcassé returned from St. Petersburg and had to
be replaced by another ambassador. Telegraphing on
January 8 [1216], Isvolsky mentions Paléologue as Delcassé's
successor, and says expressly that the choice has been made

" on the personal initiative of the President of the Republic," who has been " a close friend " of Paléologue " from their school days." It might therefore be relied on that the new appointment would bring no change in the existing policy.

But for all the contentment of the Isvolskys and Sazonovs and Poincarés, there were short moments when the rush to the abyss of world war seems, as we look back, to have been held up and interrupted. On February 12 [1267] Isvolsky turned to his Foreign Minister in " a matter which is personally very disturbing " to him. He had heard rumours that he was to be recalled and replaced by Kokovtsov. He mentioned his difficult financial situation, appealed to the " old friendship " of his superior, and asked for early information. Shortly afterwards, in view of the impending fresh elections in France, he writes [1291] that the Left parties are likely to win, and considers the possibility that Poincaré may have to resign. The most dangerous personalities in the world of high politics seemed thus to be threatened, and after what we have seen of their activities it is easy to imagine how fortunate might have been the consequences of the retirement of either of them, still more of both, in the maintenance of peace. But fate inexorably willed it otherwise. On February 25 [1274], Isvolsky thanks Sazonov for the relieving information that " the blow has passed this time over his head " and that he is to remain at his post. On March 17 Mme. Caillaux shot dead M. Calmette, the editor of the *Figaro*, and in the result her husband had to retire, and fresh wind filled the sails of the parties of the Right in their campaign against the Left [1296]. The new elections brought a great victory for the extreme Radical parties, but also showed that the nation was strongly in favour of the programme of the moderate Republicans, including the maintenance of the three years' system. On May 21 [1345] Isvolsky writes that he hopes that Poincaré will be able " to divert French internal policy into more conservative channels by a bold use of his constitutional rights." On June 3 [1357] he reports the formation of the Viviani Cabinet, and praises its leader as " a Radical of the type of Briand, Millerand, and other former doctrinaires who have learnt through experience of office and are now moderate and practical statesmen." As to that, the Millerand type is familiar to us from the records of 1912 and the sketch by Ignatiev, the Russian military attaché. It was at all events a type thoroughly to the taste of Isvolsky. On June 17 Isvolsky telegraphs, in great contentment :

In his declaration read yesterday in the Chamber, Viviani said that one of the highest tasks of the Government would be the continuance of the foreign policy which France had followed for so many years, and the development of an Alliance consecrated by the experience and sympathy of the two peoples—the Alliance of two peoples devoted to peace—and also the Entente with France's powerful neighbour. With regard to the three years' system, the Foreign Minister declared that the Government would apply this law with exactitude and loyalty. In the course of debate the Minister said that should he be still in office in the autumn of 1915 he would on no account reduce the term of service of the classes now under the colours. Despite the energetic opposition of the Socialists, the Government obtained an enormous majority, and its position is apparently thoroughly firm.

Thus all the dangers threatening the aims, now common, of French and Russian policy had happily been overcome. As has already been shown from the documents themselves, the ultimate fate of Europe was already sealed. The two Great Powers with positive aspirations, France and Russia, were agreed on the one decisive point that the realization of their aspirations was only possible by overcoming the obstacle to both represented by the Central Powers, Germany and Austria. And the two latter Powers were at the same time surrounded by an absolutely closed network of hostile aims, in which they might at any time, without realizing it, become ensnared, the moment they gave their waiting enemies the pretext for the realization of their secret purposes. That is the picture of the general situation which is revealed at the end of June 1914 by the documents.

VII

CONCLUSION

On June 28 the shots fired in Serajevo echoed across our Continent, through an atmosphere already poisoned by warlike tendencies ; and the curtain lifted on the catastrophe of 1914. With this we are not concerned here ; the prelude to this disaster has already been fully described in various important works.[1] A fact that seems worth noting is that from the beginning of July there is a big gap in Isvolsky's papers. Is this the result of a prudent holocaust ? We have no definite knowledge, but the sudden stoppage justifies the question.

The results so far attained by research show that the assassination of the Archduke Francis Ferdinand was organized by Colonel Dimitrievitch, chief of the Information Section of the Serbian General Staff. The Austrian historian Mandl brings evidence in the Vienna *Neues Acht-Uhr-Blatt* of July 27 and 28, 1924, to show that this man was working in agreement with Artamanov, the Russian military attaché in Belgrad. Should this be confirmed, it would show that the crime was prepared as a Russian blow at the Dual Monarchy, and that in it an important part of Sazonov's programme, familiar to us, for the " great solution " of the question of the Straits had been put into execution, though it may be questioned whether the military authorities did not act rather sooner than the political

[1] To mention a few only, B. W. von Bülow, *Die ersten Stundenschläge des Weltkrieges* ; Montgelas, *The Case for the Central Powers* (London : George Allen & Unwin) ; Romberg, *The Falsifications of the Russian Orange Book* (London : George Allen & Unwin) ; Morhardt, *Les Preuves* ; A. Fabre-Luce, *The Limitations of Victory* (London : George Allen & Unwin) ; Gunther Franz, *Russlands Eintrtt in den Weltkrieg*.

14

leaders wished.   However that may be, the atrocious crime
was regarded everywhere as a very grave provocation to
the Habsburg Monarchy, as is admitted even by the British
Blue Book on the origins of the world war.

I will confine myself to a short summary of the existing
evidence as to what happened between Paris and St. Petersburg immediately before the last critical days, in order to
test the results already arrived at in these pages.

From July 20 to 23 Poincaré and Viviani were in Russia
on a second visit to the Tsar.   The journey had long been
planned, and is mentioned as early as January 5, 1914, in a
telegram from Isvolsky.   Our knowledge of the externals
of the visit comes from accounts given by Poincaré [1] and
Paléologue,[2] which also enable some conclusions to be
drawn as to what happened below the surface.   The following is a short summary of their accounts.

In view of what had already happened, it is not surprising
to find the Tsar saying to Paléologue in the course of breakfast at Peterhof on July 20, before Poincaré's arrival :

" There is one question especially about which I am concerned—our Entente with Great Britain.   We must induce
her to enter our Alliance."

On his arrival in the cruiser *La France*, Poincaré came
on board the Tsar's yacht *Alexandria*, and the first discussion took place between the two.   According to Poincaré,
" Nothing was said beyond very general remarks, and I am
bound to add very banal ones, concerning the necessity of
the maintenance of our Alliance."   Paléologue, however,
writes : " Sitting on the port side, the Tsar and the President
at once began a conversation, or rather a conference ; for
it was clear that they were talking business, interrogating
one another, discussing.   As was to be expected, Poincaré
led the conversation.   Soon he is doing all the talking.
The Tsar merely assents ; but his whole attitude shows that

[1] R. Poincaré, *Les Origines de la Guerre*, in the *Revue de la Semaine
illustrée*, No. 10, March 11, 1921, pp. 136 sqq.
[2] M. Paléologue, *La Russie des Tsars pendant la grande guerre*, in the
Revue des Deux Mondes, January 15, 1922, pp. 230 sqq.

he sincerely approves, that he feels in agreement and in sympathy." It does not seem, then, that the conversation was entirely unimportant. In the evening, at half-past seven, there was a gala dinner, at which the Tsar once more listened to Poincaré, " with grave and interested attention." The President had, at all events, a great deal to say.

On the morning of July 21 the Tsar visited Poincaré in Peterhof Palace and spent nearly an hour with him. According to Poincaré's own account, the conversation was quite desultory, and there was no discussion of the possibility of war. He admits, however, farther on, in quite general terms, that in his conversations with the Tsar he tried to remove the differences of view then existing between Great Britain and Russia (over Persia). At half-past one, according to Paléologue, Poincaré went round St. Petersburg. At three he received a delegation from the French colony. At four he met the diplomats in the Winter Palace. The conversations with the representatives of the various countries were very characteristic. Not a word on politics was spoken to the German ambassador, Count Pourtalès. Paléologue gives this description of the conversation with Baron Motono, the Japanese ambassador : " In a few sentences the principle of adhesion to the Triple Entente was formulated and approved on both sides." Poincaré assured Buchanan, the British ambassador, " that the Tsar is determined to show the most conciliatory spirit in the Persian affair, and he urges that the British Government should at last realize the necessity of the conversion of the Triple Entente into a Triple Alliance." Paléologue then gives a very interesting account of the conversation between Poincaré and Count Szápáry, the ambassador of Austria-Hungary :

After a few words of condolence over the assassination of the Archduke Francis Ferdinand, the President asked Szápáry,

" Have you any news from Serbia ? "

" The judicial investigation is going on," replied Szápáry coldly. Poincaré replied,

" I cannot but fear the results of this inquiry, M. l'ambassadeur ; I remember two earlier investigations, which did not improve your relations with Serbia. . . . You will remember, M. l'ambassadeur . . . the Friedjung affair and the Prohaska affair."

Szápáry answered drily,

" We cannot, M. le Président, permit a foreign Government to prepare assassinations of our sovereigns on its territory."

Poincaré tried, in the most conciliatory tone, to point out to him that in the present condition of feeling in Europe every Government must act with redoubled caution. " With a little good will this Serbian affair can easily be settled. But it can also easily develop dangerously. Serbia has very warm friends among the Russian people. And Russia has an Ally, France. What complications are to be feared here ! "

In the next *salon* there were waiting the other representatives of foreign countries ; Poincaré merely shook hands with them. He only stopped when he came to the Serbian Minister, to whom he offered a few words of condolence.

This throws a good deal of light on Poincaré's activities. We see his effort to win over Japan to the Entente, and his impatience to bind Great Britain to the Franco-Russian Alliance. We see, in fact, the continuation of his efforts, pursued with iron resolution, to isolate and encircle the Central Powers. We also see his strange attitude towards the acute question of the day, the Austro-Serbian conflict, his open threat to the representative of Austria-Hungary, and his demonstration of sympathy for the Serbs. Poincaré himself tells us nothing of this ; but Paléologue's gossip reveals it all.

But Paléologue has yet more to tell us. According to Poincaré no one had any idea of the possibility of war while he was in Russia. Contrast with this the words with which the grand duchesses Anastasia and Melitza, the two Montenegrins, greeted Paléologue at the dinner given in Poincaré's honour on July 22 by Nicholas Nicolayevitch. Anastasia cried enthusiastically—

" Do you know, we are passing through historic days, blessed days ! . . . At to-morrow's review the bands will play nothing but the *Marche Lorraine* and *Sambre et Meuse*. . . . I have had a telegram from my father to-day, in a code we agreed on ; he tells me we shall have war before the month is out. . . . What a hero, my father! He is worthy of the Iliad. . . . Stop a minute, look at this little box—it never leaves me; it has Lorraine soil in it, Lorraine soil, which I brought over the border when I was in France two years ago with my husband. And now look at that table of honour! It is decorated entirely with thistles; I would not have any other flowers put on it. Now then! They are thistles from Lorraine! I picked a few stalks from close where I was, brought them here and had the seeds sown in my garden. . . . Melitza, go on telling the ambassador; tell him all to-day means to us, while I go and receive the Tsar."

During the meal I was sitting next the Grand Duchess Anastasia and the dithyrambics continued, mixed with prophecies.

" War is going to break out . . . there will be nothing of Austria left. . . . You will get Alsace-Lorraine back. . . . Our armies will meet in Berlin. . . . Germany will be annihilated. . . ."

Then, suddenly—" I must control myself, the Tsar is looking at me."

These words show the feeling in Russia in those critical days. The grand duchess was right about the bands; at the grand review at Krasnoye Selo, held in Poincaré's honour on July 23, the infantry marched past to the strains of the *Marche de Sambre et Meuse* and the *Marche Lorraine*. Most significant of all is King Nicholas's telegram to the grand duchess, confidently prophesying war on July 22, though Austria's ultimatum to Serbia had not then been delivered or even heard of. How well Poincaré knew how to make capital out of the bellicose excitement is evident from his farewell toast on July 23, with this final sentence : " The two countries have the same ideal of peace in power, honour, and glory ! " Paléologue adds : " The last words, which were only heard with difficulty, let loose a storm of applause. Grand Duke Nicholas Nicolayevitch, Grand Duchess Anastasia, and Grand Duke Nicholas Michailovitch glanced at me with sparkling eyes."

This scene is of importance as showing clearly how Poincaré was understood and hailed by the pro-war element while, with shrewd regard for the anxiety of the Tsar, he was ostensibly talking of peace. To influence the Tsar and put courage into him was beyond doubt the main object of his visit, and up to the last minute he pursued it with

energy and tenacity.   Immediately before his departure he
had a confidential talk with the Tsar on the bridge of *La
France*.   What was actually said is unknown, but its
purport may be gathered from what, according to the *Matin*
of August 26, 1915, Nicholas II himself said at about that
date to Jean Cruppi : " I always have a vivid memory of
the emphatic words of the President of the Republic to
me at the moment of his departure from Russia."

After all this it is impossible to believe that the secret
discussions between the leaders of French policy and the
ruling circles in Russia were so entirely devoid of reference
to the situation at the moment as Poincaré tries to suggest
to us.   There was already an indirect indication that these
discussions could not have been so innocent, for the British
Blue Book lacks the text of the telegram No. 6 of July 24
from Buchanan, the British ambassador in St. Petersburg,
though its contents are briefly indicated in the index as a
summary of the results of Poincaré's visit.   This document,
however, which was, no doubt, deliberately omitted, can be
quoted here.   It runs as follows : [1]

Minister of Foreign Affairs and French ambassador told me
confidentially result of visit of President of the French Republic
had been to establish the following points :

1. Entire community of views concerning the various questions
facing the Powers, so far as concerns the maintenance of the general
peace and balance of power in Europe, and especially in the East.

2. Resolve to take steps in Vienna to prevent a request for
explanation, or any demand equivalent to an interference in
Serbia's internal affairs, which Serbia might legitimately regard as
an attack on her sovereignty and independence.

3. Solemn confirmation of the obligations laid by the Alliance
on the two countries.

It must be borne in mind that these agreements were made
before the Austrian ultimatum was handed to Serbia.   In
view of this the " solemn confirmation " in Point 3 has
special significance.   It proves irrefutably that, in full
accord with what has already been established here in regard

[1] Retranslated.

to the attitude of the French and Russian Governments, an assurance of mutual armed assistance was given before there was any occasion for it arising out of the course of events. The French and the Russian will to war came together here at a critical moment, and from this moment on the Tsardom knew that it had its Ally at its back if in the acute Austro-Serbian conflict it resorted to force. The blank cheque for world war signed first by Poincaré in 1912 was now signed again.

From this everything else follows almost inevitably, and there is no need to recount further the familiar facts and events. For Russia and France, the Austro-Serbian conflict was a favourable occasion for the realization of their plans. If the local conflict could be made general, Germany must become involved, as Poincaré desired. And this was done by the Russian mobilization on July 30. This also avoided arousing British susceptibilities, which would be hurt by any direct settlement of the question of the Straits. Only now, when it is borne in mind what had gone before, can it be fully realized why when the disaster came things were bound to happen as they did on the Neva and the Seine.

There has been too great a tendency hitherto to isolate the crisis from the general current of history and to place it under the microscope as a sort of separate exhibit. Such a method is unsatisfactory from a historian's point of view. The causes of so momentous a process in the history of humanity as the world war are not to be ascertained by studying it only at the moment of the explosion. There must be careful research into the elements involved in the explosion ; only after this has been done can a definite historic judgment be conscientiously pronounced.

From this point of view the foregoing inquiry has attempted to contribute to the discovery of the nature of the determining forces in France and Russia. It has brought a conclusion which may be stated in very few words as follows :

Since 1911 Isvolsky had been working for world war. Poincaré joined him in the autumn of 1912. And since the end of 1913 Sazonov also had seen in European complications the road which would lead Russia to the Straits. In the great question of the responsibility for the fearful disaster which overtook Europe in 1914, these conclusions should at all events be of some value.

APPENDIX I

THE RUSSO-BULGARIAN CONVENTION OF MAY 1902

DRAFT

1. The present agreement pursues no aggressive aims, but is intended only as a counter move to the military convention concluded between Austria-Hungary and Roumania.

2. In view of what is said in Article 1, the present agreement only envisages action against Austria-Hungary and Roumania, and is not to be directed either against Turkey or against another Balkan State.

3. Russia will bring all her forces to bear to maintain the integrity and inviolacy of the territory of Bulgaria.

4. In the event of Bulgaria or Russia or both of these States together being attacked by Austria-Hungary or Roumania or both of these States, or by the Triple Alliance, the States party to the present treaty are bound to bring into operation all their forces and resources for the struggle with the aggressors, shrinking from no sacrifice to secure a complete victory.

5. Should Bulgaria be threatened only by Roumania, Bulgarian armed forces will be employed against Roumania. In view, however, of the moral and even armed support promised to Roumania by Austria-Hungary, Russia binds herself to accord diplomatic support to Bulgaria; but should Austria proceed to furnish active assistance to Roumania, Russia also will hasten to the aid of Bulgaria with the forces sufficing for the overthrow of Austria.

Should Austria-Hungary and Roumania or the Triple Alliance, without beginning war against Bulgaria, attack Russia, Bulgaria is also bound to mobilize her armed forces, to concentrate them on a plan to be elaborated, and, if Russia should request it, to take the initiative against the Austro-Roumanian troops.

6. In the event of a war between Russia and Bulgaria on the one part, and Roumania and Austria-Hungary or the Triple Alliance on the other part, Bulgaria preserves strictest neutrality towards Turkey and employs the utmost caution in dealings with her, in order not to produce complications in the general situation through a conflict with this Power.

In view of the foregoing, Bulgaria concentrates her army along the Danube for action against Roumania on a plan to be elaborated.

leaving a small part of her forces on the farther side of the Balkans to watch the frontier and preserve order and quiet in the country,

7. The plans for the mobilization and concentration of the Bulgarian army and its sections, and the plans for defence and for advance in accordance with the operations and objectives determined by the Russian General Staff, must be worked out beforehand under the direction of the Russian General Staff in collaboration with the Bulgarian Ministry of War; they will be confirmed and, if necessary, later reviewed, improved, and brought up to date by His Imperial Majesty the Tsar of Russia.

8. The supreme command over the armed forces of Russia and Bulgaria during the war, and the conduct of operations, falls in all cases on the Russian supreme commander, whether the Russian and Bulgarian armies operate together or separately, that is, in different theatres of war. His Royal Highness the Prince of Bulgaria retains the rights and the title of a commander-in-chief of his army, and will personally command it. Should His Highness wish, however, to transfer this office to any personality, the latter, and also the Chief of Staff of the army, must be selected after prior agreement with the Russian Ministry of War and with the assent of His Majesty the Tsar of Russia.

To facilitate communication with the Russian headquarters, there will be attached to the headquarters of the Commander-in-Chief of the Bulgarian army a general of the Russian army, who will have a staff officer with him. A Russian staff officer will be attached to the command of every corps or every special division of the Bulgarian army. All these persons have a consultative voice in the decision of questions of operative character.

There will be attached to the headquarters of the Russian Commander-in-Chief a Bulgarian general or staff officer, appointed by his Royal Highness the Prince of Bulgaria.

9. While war is in progress the fighting ships and transports of the Russian fleet have the right to make use of all Bulgarian ports, to provide themselves in them with consumable stores of all kinds, and to take steps for their closing and defence.

The Bulgarian war and merchant fleets are subjected entirely to the disposition of the Senior Commanding Officer of the Russian fleet; this officer has the decision, according to his own judgment, as to all operations, joint or separate, which he regards as necessary.

10. The present agreement comes into force immediately after signature and is a State secret of special importance.

(Signed) ZHILINSKY,
Major-General.

(German Foreign Office, Documents from the Russian Secret Archives, p. 11 sqq.)

APPENDIX II

MINUTES OF THE SPECIAL CONFERENCE OF
DECEMBER 31, 1913

In the Chair : The Prime Minister, Secretary of State, and Privy Councillor Kokovtsov.

Present : The Minister of War, Adjutant-General Suchomlinov, the Minister of the Navy, Adjutant-General Grigorovitch, the Foreign Minister, Comptroller Sazonov, the Chief of the General Staff, Cavalry General Zhilinsky.

For the purpose of preparing the minutes of the Conference, Chamberlain and State Counsellor Bützov and Titular Counsellor Sukin, officials of the First Department of the Foreign Ministry, were present.

Before the Conference, a humble memorial from the Foreign Minister, dated December 23, 1913, was handed to the members. At the same time there was communicated the statement prepared by the Foreign Office, consisting of the following points for discussion at the conference :

1. Even if the possibility be admitted of a German general commanding a section of the troops outside Constantinople, for instance in Adrianople, Russia cannot give her consent to the presence of a foreign general in command of a detachment in Constantinople.

2. The Foreign Office must continue the negotiations in Berlin and Constantinople on these lines.

3. Since the latest news indicates equivocal proceedings by the German Government in this matter, decisions must now be taken to provide for the possible necessity of supporting our demands by measures of compulsion.

4. The said measures of compulsion on our part might take the form of the occupation of some point in Asia Minor, e.g. Trebizond or Bayazid, with a declaration that we should stay there until our demands were satisfied.

5. After it has been clearly established what measures of compulsion we should be able to employ, a confidential interchange of views on the subject must be set on foot with the British and French Governments, since measures of compulsion can, necessarily, only be decided on after we have ascertained whether we can count on corresponding steps on the part of those two Powers.

6. In the negotiations with the said Governments, the necessity for extremely cautious and unanimous action on the part of the three Powers must be insisted on, in order, if possible, to prevent the conflict becoming more acute, as a European war might result. At the same time efforts must be made on our part to prepare France and Great Britain for the

necessity of pursuing to the end any action initiated in the common interest.

7. Should this point of view be accepted by all three Powers and the negotiations in Berlin not lead to the desired result, an understanding must be arrived at as to an ascending scale in the measures of compulsion. The following are conceivable measures :

(a) A rigid financial boycott of Turkey ;

(b) Should this method fail to produce the required effect as in the case of the Adrianople question, the three Powers might withdraw their representatives from Constantinople ;

(c) At the same time the Governments of Russia, France, and Great Britain would acquaint the Porte with the date fixed for the fulfilment of their demands, after which the measures of compulsion might begin to be put into force, with the warning that they would not be withdrawn until the demands made had been complied with.

8. Should certain preparatory steps of a military nature, such as reinforcements of troops in the Caucasus, be necessary to enable us promptly to put measures of compulsion into effect, it would be desirable to keep these steps as secret as possible. From the political point of view, however, it is clearly necessary that it shall be possible, after issuing a threat, should that become necessary, to take prompt steps to translate the threat into action.

9. The results of the conference are, in accordance with a command graciously given to the Foreign Minister, to be laid before His Majesty for inspection.

After opening the session, the Prime Minister pointed out that a week had passed since the presentation of the Foreign Minister's humble memorial to the members of the conference, and asked the Foreign Minister for information as to the latest material at his disposal on the question before the conference.

The Foreign Minister stated that the news which he had received during the last few days was scanty and contradictory, and communicated to the conference the contents of a secret telegram of December 29 from the Russian ambassador in Constantinople, stating that General Liman is to have the highest Turkish rank but one, and therefore will give up the command of the 1st army corps, remaining Inspector of the War School and Chief of the Military Mission. This seems good news ; it does not, however, entirely agree with the contents of a telegram of December 30. This latter states that Liman's withdrawal from the command of the 1st army corps is not yet an accomplished fact, and calls for a less optimistic view of the position. Should the news contained in the former telegram correspond with the facts, this conference could be regarded as not so pressing, and the discussions of the situation would be merely of an academic character. The Minister considered it desirable, however, that the conference should first discuss the points communicated by him to the members.

The Prime Minister expressed the view that the object of this conference is to determine the position which the Imperial Government would have to take up in any turn that events might take. Proceeding to an examination of the statement supplied by the

Foreign Office, Secretary of State Kokovstov pointed out the necessity of being clear in the first place as to the solution of the question of the German Military Mission in Turkey which could be recognized by Russia as admissible, and as to the things to which we must in any circumstances object. The basic proposition is expressed in Point 4, which must serve as the cue for the further discussion. The Prime Minister stated that the standpoint of the Imperial Government was first established during the negotiations in Berlin in October 1913. Secretary of State Kokovtsov believed it to be the moral right and the duty of the Russian Government not to move from that standpoint. As the substance of the said negotiations might not be known to the Ministers of War and of the Navy, or to the Chief of the General Staff, Secretary of State Kokovtsov considered it necessary to acquaint the conference with the details of the negotiations as set down in the humble report of the Prime Minister on the subject. In the conversations with the German Emperor and the representatives of the German Government he had declared that Russia could not remain indifferent in face of the exercise by a foreign officer of the command over a detachment of troops in Constantinople, since this would give one Power a position of advantage in Turkey, altering the whole complexion of the Near Eastern question. Reverting to Point 1, the Prime Minister declared that he regards it as necessary still to adhere to the views then expressed by him to the German Emperor.

The Foreign Minister communicated to the conference the contents of the secret telegram just arrived. In connexion with the possible withdrawal of General Liman from the command of the 1st army corps, referred to in the telegram from the ambassador in Constantinople, the Minister asked what attitude should be adopted towards the command by a German officer of a division not stationed at Constantinople itself but at Scutari, since a solution of this nature was known to the Russian representatives at Berlin and Constantinople to have been already under consideration.

The Prime Minister, the Ministers of War and of the Navy, and the Chief of the General Staff gave their opinion that such a turn of affairs would not be admissible. General Zhilinsky remarked that, if a German officer had command even of no more than a division, Germany would dominate the Straits. As to this, Secretary of State Kokovtsov pointed out that the possibility of German officers commanding the forts protecting the Straits had now passed away, and that it might now be regarded as established that the command of these defences would in any case fall to Turkish officers. This drew from the Minister of the Navy the remark that, under the pretext of the lack of a commanding officer for some detachment of troops, a German officer might nevertheless prove to be in acting command.

The Prime Minister drew attention to the connexion between the wording of Point 1 and the news received as regards the possibility of the nomination of General Sanders as Inspector of the Turkish Army, and to the necessity of determining the attitude of the Government to such a solution ; for this purpose the meaning of the expression " Inspection " must first be settled.

The Chief of the General Staff remarked that there are in Turkey four Inspectorships of a territorial character, which correspond to the position of the commandant of a military district.

The Prime Minister stated that, should General Sanders be given, instead of the general inspection of the Turkish army, an Inspectorship in the territorial sense, equivalent to the command of the troops in a military district, such a solution would be still less acceptable to Russia than the command of an army corps. This rendered it unnecessary to decide beforehand whether we should raise objections to the transfer to a German general of a territorial Inspectorship anywhere, or only in Constantinople itself and the districts bordering on the Caucasus, i.e. in the eastern parts of Asia Minor. The Prime Minister was therefore of the opinion that, in consequence of the changed circumstances, Point 1 must be extended to indicate that the Inspectorate to be conferred on General Sanders could only be regarded as admissible if by " Inspectorate " was to be understood a general inspection of the army and not a territorial command.

In this opinion all participants in the conference agreed.

In the view of the Minister of War, all the conditions of the activity of the German Military Mission which were down for discussion were only subsidiary matters. The root of the matter was that there should be no doubt that the arrival of General Sanders at Constantinople does not signify a return to the system of von der Goltz Pasha and his instructional duties. To the knowledge of the War Office, the former instructors were the poorest element in the German army. The arms and ammunition, too, with which Germany supplied Turkey before the Balkan war, were by no means of high quality. Now General Sanders is accompanied by forty persons chosen from among the best officers of the German army, and some sixty further men of this type are being sought for. In the view of Adjutant-General Suchomlinov it must be realized that the present military mission has quite other tasks than were performed by von der Goltz Pasha. The intentions of Germany in taking energetically in hand the organization of the Turkish army are evident. The Turkish troops, whose qualities the German Military Mission will have to develop, will be stationed on our Caucasian frontier and naturally intended for use against Russia. The War Minister thought it dangerous to lose time, and desirable to take measures of protection against the change of affairs to Russia's disadvantage which he had depicted. Since it is impossible to count on Germany's voluntary renunciation of the work begun, and since on the other hand the hopes which had arisen of a hostile attitude in the Turkish army towards the German Military Mission have proved unfounded, in spite of the wholesale discharges of Turkish officers, the Minister would like information as to the possibility of persuading Turkey to dispense with the Military Mission.

The Foreign Minister expressed the conviction that any advice given by us in Constantinople would remain without result in the absence of pressure. The Minister hereupon requested the conference to proceed to the discussion of means of bringing compulsion to bear on Turkey, mentioning that in the conversations with the French and British ambassadors in St. Petersburg he had suggested that there should be some sort of definite scheme of steps that might be taken by the Entente Powers. In the first place it appeared possible to resort to financial pressure on Turkey. With a sincere intention on the part of all three Powers to carry it out, a real result might be hoped for, since Turkey needs enormous amounts of money, running into hundreds of millions, and small chance supplies like the loan from the banking firm of Perrier & Co. could not amount to any effective support for her disordered finances. It must, however, be borne in mind that the French Government, though anxious to do so, might prove unable to carry out a rigid financial boycott of Turkey, since it was not always in a position to influence French financial circles in the desired direction. Secondly, should the financial measures fail to produce the desired effect on Turkey, a programme must be worked out involving methods of exercising direct pressure on the Porte. We for our part must determine what sort of proposals Russia could bring forward, and it was for this purpose that the Foreign Office had elaborated the statement which was now before the conference for discussion.

The Prime Minister asked the Foreign Minister, before the discussion of the said means of pressure, to permit him to lay stress on two matters of primary importance in determining the line of further action; these appeared to Secretary of State Kokovtsov to be as follows:

1. The German Government is looking for a way out of the situation created by Russia's demands. In this connexion the Berlin Cabinet points to the necessity, in the interest of a satisfactory solution of the question, of Russia's avoidance of any categorical declaration, of the character of an ultimatum to Germany, as this might compel Germany to adhere still more firmly to her standpoint, since regard must be had to the difficult position of the German Government in the face of public opinion in its own country.

2. The negotiations with the Berlin Cabinet, which have now been going on for two months, should be continued until the Imperial (Russian) Government is convinced that it is impossible to attain the object indicated in this manner.

The Foreign Minister supported the views formulated by Secretary of State Kokovtsov, and stated that he had at the same time pointed out, in his negotiations with the German ambassador in St. Petersburg, that it is impossible for the Russian Government to put off the decision of the question of the German Military Mission at Constantinople for long.

Proceeding to the measures for bringing further pressure to bear, Secretary of State Kokovtsov considered it necessary to make it clear that the steps envisaged in Point 7 are proposed by the Foreign Office to be taken in the closest association with the other Powers of the Triple Entente. Before any decision is come to, the Imperial Government must know to what extent it will receive the support of France and whether active participation by Great Britain in the pressure on the Porte can be relied on.

The Foreign Minister confirmed that his scheme of contemplated pressure was in fact subject to the collaboration of all the Powers of the Triple Entente, and pointed out that it seems still to be uncertain how far Great Britain would be prepared for energetic action. As regards France, the Russian Government may count on effectual support to the uttermost limit. M. Delcassé has assured the Minister, in the name of the French Foreign Minister, that France would go as far as Russia may wish.

The Prime Minister believed it to be necessary, while continuing the negotiations in Berlin, to ascertain at the same time the degree to which the London Cabinet would take part in measures that might be adopted by the Powers of the Triple Entente. Secretary of State Kokovstov remarked on the peculiar position of Great Britain in the question of the German command in Constantinople owing to the presence of the British admiral as Instructor in the Turkish capital. Great Britain has so far, in the view of the Prime Minister, given no real support to the efforts of the St. Petersburg Cabinet, and has indeed made it easier for Germany to offer resistance to Russia's objection, by her retention of Admiral Limpus in Constantinople. It was possible for Germany, in the negotiations for the recall of General Sanders from Constantinople, to appeal to the fact that the centralization of oversight over the Turkish fleet in the hands of the British admiral had not aroused the apprehension of a single Power. When Count Pourtalès brought forward this argument about the admiral, the Prime Minister had replied to him that Russia could not attach any importance to the fact of a command over a virtually non-existent fleet.

In reply to the remarks of Secretary of State Kokovtsov, which were supported by the Ministers of War and of the Navy, and were to the effect that it would be desirable in the first place to press Great Britain to recall the admiral, the Foreign Minister stated that Sir Edward Grey had already declared himself prepared to do this, and that such a decision on the part of the Government of Great Britain would in any case be obtainable should this be desirable to facilitate success in Berlin. The Minister, however, feared that Admiral Limpus might be replaced by a German commander, and drew attention on the other hand to documents in his possession, which justify the assumption that if the British admiral were recalled Germany would still decline to withdraw from the position which she has taken up on the question of the Military Mission. The Berlin Cabinet would, on the contrary, oppose the recall of Admiral Limpus, and would see in it nothing but a measure for exercising effective influence, which would merely strengthen Germany's resistance.

Returning to the matter of a definite scheme of action to be taken by the Entente Powers, the Minister considered that, should the negotiations in Berlin end without result, they would have to be transferred to Constantinople, the influence of the Powers being brought to bear on Turkey.

The Prime Minister referred to the means of pressure mentioned in the points set down by the Foreign Office, viz. financial boycott, recall of diplomatic representatives, and military measures, and observed that Turkey must be the direct object of this pressure, but that the ultimate goal would be the termination of the treaty between the Porte and Germany. Since in this way the interests of Germany would be affected, these measures were likely to provoke her intervention.

The Foreign Minister drew the attention of the conference to the possibility of obtaining success through energetic and at the same time cautious and unanimous action on the part of the three Powers, without, in the Minister's view, at all necessarily bringing war with Germany. In reality, a Russian initiative supported only by France would not appear particularly dangerous to Germany. The two States would hardly be in a position to deal Germany a mortal blow, even in the event of military successes, which can never be predicted. A struggle, on the other hand, in which Great Britain participated, might be disastrous to Germany, who clearly realizes that if Great Britain were drawn in, the result might be social disturbances of a catastrophic nature within her frontiers in less than six weeks. Great Britain is dangerous to Germany, and in the consciousness of this is to be found the explanation of the hatred with which the Germans are filled in the face of Great Britain's growing power. In view of this it is essential that before taking any decisive steps the Tsar's Government shall assure itself of the support of the London Cabinet, whose active participation does not seem, in the Minister's view, to be certain. There seems no doubt that Great Britain would intervene in the event of Russian and French ill-success in the military operations. This intervention might be directed either towards the ending of the European conflict, a purposeless one from the point of view of British interests, or towards the support of those States whose defeat would be contrary to the aims of British policy. About the necessity already noted for the Imperial Government to act only after an assurance of Great Britain's active participation, there can be no doubt, and this is the precarious element in Russia's situation in

15

this matter. The Minister informed the conference that, in the conversations with the British ambassador in St. Petersburg, he had mentioned the possibility of influencing the Porte as indicated in Point 4. In reply to the suggestion that Russian troops could be landed to occupy Trebizond, while Great Britain might occupy some point along the coast in Turkish territory, e.g. Beyrout or Smyrna, Sir George Buchanan expressed doubts of the practicability for Great Britain of operating with the fleet alone in the event of fighting being necessary to hold the occupied position, for which purpose a considerable force of troops would have to be landed.

The Chief of the General Staff expressed the opinion that in this case it can only be a question of a naval action, since, owing to the difficulty of transport, it would be impossible for Great Britain to carry out a military occupation.

The Minister of the Navy indicated the easy practicability of an occupation exclusively by the fleet, under the protection of the ships' guns.

The Prime Minister was of the opinion that such measures would inevitably be followed by war with Germany, and put the question : Is war with Germany desirable, and can Russia wage it ?

The Foreign Minister, in reply hereto, agreed in the view of Secretary of State Kokovtsov that in principle a war with Germany would be undesirable. As to the question whether Russia would at present be in a position to fight against Germany, the Minister did not consider himself called upon to decide this.

The Minister of War and the Chief of the General Staff declared categorically the complete readiness of Russia for a duel with Germany, not to speak of one with Austria. Such a duel is, however, hardly probable ; those Powers would be much more likely to have to deal with the Triple Entente.

The Prime Minister returned to the steps which might be chosen in order to avoid what he regards as an inadmissible risk, and expressed the view that the financial boycott of Turkey, as a measure which would not entail the danger of a war with Germany, deserves serious consideration. No exaggerated hopes must, however, be set upon any thorough execution of this measure on the part of the French holders of Ottoman paper. The material losses of the latter if Turkey were to suspend payment of coupons would be likely to cool down even the most ardent patriotic efforts of the French. As to direct methods of compulsion, among which the capture of Trebizond was mentioned, Secretary of State Kokovtsov holds it to be desirable to refrain from them, since they would be risky and difficult to realize, as had been established when similar measures were discussed in the summer of 1913, when the occupation of Trebizond was proposed in connexion with pressure on Turkey in the matter of Adrianople.

The Foreign Minister drew the attention of the conference to the ease with which supplies to Asia Minor through the port of

Trebizond could be stopped; this would be felt very seriously in Turkey.

Adjutant-General Grigorovitch supplemented this suggestion by pointing out that it would be quite practicable first to capture Sinope, which could be used as a base, and so enable supplies through the Black Sea port to be stopped.

Secretary of State Kokovtsov again pointed out the inevitability of German intervention if operations of this sort were carried out. The measures in question—stoppage of supplies, a naval demonstration, or the occupation of Bayazid, which would be dangerous in itself, in view of the impossibility of evacuating the place—represent at bottom methods of bringing material pressure on Turkey in order to secure her renunciation of the German mission, and this might easily bring Germany into the field.

The view of Secretary of State Kokovtsov was not entirely shared by the Foreign Minister, who for his part considered that there was a possibility of non-intervention by Germany. On the other hand, he considered it necessary to reckon on some measure of British participation in our action and to bear in mind that, in the event of our occupying Trebizond, Erzerum, where the bulk of the military forces is concentrated, would be cut off and the whole of Asia Minor threatened by Russia. The suggested occupation of Bayazid would, in the Minister's view, be a very effective measure, which might deter Germany from interfering. These views, which were shared by the Ministers of War and of the Navy, and by the Chief of the General Staff, drew from the last named the statement that the occupation of Bayazid cannot be put forward as an isolated measure, since it would in any case involve the mobilization of the Caucasus command. The military forces of Turkey in the district adjoining the Caucasus consist of an Army Corps restricted to 23 battalions. A battalion and a half are at present stationed in Bayazid. In view of the serious importance of this flanking-point (an attack on it has been the prelude of all our latest wars against Turkey), it would not be possible to take it without fighting, and a movement in this direction would be tantamount to the opening of warlike operations against Turkey. Moreover, restriction to the occupation of this one point could not, in the view of Cavalry General Zhilinsky, be looked upon as a practical proposition. Ardos, Deribaba, and Karaderbent would have to be occupied at the same time. Here the Chief of the General Staff emphasized the fact that such an occupation, as a demonstration not accompanied by a general advance, need not involve the necessity of strengthening the Caucasian theatre of war by drawing troops from the other districts of Russia, a reinforcement which is part of the general plan of mobilization in the event of a war with Turkey. For the contemplated operation of an occupation of Bayazid this measure would not be necessary, since even if Russia restricted herself to bringing the number of the troops of the Caucasus command up to the pitch of readiness for war, she would still have troops available which were numerically superior to those of the Turkish Army Corps. The Chief of the General Staff added that the arguments which he had put forward were based on a consideration of the present position of Turkey, who is busily arming on her other front to fight Greece. To prevent Turkey getting troops to Asia Minor through the Black Sea, Constantinople would have to be threatened by bringing our Black Sea Fleet to the Bosphorus.

In the view of the Foreign Minister, the demonstration at the Bosphorus might also play a part in another respect ; it might cause a panic in the capital, and a revolution which might at the same time solve the question of the German Military Mission.

The Foreign Minister repeated that the measures of compulsion against Turkey were contemplated only in the closest co-operation with France and Great Britain, and wanted to know what attitude the Government was to take up in the event of the active support of England and France having been assured.

Secretary of State Kokovtsov, who considered that a war at the present moment would be the greatest misfortune for Russia, expressed the opinion that it would be most undesirable to entangle Russia in a European conflict—a view which was shared by the other members of the conference.

The Foreign Minister foresaw the possibility of a failure of the negotiations, and asked what should be decided in that case.

The Prime Minister declared that he was ready, while striving to avoid steps which might involve the risk of military complications, to decide in favour of the financial boycott, although it offers no sufficient guarantee of success in reaching the goal. He repeated that the interestedness of French holders of Turkish Government paper will be of considerable importance in this matter. Secretary of State Kokovtsov drew attention, with the object of making it easier for the French Government to pursue a rigid financial boycott of Turkey, to the possibility of Russia pledging herself, on some basis or other, to share with France the responsibility for the due payment of coupons for holders of Turkish paper which has been issued in the past on the Paris market.

The Prime Minister drew up the following statement of the sense of the conference :

1. It is necessary to continue the representations in Berlin as to the inadmissibility, from the standpoint of Russian interests, of a German general commanding a detachment of troops in Constantinople, or of an Inspectorship, in the sense of the command over a particular district, being given to him, although it is recognized as admissible that a commission for general inspection of the Turkish army should be conferred on the head of the German Military Mission.

2. The negotiations with Berlin are to be continued until their lack of success becomes quite clear.

3. Hereupon, recourse must be had to the proposed measures of pressure outside Berlin, in agreement with France and England.

4. Should the active participation of both France and England in steps in common with Russia not be assured, it does not appear possible to adopt means of pressure which might lead to a war with Germany.

(*Signed*)

    KOKOVTSOV,   W. SUCHOMLINOV,   W. GRIGOROVITCH,

                   SAZONOV,   J. ZHILINSKY.

(M. Pokrovsky, *Drei Konferenzen—Three Conferences—*pp. 32 sqq.)

APPENDIX III

MINUTES OF THE SPECIAL CONFERENCE OF FEBRUARY 8, 1914

[On the original, in the Tsar's handwriting :

" I entirely approve of the resolutions of the Conference.
" TSARSKOYE SELO,
" *March* 23, 1914."]

In the chair : The Foreign Minister, Comptroller Sazonov.

Present : The Minister of the Navy, Adjutant-General Grigoro-vitch, the Chief of the General Staff, Cavalry General Zhilinsky, the Imperial Ambassador in Constantinople, Comptroller Giers, the deputy Foreign Minister, Comptroller Neratov, the Quarter-master General of the General Staff, Lieutenant-General Danilov, the second Chief Quartermaster of the General Staff, Major-General Averyanov, Captain Nenyukov as representative of the Chief of the Naval General Staff, the Head of the Near East Section of the Foreign Ministry, Chamberlain Count Trubetskoi, the Chief of the Second Operations Section of the Naval General Staff, Commander Nemitz.

There were present to prepare the minutes of the special con-ference : the deputy Head of the Near East Section of the Foreign Ministry, Chamberlain Bützov, and the Vice-Director of the Secre-tariat of the Foreign Ministry, Chamberlain Basili.

At the opening of the sitting the Foreign Minister reminded those present at the conference that in the humble memorial, familiar to them, which he had submitted in the preceding November, he had felt it his duty to submit for the All-Highest's most gracious decision the considerations that in connexion with the change in the political situation account must be taken of the possibility of the occurrence, perhaps even in the immediate future, of events which might radi-cally alter the international situation of the Straits of Constantinople, and that it was therefore necessary to proceed without delay, in collaboration with the appropriate departments, to the preparation of a programme, elaborated in every direction, which should aim at the assurance of a solution in our favour of the historic question of the Straits. S. D. Sazonov added that H.M. the Tsar had been pleased most graciously to approve the views set forth in the above-mentioned memorial, and to permit it to be placed before the special conference for discussion.   Accordingly the Minister had requested the Ministries of War and of the Navy, as the authorities mainly concerned in the questions dealt with in this memorial, to take part in the discussion, in order to be able to lay a further report before His Imperial Majesty.   The Foreign Minister took advantage of the presence in St. Petersburg of the Imperial Ambassador in Constantinople to invite him to take part in the discussion.   The Foreign Minister stated that at the moment there seemed to be little likelihood of the occurrence of important political complications, but remarked that it was, nevertheless, impossible to guarantee the maintenance of existing conditions in the Near East, even for the immediate future.   With regard to this, S. D. Sazonov expressed the firm conviction that should events result in the Straits slipping from Turkey's control, Russia could not permit any other Power to establish itself on their shores.   Russia might thus be compelled to seize possession of them, in order then to secure in one shape or another a state of things along the Bosphorus and the Dardanelles corresponding to her interests.   The Minister remarked that the success of this operation would depend in a large degree on the rapidity with which it was carried out, and referred to the necessity of providing in the accomplishment of this task for a landing operation in addition to the activities of the naval forces.   S. D. Sazonov asked the members of the conference to make clear what has already been done, and what more can be done and needs to be done, in order to prepare for our action at any time in the Straits.   The Minister recommended that the following questions should be taken in order, in correspondence with the five points dealt with in his humble memorial:

1. Measures for expediting the mobilization of a sufficiently strong landing force.

2. Measures for equipping the lines of communication required for this.

3. Measures for increasing our means of transport to the level of the requirements for a landing operation.

4. Measures for bringing the Black Sea Fleet up to a state in which it would be superior in strength to the Ottoman Fleet, so as to be able to fulfil, jointly with the army, the task of forcing a way through the Straits, in order to occupy them provisionally or, in case of need, permanently.

5. The question of the construction of the so-called mountain pass railway in the Caucasus, which cannot be separated from the other measures for strengthening the means of defence in the waters of the Black Sea and along the Turkish borders.

The landing army, its composition and its mobilization.

1. On the proposal of the Foreign Minister, the Conference turned

first to the discussion of the question of the landing army, its composition and its mobilization.

The Chief of the General Staff pointed out first that for the seizure of the Straits a fairly considerable number of troops and a strategic development of the operation would be necessary. Proceeding to the consideration of the troops which could be availed of for the landing operation, Cavalry General Zhilinsky stated that the nearest troops for the purpose, namely the 7th and 8th army corps, stationed in the Sevastopol and Odessa commands, were proposed to be used. To clinch the operations it would probably be necessary to bring up two more army corps from the inland commands. The Chief of the General Staff then pointed out that the first detachment of the landing army, which must land in a body, must be at least of the strength of an army corps, that is 30,000 to 50,000 men, as a smaller number of troops could easily be overpowered. J. G. Zhilinsky made the reservation, however, that in view of the great difficulties of a landing operation the first detachment of troops could only be limited to one army corps under specially favourable circumstances, that is if no great opposition was to be expected. It was proposed to form the first detachment, as a combined army corps, out of the nearest sections of the 7th and 8th army corps, namely the 13th division, stationed in Sevastopol and Simferopol, and the 15th division, stationed in Odessa, with the 4th artillery brigade. The Chief of Staff pointed out the connexion between the number of troops required for seizing the Straits and the political and strategical development of this operation, and touched on the question of our possible opponents in the matter. First must be mentioned the Turks. They have at present seven army corps at their disposal around Constantinople. Under Enver Pasha's new plan, the execution of which is, for that matter, very doubtful, they propose to station three army corps along the European shore of the Straits.

The Foreign Minister remarked with reference to this that our seizure of the Straits might also be opposed by Greece and Bulgaria. In view, however, of their historical enmity and their present conflicting interests, there was a good deal of reason to suppose that if one of these States were to come out as our enemy the other would range itself on our side, so that they would cripple one another.

Replying to the question whether in such an event we could count on support from Serbia, S. D. Sazonov said that it could not be assumed that our operations against the Straits could take place without a general European war, and that it was to be assumed that under such circumstances Serbia would direct all her forces against Austria-Hungary.

The Chief of the General Staff stressed the great importance for us of Serbian action against Austria-Hungary in the event of our armed collision with the latter. According to his information, Austria-Hungary would have to send four to five corps against

Serbia. General Zhilinsky here pointed out that from a military point of view it would be an important question what attitude Roumania would take up in the event of a general European war.

To this S. D. Sazonov replied that Roumania, although not formally a member of the Triple Alliance, had undoubtedly concluded a military agreement with Austria, directed against us. This was confirmed by the Imperial Ambassador in Constantinople, who had been in Roumania's confidence in the course of his former service. The favourable turn in Roumanian policy and public opinion now to be observed, however, justified, in the view of the Foreign Minister, a certain doubt whether in the event of our being at war with Austria, Roumania would actually come out against us ; we were, however, without positive material for judging as to this. Returning to the question of our possible opponents in the Straits, S. D. Sazonov pointed out that in the event of our coming into collision with the Triple Alliance, Germany and Austria would send no troops towards the Straits, and that at the worst Italy might send landing parties, though it would be dangerous for Italy to expose her frontiers to attack from France.

With reference to what the Foreign Minister had said concerning the general situation in which a decision of the question of the Straits might be expected, the Chief of the General Staff expressed his conviction that the struggle for Constantinople would hardly be possible without a general European war. Cavalry General Zhilinsky regarded it, therefore, as his duty to emphasize that the dispatch of troops for an expedition against the Straits and even the possibility of such an operation would depend on the general situation at the beginning of the war. In J. G. Zhilinsky's view, the army corps proposed to be devoted to this expedition could only be sent against Constantinople if no fighting took place along the western front or matters stood well there. Otherwise these troops would have to be sent to the western frontier, for a successful struggle on the western frontier would also mean success in the question of the Straits. According to the war plan drawn up to meet the eventuality of a battle on the western front, all the troops from the inland commands must be brought up to join the troops operating on the western front ; it would, therefore, unfortunately be impossible to find troops from the inland commands in the Empire to send to this front to replace the southern army corps proposed to be used for the landing operation, in order to make it possible to send this army corps to Constantinople whatever the circumstances. The Foreign Minister asked whether the situation would be altered in this respect by the increase in our army now in progress ; the Chief of the General Staff replied that this increase would consist only of the formation of two army corps in 1915 and 1916. These army corps will be stationed on our western frontier and serve only to balance the recent increase in the German and Austrian armies. Apart from this, the formation of two new army corps obviously cannot compensate for the dispatch of four army corps to Constantinople, as would be necessary for such an expedition.

From what the Chief of the General Staff had said, the Imperial Ambassador in Constantinople inferred that, should operations take place on our western front on the outbreak of war, it would be impossible to be sure whether the landing troops required for the seizure of the Straits would be available, and whether it would be possible for the expedition to take place at all when the moment arrived for it. M. N. Giers emphasized that it would be desirable to set apart specially the troops required for the landing operation, with provision for their being diverted and used for another purpose, if required, and he suggested the question whether it would perhaps be possible to assign the army corps stationed in the Caucasus for the operation against Constantinople. In favour of such an arrangement the Imperial Ambassador in Constantinople adduced the consideration that in the event of anarchy in Constantinople there would be no fighting along our Turkish frontier, and that our Caucasian corps would be free.

Cavalry General Zhilinsky considered that the idea put forward by M. N. Giers was not practicable, since in the view of the military authorities an expedition to Constantinople would not save the Caucasian frontier from fighting. A large part of the Turkish forces are in Asia Minor. Under Enver Pasha's plan it is intended to leave only three army corps in the European parts of Turkey. In the event of a landing operation in the Straits, our task must consist in preventing a concentration of the other army corps around Constantinople, and diverting them to the Caucasian frontier. Our three Caucasian army corps must, therefore, be mobilized in addition to beginning the landing operation.

The Quartermaster-General of the General Staff, Lieutenant-General Danilov, added to what had been mentioned that it was also, in his view, impossible to assign the troops stationed in the Caucasus for the landing operation because, in consequence of the local conditions, mobilization in the Caucasus was a very lengthy operation. The Caucasian railway network is too scanty, the local Russian population is small, and the troop formations have to be filled up largely with reservists from the inland Governments. For these reasons the mobilization in the Caucasus extends at least to three weeks. The Quartermaster-General proceeded to express his view that it is quite impossible to assign certain troops exclusively to an expedition to Constantinople. He was convinced that, apart from the difficulty of the task of carrying out the seizure of Constantinople, we must always bear in mind the necessity of directing our whole forces westwards to meet Germany and Austria, however many troops we may have, even if there were very many more than at present. The only good strategy is strong strategy. The war on our western front would demand the utmost application of all the forces of the State, and we could not dispense with a single army corps in order to leave it behind for special tasks. We must direct our energies to ensuring success in the most important theatre of war. With victory in this theatre we should secure favourable decisions in all secondary questions. With a battle proceeding or expected on the western front, the setting apart of four army corps for the landing operations in the Straits must, in General Danilov's view, be regarded as indefensible and impossible. The preservation of Constantinople from seizure by a third Power must be a special task of our policy.

The Chief of the second Operations Section of the Naval General Staff, Commander Nemitz, disagreed with this view of the question. He fully recognized the correctness of the rule that it is necessary to be strong against the enemy in the chief theatre of war, and therefore to sacrifice less important tasks ; and he would associate himself with the inference drawn by Adjutant-General Danilov, if we had against us on the road to the Straits and Constantinople the same principal opponent as on the western front, that is, the German and Austrian forces. Then our one task would obviously be to beat the German and Austrian armies, when we should dictate our will in Berlin and Vienna and should receive the Straits. Actually, however, the naval general staff sees the situation in another light. On the road to the Straits Germany and Austria are not our only serious opponents. However successful our operations on the western front might be, they would not give us the Straits and Constantinople. Other countries' fleets and armies could occupy them while the battle on our western front was proceeding. Commander Nemitz was, therefore, of the opinion that simultaneously with the operations on the western front we must occupy Constantinople and the Straits with an armed force, in order at the peace negotiations to have the accomplished fact of our seizure of them. Only in such a case would Europe consent to a solution of the question of the Straits under the conditions which we require. If it is impossible to set apart the needed number of troops out of the present strength of our army, then, in Commander Nemitz's view, three new army corps should be formed specially for this purpose. Such an additional sacrifice for armaments cannot be admitted to be beyond Russia's strength if it would ensure the attainment of our historic tasks.

In reply to the arguments of Commander Nemitz, the Chief of the General Staff pointed out that his idea of procuring still more army corps for the Constantinople expedition was impossible of realization at present. In the desire to define more precisely, after the discussion which had taken place, the attitude of the Ministry of War towards the question of assigning troops for the landing operations in the Straits, J. G. Zhilinsky added further to what he had already said. He is convinced that in the eyes of every Russian the Straits are of such enormous importance that it may certainly be said that should there arise a danger of their transfer from Turkey into other hands, we cannot refuse to take possession of them, and should accordingly at once send an army to land at Constantinople. It is to be assumed that this will only be able to occur during a crisis which would lead to a general European war. But the war in the Straits for Constantinople may precede the collision on our western front. In the view of the Chief of the General Staff, it is very probable that this is what would happen. In such a case there can, of course, be no question of diverting the landing army to which this duty has been assigned. This could only arise if the war began with operations on the German and Austrian frontiers and demanded a concentration of all forces on the western front. As already mentioned, if operations are begun for seizing the Straits, it is proposed to assign this duty to the 7th and 8th army corps. These army corps are, however, also included in the war plan for the western front. In this case the first of these army corps would be incorporated in the army operating against Austria, while the second is proposed to be employed in the operations against Roumania. Only in the event of Roumania's neutrality could the 8th army corps remain free.

At the desire of the Foreign Minister, the Chief of the General Staff proceeded to deal with the duration of a mobilization of the troops proposed to be used for the landing operation. The 13th and 15th divisions and the 4th artillery brigade, forming the first detachment of the forces intended for the landing army, consist of companies 60 strong, and their mobilization, without the artillery parks, would last five days. The remainder of the troops belonging to the strength of the 7th and 8th army corps consist at present of companies 48 strong, and are therefore mobilized in eight to nine days. The same time is required for the mobilization of the two other army corps by which in case of need the landing army could be strengthened. Under the new plan for strengthening our army all infantry units can in the shortest space of time be brought up to a company strength of 60. The period of their mobilization would thus be reduced to five to six days, as with the increase of the strength of a company the mobilization area is reduced. Should it be recognized to be necessary, the preparedness for war of the troops intended for the Constantinople expedition can be further increased, the company strength being raised to 84 or even 100. The new plan for the increase of the army prefers the introduction of this maximum to the increase of certain units, as enabling the military authority at its own discretion to bring up any units to this strength. An intensive increase of this sort is, however, primarily needed in the armies stationed along our western frontier. As, however, it might prove necessary (for instance, in the event of an outbreak of anarchy in Constantinople) to transport in the shortest possible time the first section of the landing armies destined for the Constantinople expedition, that is, the 13th and 15th divisions and 4th artillery brigade, these troops could, should special All-highest directions be issued to this effect, be included in the troops whose strength is to be increased to 84, and this would still further reduce the period of mobilization. J. G. Zhilinsky would, however, in order to extend this measure to the two first divisions or to the whole of the 7th and 8th army corps, regard it as possible to adopt the measure only in the last resort, as such a strengthening of this army corps could only take place at the expense of the troops stationed on the western front, whose strength is a matter of special anxiety to the military authority. The Chief of the General Staff pointed out that what had been said referred only to the infantry, and proceeded then to the question of the mobilization of the artillery. Up to now our artillery contained in peace time only trains with four guns and two munition wagons in each battery. In consequence, mobilization lasted 18 days. Under the plan now being put into execution for the strengthening of the army, the number of trains in the artillery will be substantially increased. In all frontier commands trains with six guns and twelve munition wagons are provided for each battery. With such a strength the artillery can proceed as early as the second or third day of mobilization. In the inland commands the batteries will have trains with four guns and four munition wagons, and will be mobilized in 12 to 14 days. As the Odessa command is included in the inland commands, the artillery of the 7th and 8th army corps forming it will not be much better off after the reform has been carried out in regard to rapidity of mobilization. Should it therefore be regarded as necessary to increase their preparedness for war, the number of trains could, assuming All-highest directions, be increased in the case of the artillery of the Odessa command in the same way as is provided in the case of the frontier commands ; this could of course only be effected at the cost of certain artillery sections in these commands, or by the increased peace strength being put into force for the troops of the landing corps.

As regards the cavalry, it is always in a condition of mobilization. It is, moreover, intended to introduce a regiment of cavalry into each army corps of the landing army.

Summing up, Cavalry General Zhilinsky pointed out that with the putting into execution of the measures already decided on and shortly to be carried out, the infantry troops assigned to the landing army will be mobile in five to six days, the artillery in twelve to fourteen days, and that in the event of the All-highest assent being given the duration of the mobilization of the infantry troops of the first section of the landing army, that is the 13th and 15th divisions and the 4th artillery brigade, will probably be reduced to three to four days, and the mobilization of the artillery of the 7th and 8th army corps could be similarly expedited.

As to the time required for the transport of these troops to the ports for embarkation, the embarkation of the 13th and 15th divisions and the 4th artillery brigade, stationed at Odessa and Sevastopol, and in part at Simferopol, could take place at once.   The transport of the remaining troops of the 7th and 8th army corps would not take more than two to three days.   The transport to the ports of the two other army corps from the inland commands would take about six days.

According to the information in the hands of the Chief of the General Staff, the preparation of the means of transport required for the landing operations would, in view of the poor development of these means in the Black Sea, require rather more time than the mobilization of the landing army according to the calculation presented.   General Zhilinsky considered, therefore, that so long as there existed no possibility of a more rapid mobilization of transport, there was no reason to take further measures to put the army corps destined for the Constantinople expedition into a higher state of preparedness for war, especially as this could only be done at the cost of the preparedness for war on the western front.   Should it appear necessary when transport had been improved to shorten further the duration of the mobilization of the landing army, this could, as mentioned, be effected by the military authorities on their own initiative.

The Minister of the Navy confirmed the correctness of what the Chief of the General Staff had said as to the duration of the preparations for the transport operations ; concerning this he would give full details when this matter came up for discussion.   At present, in any case, the embarkation of the first section of the landing army could not be completed under ten days.   Should it prove possible to shorten this period, the Ministry of the Navy would not fail to inform the General Staff.

The lines of communication needed for the transport of the landing army to the ports of embarkation.

2. The Conference then proceeded to the question of the lines of communication needed for the transport of the landing army to the ports for the purpose of embarkation.

With reference to this, the Chief of the General Staff mentioned that the existing railways were on the whole sufficient for the requirement indicated, and that the lines leading to Odessa were at present being further developed.   Of these new lines, the most important in this command appeared, from the point of view of the Ministry of War, to be the Bachmatch–Odessa and Ekaterinoslav–Cherson lines.   The former is already nearly ready, the plans for the construction of the latter are drawn up.   As regards the railways, therefore, the situation may, from the point of view of the landing operations against Constantinople, be regarded as satisfactory.

The means of transport needed for the landing operation.

3. The Conference then turned to the examination of the question

of the means of transport needed for the transport of the landing army to the Straits.

The Minister of the Navy emphasized first that, under the existing circumstances, the conditions for the carrying out of this operation are not too satisfactory. The main difficulty lies in the serious shortage of means of transport in the Black Sea. To this must be added that these means of transport are not suited to the purposes of the transport of troops, and that no proper organization for the commandeering and mobilization of the ships lying in the Black Sea exists. The conveyance of a sufficiently strong landing force in a short space of time could, as the Minister of the Navy showed, only be assured after a number of measures had been carried out by the joint efforts of several departments. Adjutant-General Grigorovitch here requested Commander Nemitz, the Chief of the second Operations Section of the naval general staff, to give the Conference further details on this question.

Commander Nemitz pointed out that the duties in connexion with transport operations in the Black Sea had hitherto belonged to the staff of the Odessa command, and had only recently been transferred to the naval department. The preparations for the embarkation of the first section of the landing army would, he said, under present conditions take at least ten to twelve days, so that it must be reckoned that between the date of the declaration of mobilization and that of the landing at least two weeks would pass. If the transport ships returned promptly to the places of embarkation, it would be at least a week after the departure of the first troops before they could begin the second journey. The number of troops that could be transported in one passage is to be estimated under present conditions at only one division of war strength, that is, in all about 20,000 men. This number could at present be increased to an army corps at war strength if an organization were set up to mobilize for transport purposes the whole of the merchant shipping in the Black Sea.[1]

In the course of two or three years, with steady organization, preparations could be made for the embarkation of a still greater number of troops, that is, two or three army corps, in a single passage. For this the first necessity is to make use not only of the Russian but of all other ships in the Black Sea, which could not be done without first setting up the required organization. The principal means of assuring the transport of so considerable a landing army must be sought in the development of our merchant fleet in the Black Sea. This can only be secured by concordant and energetic activity in the Ministry of Finance, the Ministry of Commerce and Industry, and the Ministry of the Navy, and demands a series

[1] In this connexion it must not be forgotten that it would not be possible to employ the whole strength of our Black Sea merchant fleet for the landing operation, but only the vessels actually in the Black Sea at the time of mobilization.

of measures, of which the most important would be an agreement between the Government and the State-supported shipping companies, especially the Volunteer Fleet, for an increase in their fleets, the new ships being such as satisfy the special requirements of the transport of troops. If the fleets were increased by fifteen such transport ships, of the required tonnage, this would enable the number of troops that could be transported in one passage to be increased by one army corps.

The Head of the Near East Section of the Foreign Ministry laid stress on the importance to the whole State of an increase of our merchant fleet in the Black Sea. Its development is needed not only from the point of view of our military requirements, but also on account of urgent economic considerations. Unfortunately, to the present day nearly 59 per cent. of our enormous exports through the Black Sea has been carried in foreign ships, and scores of millions go every year into the pockets of foreigners for the transport of our goods. The ambition to free ourselves from foreign control in this respect is a further justification of the financial sacrifices which would be called for by an early strengthening of our merchant fleet in the Black Sea.

On the proposal of the Foreign Minister the Conference resolved that it is desirable that the Government should without delay consider the elaboration of measures for the development of our merchant fleet in the Black Sea.

M. N. Giers returned to the question of the period required for carrying out the transport operations. In the view of the Imperial Ambassador in Turkey, the period of two weeks mentioned by Commander Nemitz for the arrival of the landing army in Constantinople might in any case be excessive. An expedition to Constantinople might, for instance, be called for by an outbreak of anarchy in the Turkish capital and the danger of a massacre. In such a case it would be necessary to expedite the action. M. N. Giers therefore asked for information as to the extent to which the carrying out of the landing operation could be expedited by appropriate preparations.

The Chief of the second Operations Section of the naval general staff replied that in this respect everything depends on the degree of adaptation of the merchant fleet for transport operations, and of the preparation for mobilization. If the ships of the Volunteer Fleet were correspondingly mobilized, a division at war strength could be got to Constantinople within a week.

The Foreign Minister expressed the desire that the whole of the first section of the landing army, that is, the combined army corps, of which the mobilization is planned, should be expedited from three to five days and at once embarked, in order so to reach the Bosphorus four to five days after the declaration of mobilization.

In this connexion the Chief of the General Staff drew the attention of the Conference to the importance of having the ships which might be called upon to transport troops suitably equipped in peace time. It is important to supply them with collapsible horseboxes, portable cookers for preparing food, davits for slinging small boats, and so on. It is of special importance to attend to the equipment of ships for the transport of artillery, bearing in mind also that this is being reorganized. The corresponding equipment of the ships must be made the duty of the companies subsidized by the State. It is also necessary to prepare and maintain in the storehouses in the various ports various articles necessary for landing operations.

The Minister of the Navy emphasized that very little had so far been done towards the equipment of ships for the purpose of the transport of troops, and stated that many useful suggestions as to this would be afforded by the impending test landing operation in the Black Sea. This operation will also afford information as to the minimum length of time required. It is intended during the summer manœuvres to convey to the Caucasian coast in two convoys a division at war strength, that is, 20,000 men. Half of these troops are to be landed in harbour and the rest on an unembanked shore. In the first case the landing conditions will in some degree resemble the conditions under which our landing troops would have to land in Bulgaria if a Bulgarian port were used. In the second case there will be a certain analogy with the landing of our troops directly on the Turkish shores, with no support from the land. Unfortunately, financial considerations render it impossible to carry out this test on a large scale, as this would require a large number of ships, which would be too expensive and a burden on our merchant shipping.

The Chief of the General Staff expressed the view that in order to expedite the preparation of landing operations it would be more serviceable always to have special military transport vessels at disposal.

The Minister of the Navy stated that this would entail heavy expenditure both on acquiring transports and on their maintenance. These ships would be a deadweight on the navy, while already there are many, especially among the members of our legislative bodies, who regard our navy as insufficiently ready for action.

In the view of the deputy Foreign Minister, the last consideration should not be advanced against the incorporation of a number of transports in the Black Sea Fleet, as these ships would be designed for the performance of a definite and purely military duty.

With regard to what the Minister of the Navy had said, Commander Nemitz added that the naval general staff is at present studying the question of acquiring a small number of suitable vessels for equipment for the transport of horses. As the conveyance of horses is particularly difficult, this step might substantially expedite the landing operation.

16

The Naval Forces in the Black Sea.

4. From the discussion of the measures needed for the strengthening of our merchant fleet in the Black Sea sufficiently to meet the requirements of a landing operation for the seizure of the Straits, the Conference proceeded to the question how our naval forces in the Black Sea could be rendered superior to the Ottoman navy, and how they could carry out the forcing of the Straits jointly with the army, in order to obtain possession of them. The deputy Chief of the Naval General Staff reported on the relation of our naval forces in the Black Sea to those of the Turkish navy at the present time and in coming years. Up till now our fleet has certainly been predominant in the Black Sea. In the coming autumn, however, the Ottoman fleet will be increased by two large battleships : the *Reschad V*, ordered from Great Britain by Turkey, and the *Rio de Janeiro*, which she recently acquired in Brazil. Unfortunately we are unable at present to set a single dreadnought against these ships in the Black Sea, and the mastery of the Black Sea will thus pass shortly to Turkey. The impending increase of the Turkish navy is very much to our disadvantage, especially from the point of view of the operation under discussion of the seizure of the Straits. So long as the Turkish fleet has the mastery of the Black Sea, it will be impossible to attempt the landing operation, without first having removed the predominance of the Ottoman naval forces. As, however, it might prove impossible for the Russian Black Sea fleet to destroy the Turkish naval forces in the period in question, the possibility of a landing operation would no longer exist, so long as our naval forces have not the preponderance. The unfavourable proportion between our own and the Turkish naval forces will begin to change in the summer of 1915, provided that there is no fresh increase in the Turkish navy through the acquisition of fresh completed ships of the line, which, as past experience has shown, is hardly likely to be prevented by financial difficulties. In consequence of exceptional measures taken by the naval department it has proved possible so to hasten the construction of the dreadnoughts in our Black Sea dockyards that it may be expected that the *Imperatritsa Maria* and the *Alexander III* will be completed by June 1 and September 1, 1915, instead of in 1916, as was provided in the contracts. Captain Nenyukov mentioned the existing opinion that the Turkish dreadnoughts are superior in fighting power to the dreadnoughts under construction for the Black Sea fleet, and stated that the former have not in fact any advantage over the latter. Certainly, the Turkish ships have $13\frac{1}{2}$-inch guns, while ours have 12-inch guns. If the ammunition were of equal quality, the artillery of the Turkish ships would be greatly superior to ours. But the Turkish navy is supplied with British ammunition, much less powerful than our ammunition of equal calibre. It may, therefore, be said that the two Turkish dreadnoughts could

about be held in check by our *Imperatritsa Maria* and *Alexander III* when they come into the fighting-line in 1915. We shall then have superior forces owing to the rest of our fleet, that is, the four existing and comparatively recent armoured ships, *Panteleimon, Joann Slatoust, Jevstafi,* and *Tri Svatitelya,* which have substantial superiority over the forces which Turkey has at present, before the addition of the dreadnoughts. At the end of 1915 our Black Sea fleet will be further strengthened by a third similar dreadnought under construction, the *Katharina II* ; also in 1916 by two cruisers. Finally, it has been decided to lay down a fourth battle cruiser of similar type to the three already mentioned ; this will be completed in 1917, and will complete the formation of a full squadron of dreadnoughts. In addition to this fourth ship, it has been decided to build two cruisers, eight mine-layers, and six submarines, which are to be completed in 1917. How far these vessels will assure us the mastery of the Black Sea depends on the further development of our own and the Turkish naval armaments. The Turkish programme provided for the acquisition of six capital ships and twelve ocean-going torpedo-boat destroyers. The realization of this programme is, of course, as yet very uncertain.

The Minister of the Navy stated with reference to this that the naval department has provided for a further important increase in our Black Sea fleet in coming years by the construction of a second squadron of battle cruisers of the latest type.

The Conference took note of this statement with great satisfaction, and expressed the hope that the intentions of the naval department may be realized as soon as possible.

The Minister of the Navy proceeded to explain how it was that we failed to avert the alienation by Brazil of the dreadnought *Rio de Janeiro* to Turkey, with its unfortunate results for us. At the time the naval department had raised the question of the purchase of this ship by Russia ; later, the news came from English sources that the ship would not be sold. The Brazilian Government's altered decision was probably due to pressure put upon it in some form or other. The naval department is now doing its utmost to prevent other vessels which might be bought by Turkey from coming into her possession. According to information to hand the Argentine Government may possibly be ready to sell the *Rivadavia* and *Moreno,* now under construction in the United States of North America ; the Chilean Government also seems inclined to sell two dreadnoughts of the *Amirante Latorre* class, which are also under construction. As there are no other important units at present in the market, the purchase of these would remove the possibility of a further increase at present in the Turkish navy, and would also expedite the development of our own naval forces. His Majesty has been pleased to concur in these views and to command that the battle cruisers for sale abroad shall be bought. The means for this can be secured by the application of Article 117.

The naval department is at present occupied in ascertaining what ships can be acquired and under what conditions. The ships bought abroad could form the nucleus of a Mediterranean squadron whose strategic duty would be to compensate for the Turkish predominance over our fleet in the Black Sea.

The Imperial Ambassador in Constantinople expressed his great satisfaction at the decision to acquire the purchaseable dreadnoughts.

The Foreign Minister concurred. He also mentioned the importance of the appearance of our ships in the Mediterranean as likely to divert Turkish ships from the Black Sea.

The Ambassador in Constantinople pointed out that the acquisition of the two battle cruisers had had a great moral effect in favour of the Turks, and that account must be taken of this as well as of the strengthening of their material resources.

The Minister of the Navy stated that the Turks would be unable at once to acquire familiarity with such complicated ships as the modern dreadnoughts. They would have to engage foreigners to command the ships, and the completion with officers and crew would take at least three months.

The Railways in the Caucasus.

5. The Conference proceeded to the last of the points down for discussion, the question of the railways in the Caucasus, and especially the so-called mountain-pass railway.

The Chief of the General Staff pointed out that in the interest of the defence of the country the construction as soon as possible of a mountain-pass railway over the ridge of the Caucasus range is urgently required. So long as this railway is not in existence, if war should break out on our Turkish frontier our army would have no adequate communication with the country in its rear. The Black Sea railway could not take the place of the mountain-pass railway, and is no more than an emergency resource. It is exposed to the danger of destruction from the sea, and it ends in a *cul-de-sac* at Mount Suram. The construction of the mountain-pass railway is also required in order to improve the conditions of mobilization in the Caucasus, since, as already mentioned, mobilization takes too long there, for local reasons. As, in the event of a struggle for Constantinople, a collision on the Turkish frontier must be regarded as inevitable, the construction of the mountain-pass railway, necessary to meet this emergency, must be included among the measures required in preparation for our offensive on the Bosphorus.

The Head of the Near East Section of the Foreign Ministry remarked that complications on the Turkish frontier might occur, even without the struggle for the Straits, through unrest in Armenia. Count Troubetskoi added that after the mountain-pass railway has been built the construction of railways in Turkey in the districts bordering on the Caucasus will lose its danger for us. It is no longer possible to follow a policy of leaving these districts without communications. We must show ourselves prepared to see a whole network of railways built in Asia Minor, and must ourselves take in hand the construction of railways in the border zone. Common sense requires that we should complete the mountain-pass railway by the time when the Turkish railways approach our frontier. The building of the mountain-pass railway must be taken in hand at once.

The Chief of the General Staff pointed out that in addition to the mountain-pass railway several strategic railways are required in Transcaucasia :

1. A continuous double-track line from Tiflis via Kars and Sary-kamish to Karaurgan—on the Turkish frontier—which is already in hand.

2. It would be very useful to build a line from Michailov station via Borshon to Kars, with a branch to Olty, which would provide the Black Sea Railway with an outlet to Kars.

3. A line from Batum to Kars might also be useful ; as far as is known, private capitalists are ready to undertake its construction.

*   *   *   *   *

After the conclusion of the survey of the most important questions which have become acute for us through the necessity of a deliberate preparation for a seizure of the Straits, which may possibly soon be required, the Conference, on the proposal of the Foreign Minister, expressed the general desire that the Government should cause all measures to be taken by all the authorities concerned which are required for the technical execution of this task. Proceeding to the concrete measures, the necessity of which had been made clear by the representatives of the departments interested in the course of the preceding discussion, the Conference regarded it as desirable that in the first place the following measures should be carried out, namely :

1. The landing troops of the 13th and 15th divisions and the 4th artillery brigade, destined to form the first section of the Constantinople expedition, should have a company strength of 84.

2. The artillery sections of the Odessa command should have their trains strengthened as is proposed for frontier commands in peace time, that is, trains with six guns and twelve munition wagons.

3. The Ministry of Finance, the Ministry of Trade and Industry, and the Ministry of the Navy must make every effort to carry out the most urgent and effective measures for strengthening our means of transport in the Black Sea. In particular, the Government must conclude an agreement with the State-supported steamship companies for an increase of their fleets by means of ships corresponding both in method of construction and in equipment to the special needs of the transport of troops.

4. The naval department must in the immediate future find means of reducing the time required for the conveyance of the first section of the landing army, of the dimensions of an army corps, to four to five days, calculated from the day of the issue of a command to this effect.

5. Our Black Sea fleet must in as short a time as possible be strengthened by a second squadron of the most modern and powerful battle cruisers ; and,

6. In as short a time as possible the construction must be completed of the continuous double-track line from Tiflis via Kars and Sarykamish to Karaurgan, and the mountain-pass railway must be built.   It is also necessary to build a line from Michailov station via Borshon to Kars, with a branch line to Olty ; the construction of a railway line from Batoum to Kars by private capitalists is also desirable.

The Conference requests the Foreign Minister to lay these proposals before His Majesty for his gracious approval.

(*Signed*),

SAZONOV,   J. GRIGOROVITCH,   J. ZHILINSKY.

(M. Pokrovsky, *Drei Konferenzen—Three Conferences—*pp. 46 sqq.)

APPENDIX IV

FRANCE'S WAR AIMS

Telegram from Isvolsky to Sazonov, Bordeaux, September 30/ October 13, 1914, No. 497.

Refers to your telegram No. 2935. Personal. I have had an opportunity to speak personally, on my own initiative, with Delcassé, on the question raised in that telegram. He said to begin with that it is too soon yet " to sell the bearskin," and that he had so far avoided discussing the question with his colleagues, but admitted that it was as well that the Allies should mutually ascertain one another's views and wishes in good time. He is convinced that this can give rise to no differences of opinion between Russia, France, and Great Britain. He has himself spoken very frequently to you, with entire openness, and has been able to convince himself that the aims followed by Russia and France are identical. France seeks no territorial gains for herself in Europe, of course with the exception of the restoration of Alsace and Lorraine. In Africa also she is making no effort to obtain fresh acquisitions, and will content herself with destroying the last remains of the Algeciras Act and rectifying certain colonial frontiers. Thus, France's principal aim—and in this respect all three of the Allied Powers are entirely at one—is the destruction of the German Empire and the weakening as far as possible of the military and political power of Prussia. One must work to give the various German States themselves an interest in this. It is too soon to discuss the details of the future constitution of Germany. Great Britain will probably demand the restoration of an independent Hanover, and naturally neither Russia nor France will oppose this. Schleswig-Holstein must go to Denmark, despite the ambiguous attitude of the Danish Government. Great Britain also seeks no conquests in Europe, but will demand colonial expansion at Germany's expense, and France makes no objection to this. As regards Russia, her territorial demands are a matter of course in their general lines, and it goes without saying that France agrees in advance. Russia will also, of course, demand the freedom of the Turkish Straits, with adequate guarantees, and in this question Russia is assured of far-reaching support from France, who is able in this matter to bring useful influence to bear for us on Great Britain. Remainder follows.

Telegram from Isvolsky to Sazonov, Bordeaux, September 30/
October 13, 1914, *No.* 497.

Continuation. Personal. Very confidential. Delcassé then re
ferred to the negotiations which took place in St. Petersburg in
1913, and earnestly asked me to draw your attention to the fact
that the demands and aspirations of France remain unaltered,
with the addition only of the necessary destruction of the political
and economic power of Germany. The latter point is a sheer
necessity in view of the existing situation, and especially in view of
the participation of Great Britain in the war, and the French Government lays stress on the need for attaining this aim, in the
assumption that this is of equal importance not only for France
but for the other Powers and even for the whole world.

Telegram from Isvolsky to Sazonov, Bordeaux, September 30/
October 13, 1914, *No.* 498.

Continuation of my telegram No. 497. Delcassé was least definite
about the future of the Austro-Hungarian Monarchy. This question
is of much less interest to the French than the fate of the German
Empire. It must also be borne in mind, despite the assurances
of Delcassé to the contrary, that the French have without question
some sympathy towards Austria-Hungary, based on the entirely
mistaken idea that Austria-Hungary is endeavouring to make
herself independent of Germany, and that Austria-Hungary did
service to France at Algeciras. The same sympathy exists, only
in a still stronger measure, in Great Britain also, as the last Blue
Book, with Bunsen's reports, shows. It seems to me, therefore,
most desirable to acquaint both the Paris and the London Cabinet
with our view in this question in good time and with unmistakable
clearness. I am letting no opportunity pass, though speaking for
myself only, to point out emphatically here that it is necessary
to make an end of the Habsburg Monarchy, which is an entire
anachronism, and to summon the various nationalities which make
up the Monarchy, with the exception of the Poles, to an independent
political existence. This inevitably raises a whole series of exceedingly difficult political, geographical, and ethnographical questions,
on which people here have few ideas and those often wrong. One
of these, and perhaps the most important, is the future shape of the
Serbian Kingdom. I am working here for a unified, strong Serbo-
Croat State, including Istria and Dalmatia, in order to provide
a necessary counterweight to Italy, Hungary, and Roumania. To
this end I have introduced Supilo, the well-known Serbo-Croat
politician, formerly a Deputy in the Hungarian Parliament, who
has come here, to Delcassé ; Supilo is an enthusiastic supporter
of this line of thought. My arguments appear to have been not
without effect on Delcassé, but I think it is most desirable to acquaint

him in full detail and in an authoritative manner with our project for the future of Austria-Hungary. Delcassé asked me, among other things, where, in my view, the future congress should take place. I replied that this would probably be determined at the last moment, but that in my personal opinion there is no reason why the peace negotiations, or even the preparatory exchange of views between the three Allies, should necessarily take place under the ægis of Sir Edward Grey, who was the link between the Powers of the Triple Entente and the Triple Alliance right up to the war, and as such is not now needed at all. If you do not want to concentrate the negotiations in your own hands, it seems to me to be best to leave their direction in Delcassé's hands; he inspires complete trust both in London and in St. Petersburg, and has all the requisite personal qualities.

Telegram from Isvolsky to Sazonov, Bordeaux, September 30/ October 13, 1914, No. 498.

Continuation. Very confidential. Will you please inform me urgently what money I can have at disposal for organizing propaganda for the idea mentioned above? I feel it my duty to draw your attention to the fact that at the present moment this will hasten a decision of Roumania and Italy in our favour, while in future it will form an important counterweight against these two States.

(*Berliner Tageblatt*, December 28, 1922, No. 589.)

INDEX